SAMUEL SLOAN

SAMUEL SLOAN

Architect of Philadelphia
1815–1884

Harold N. Cooledge, Jr.

Alumni Professor of Art and Architectural History
College of Architecture, Clemson University

upp

University of Pennsylvania Press

PHILADELPHIA 1986

FRONTISPIECE: First Baptist Church, Greenville, South Carolina;
original drawing (Reproduced with permission of the
Downtown Baptist Church, Greenville, South Carolina)

Library of Congress Cataloging-in-Publication Data

Cooledge, Harold N.
  Samuel Sloan, architect of Philadelphia, 1815–1884.

  Bibliography: p.
  Includes index.
  1. Sloan, Samuel, 1815–1884—Catalogs. 2. Sloan,
Samuel, 1815–1884—Criticism and interpretation.
I. Title.
NA737.S54A4 1986   720′.92′4   85-22496
ISBN 0-8122-8003-2 (alk. paper)

Printed in the United States of America

Contents

Illustrations

Introduction and Acknowledgments

Samuel Sloan, Architect of Philadelphia, was born and reached his early maturity in that period of American cultural history which has been called the "Age of Jackson." Although he lived and worked for thirty years after the period's close, its values and ideals continued to be his own until his death. Some men are so entirely in accord with a particular social environment that only while it lasts can they function successfully. Within it, however, they are completely assured, knowing instinctively what forces of political action and reaction, what social crosscurrents, what tides of public taste are cardinal for their time and place. Samuel Sloan was such a man. Almost a Jacksonian archetype, he was a country carpenter who became an architect of national prominence, a natural politician of unbounded confidence and uncertain ethics, an opportunist, conceited and hungry for acclaim, a driving worker, and a showman who knew how to advertise himself. But withal, he was talented, quick to learn, inventive, and more understanding of the native demands upon architecture in the United States than the majority of his contemporaries.

Sloan's identification with his society in the immediate pre–Civil War decades was so complete that he often understood his clients better than they understood themselves—their pride of accomplishment, their desire for recognition, their fear of social error, their mixture of boldness and timidity, and their worship of "success." He sometimes found amusing their subservience to the fads and fashions of the day—the pronouncements of the taste-makers and the dicta of the theorists—but he did not hesitate to use those fads and fashions in giving the needs and dreams of his clients architectural form. His own convictions about the practice of architecture were an outgrowth of this craftsman background and his absorption into the commercial, speculative world of mid-century Philadelphia, which city was always his particular "place."

Sloan's adaptation to that world brought him sudden success in the decade of the 1850s, and equally sudden obsolescence in the post–Civil War period. Like any overspecialized organism, he paid the penalty for too complete an identification with too specific an environment. When that environment changed he could not change, and so he became estranged and isolated. His talent did not so much decline as it remained static, while the world grew away from him and quickly forgot him. In this he was not alone, for other architects and taste-makers of the Jacksonian Age found themselves looked upon as old-fashioned and out-of-date after the Civil War. Those who could accept a change of role—from practitioner to administrator, or from leader to "elder statesman"—maintained their status, and like Thomas U. Walter became revered figures in the developing "profession" of architecture. Some, like Alexander Jackson Davis, became misanthropes who spent their remaining years trying to confirm and substantiate their former importance. Sloan, who was a doer not a philosopher, could not understand why he was superseded by men, many of whom he had trained, who frequently used techniques and ideas he had originated.

Within a decade of his death, Sloan's name and accomplishments had been forgotten, which is surprising when the number, variety, and distribution of his executed commissions is examined. At his death in 1884 he had designed or remodeled a major hospital in every state at that time in the Union; over twenty churches had been erected from his plans; more than fifty public and private schools and numerous public and commercial buildings had come from his office; and the number of residences of all types for which he was the architect cannot be accurately determined, but it must have been in the hundreds. Why, with such a body of concrete evidence to his life and work, Sloan was so quickly forgotten is puzzling. Perhaps it was the transitional nature of his work and career, the mixture of pre- and postindustrial elements in both his designs and his practice, that made him hard to distinguish from among the body of his peers. There were so many others of like nature, if less ability, in the immediate prewar decades. Perhaps it was his ambiguous relationship with the newborn American Institute of Architects, his individual rather than institutional understanding of architecture as a profession. Perhaps it was just the memory of his highhandedness, his unforgiving temper, and roughshod ambition.

Whatever the reason for his vanishment, Sloan's many contributions to the progress of American architecture were not reconsidered until the middle decades of the twentieth century. The present study of his life and work was initiated, and continuously supported, by those scholars and historians who rediscovered Sloan—such men as George B. Tatum, Charles E. Peterson, and Henry Russell Hitchcock. To them, and to the literally hundreds of others in historical societies, state archives, and religious foundations throughout the United States who gave of their time and effort in the search for Samuel Sloan, this writer is deeply indebted. He is likewise beholden to those who gave encouragement and aid over the thirty years of preparation; to Adolf K. Placzek, Avery Librarian Emeritus; to Catherine W. Bishir of the North Carolina Department of Cultural Resources; to the late Elizabeth Biddle Yarnall and the late Isabelle Ward Pollard; and to John Mass of Philadelphia.

Some individuals and organizations without whose aid the research for this study could not have been accomplished are due particular thanks. They are:

In Pennsylvania: Nancy J. Halli and the Historical Society of Pennsylvania; Rosemary B. Phillips and Rita M. Moore and the Chester County Historical Society; Anna Coxe Toogood and Mark Frazier Lloyd and the Germantown Historical Society; Sandra L. Bullock and the Delaware County Historical Society, Inc.; Isabel W. Pons and the Annie Halenbake Ross Library of Lock Haven; Mr. and Mrs. David L. Reed of the United Methodist Home, Lewisburg; Albert W. Fowler and the Friends Historical Library, Swarthmore College; Judith Diehl of Shippensburg State College; Samuel J. Dornsife and Rebecca L. Huss of Williamsport; Richard L. Arnold of Carlisle; Roger W. Moss Jr. and the staff of The Athenaeum, Philadelphia; Sandra M. Matt and the Lancaster County Historical Society; Robert F. Looney and The Free Library of Philadelphia.

In New Jersey: Gail Greenberg and the Camden County Historical Society; Carl L. West and the Cumberland County Historical Society; Mrs. Joseph W. Hahle and the Historical Society of Riverton, Inc.; Zara Cohan of Kean College, Newark.

In North Carolina: William B. Bushong, Charlotte V. Brown, and the entire staff of the "Architects and the Builders in North Carolina" project; Carmine A. Prioli of North Carolina State University; Mattie Russell, Curator Emeritus of Manuscripts, Duke University Library.

In Alabama: Milo B. Howard of the State Department of Archives and History; Robert D. Thorington of Montgomery.

In South Carolina: Charles E. Lee and the staff of the Department of Archives and History; and the late Walter Petty of Columbia.

In the remaining states: Almon J. Durkee, State Architect, Lansing, Michigan; Dorothy Sheehans, Coordinator of Special Services, St. Peter Hospital, St. Peter, Minnesota; Mildred Askell, Hallock Medical Library, Middletown, Connecticut; Mrs. Ina May McAdams, Austin, Texas.

For genealogy: Mr. and Mrs. Ralph T. Sloan, Media, Pennsylvania; Anna E. Baker Thompson and Ewing J. Harris, Bolivar, Tennessee; Martha C. Adams, State Library, Nashville, Tennessee.

The final preparation of the manuscript for this work would have been impossible without the skill with the mysterious computer of Linda S. Stegall and Pamela J. Purcell, to whom the writer is unrepayably indebted.

CHAPTER I

The Social Context

Every art technique has a social context. As society changes techniques change, along with the media and the modes of recording experience. So a style becomes an index to the structure of contemporary consciousness and to the prevailing attitude toward experience in the contemporary world.

Wylie Sypher   *Four Stages of Renaissance Style*

Before the end of George Washington's first term as President of the United States, the traditional eighteenth-century bases of economic and social Estate had begun to erode under the impact of the technological revolution. Alexander Hamilton's *Report on Manufactures* of 1791 was a tacit admission that the days when wealth and status were determined by "real" property were over. Throughout the Federalist period, repeated attempts were made to incorporate a rising aristocracy of industry and commerce into the Jeffersonian dream of an agrarian America, but the War of 1812 revealed Jefferson's idyll as utopian romance.[1]

After the close of that war, after 1815, the rate of change in the social environment of the United States increased so sharply that the constitutions of the original thirteen states rapidly became obsolete and had to be revised or rewritten. Massachusetts, recognizing that her statutes had been formulated by and for a society that no longer existed, began their revision in 1820. By 1849 the constitutions of all thirteen original states had been rewritten. Only minor adjustments were made by the slaveholding states, for they remained largely agrarian, and a dominant minority of their citizens continued to look upon the values of pretechnological society as an ideal. This ideological split between the North and the South threatened the unity of the United States, and some resolution was imperative if they were to continue as an effective political entity. The Civil War was that resolution, a climax and conclusion to fifty turbulent years, 1815–1865, during which the nation had reformed both its written and unwritten laws, discarded many of its old values, and begun to build a new social context.

The foremen of this rebuilding came from every walk of life, were various and diverse in their interests, and often neither knew nor knew of one another. The most influential, however, were those most in the public eye or ear or pocketbook: Andrew Jackson, Nicholas Biddle, Horace Mann, Francis Cabot Lowell, Dorothea Lynde Dix, Andrew Jackson Downing, Horatio Greenough, Ralph Waldo Emerson. All these were profoundly convinced of the unique qualities of the United States and its mission to display those qualities in politics, finance, education, industry, institutional care, architecture, and philosophy. Because of that conviction, they—and many others of like mind if less fame—helped turn the focus of American culture upon itself, contending that there could be, *should* be, an American way of life, differing from, if derived from, its European heritage. Their words and actions changed the economic and social environment of the United States: the "frontier" politics of Jackson, the speculative finance of Biddle, the educational systems of Mann, the industrial organization of Lowell, the crusading philanthropy of Dix, the practical aesthetics of Downing, the liberal parochialism of Greenough, and the creative eclecticism of Emerson.

Of these, Downing and Emerson had the greatest influence on the course of architecture in the United States. Both men promoted creative eclecticism as the method whereby Americanization of the nation's culture could be achieved. Downing transmitted an Americanized version of the Romantic Picturesque through his popular books, adapting the methods of Uvedale Price, Humphrey Repton, Thomas Rickman, and Richard Payne Knight to the local peculiarities of the nation and giving reasons for the changes he made in these English sources. Emerson's medium was the lecture platform, where he was supreme. It was said of Emerson, "He was a follower of none, an original borrower from all,"[2] because of his happy assimilation of all that the past had to offer, transposing it for the vernacular culture of the United States.

Architecture in all periods of rapid socioeconomic change tends to be revivalistic. The architectural forms and symbols of the immediately preceding period are associated with a way of life whose values have become partially, or wholly, invalid. A new architecture cannot emerge until a new way of life, with its new values, has stabilized and identified its own particular forms and symbols. Random and disconnected elements of a new architectural vocabulary may appear and be employed in the transitional period, but there is not enough grammar—enough generally accepted criteria—to put them together coherently. Hence, the architect turns back to the forms and symbols of earlier periods whose values he supposedly knows, or about which he knows so little that they can be interpreted to fit his needs.

In 1815 the values of Classical and Renaissance civilization, and the architectural styles that reflected them, were supposedly fixed and understood. Understanding of the Middle Ages was, however, casual and highly personal, influenced by the writings of such men as John Carter, Paul Decker, and Batty Langley, and its architectural forms and symbols were ideal for personal reinterpretation. Revivals of the Classical, Renaissance, and Medieval styles had appeared in Europe almost a century earlier, coincident with the first social disruptions of the technological revolution. When these fashions were transposed to the United States, the results were never wholly satisfactory. Imported European designs did not take into account the functional demands of the American citizen. Even hybrid styles—like the Anglo-Italian—did not, in their European form, fit the needs of life in the United States. The American architect-builder was faced with a paradox. He was asked to adapt European prototypes to his local environment, incorporating such new inventions and materials as his clients demanded for economy or creature comfort, without so altering the visual aspect of the buildings that their associative values were lost or obscured.

Attempts to resolve this paradox resulted in what has been called "eclecticism," wherein a functional core—based on contemporary demands and utilizing contemporary technology—was enclosed in a shell of some historical style, or mixture of styles. The eclectic architect was often well aware that the forms and symbols of this shell had no sound value relationship to his own environment, and concentrated his attention on the solution of core problems, applying the visual elements of the shell with a casual, sometimes careless, hand. The failure of European models to satisfy American needs initiated a struggle for native expression, and many contemporary observers were aware of this struggle and hopeful of its outcome.

From the turn of the century a succession of essayists and orators had encouraged progress toward an American way of design, not only of buildings but also of their furnishings and the development of their grounds. During the 1840s, Andrew Jackson Downing, Horatio Greenough, and Ralph Waldo Emerson—each appealing to a different sector of the American public, but all having complementary views of the need for "Americanization"—began to exert strong influence on taste in the United States. By the decade of the 1850s, their effect on architectural criticism was extensive. The *Atlantic Monthly* for January 1858, in an article entitled "Notes on Domestic Architecture," made the following analysis:

> But whether we are content or not, it is evident that all hope of improvement lies in the tendency, somewhat noticeable of late, to the abnegation of exotic styles and graces. We have survived the Parthenon pattern, and there seems to be some prospect that we shall outlive the Gothic Cottage. Even the Anglo-Italian villa has seen its palmiest days apparently, and exhausted most of its variations. We are in an extremely chaotic state just now, but there seems to be an inclination toward more rational ways, at least in the plans and general arrangement of houses. They are to be lived in, not looked at, and their beauty must grow naturally from their use as the flower from its stem, so that it shall not be possible to say where the one leaves off and the other begins.[3]

The last sentence of this passage is nothing less than an earlier and more florid expression of Louis Sullivan's epigram "form follows function."

It is significant that the subject of the *Atlantic* article was domestic architecture. A conviction that the private dwelling—in all its variations from cottage to mansion—should be the principal concern of architecture was widely held throughout the United States for most of the nineteenth century. In 1864 the *Continental Monthly* stated flatly: "To begin with, great public buildings will never form a distinguished feature of American architecture. It is to be pre-eminently a domestic style."[4] This judgment, a holdover from the pretechnological era, continued in force until the mid-1870s and restricted the vision of many practitioners to the narrow range of residential scale in both the form and decoration of buildings despite revolutionary advances in the design and construction of institutional, commercial, and industrial architecture. As a result, design criteria for the private dwelling were applied as general criteria to all architecture. Clients wished to have the cake of fitting visual style while eating it in convenient and comfortable surroundings. Consider a passage from Samuel Sloan's *The Model Architect* (1852):

> Let everyone arrange his dwelling so as to secure the greatest amount
> of convenience, and then exercise his judgement in decoration. We
> hold that, in a manner, each building is an independent being, and if it
> is consistent with itself, both internally, and as to its purpose, then no
> fault can be found with it on that score.[5]

This approach to architectural design was an example of that "in-
clination toward more rational ways" that the *Atlantic* found hopeful
in 1858.

The architectural criterion identified with such rationalism was
Convenience, and the word is so used in Sloan's passage. Downing,
in *Cottage Residences* (first issued in 1842, exactly ten years before
Sloan's book), had followed the terminology of English writers, such
as Richard Payne Knight and Uvedale Price, in calling this critical
element of design "Fitness or *usefulness*."[6] However, in defining the
term "Fitness," Downing used the word "convenience" in much the
same way Sloan was to use it, as in this example:

> *Fitness*, or use, is the first principle to be considered in all buildings.
> Those, indeed, who care very little for any other character in a dwell-
> ing, generally pride themselves upon the amount of convenience they
> have been able to realize in it; and nothing could be in worse taste
> than to embellish or decorate a dwelling-house which is wanting
> in comfort, since the beautiful is never satisfactory when not allied to
> the true.[7]

In his further explanation of "Fitness," Downing made it obvious
from the examples cited—relationship of rooms, location of service
areas, mechanical equipment (dumbwaiter, speaking tube, and rotary
pump)—that "Fitness," or "convenience," was equated with maxi-
mizing the ease and rapidity of circulation so as to ensure physical
comfort. By the time that Sloan composed *The Model Architect*, the
paramount criterion in architectural design was Convenience, while
Fitness had become the term used for Downing's earlier criterion,
"Purpose, *the beauty of propriety*."

This shift in terminology was indicative of the shift in social environment which had taken place between 1842 and 1852. Over that
decade the craze for speculation—which had brought about the financial crisis of 1837—revived, and began its climb toward a frenetic
climax in the mid-1850s. The speculator, so distrusted by Jefferson,
was encouraged by the fiscal policies of Andrew Jackson, and at the
close of his presidency paper wealth had opened the way to political
power and social status in a way formerly possible only for those who

owned "real" property. By mid-century, speculative wealth had far surpassed "real" property as the base of economic and social Estate in all sections of the country except the agrarian South.

Commercial speculation, in which area Philadelphia was preeminent, operated in large part on borrowed capital, and the rapid turnover of goods was vital to success. Hence the Yankee maxim "Time is Money" was spoken with true conviction, and a pecuniary evaluation of time spread to every level and function of society. D. Morier Evans, an English economist writing in 1859, summarized the European opinion of this American attitude:

> It may be here remarked that the Americans, beyond any other people on the face of the globe, "calculate" on the value of time—and time is an element of strength on which they largely depend. . . . In fact, knowing the resources of the country, and looking to their future development, they are in a manner and from a European point of view, reckless of the present.[8]

For the mid-nineteenth-century American, to "spend time" unremuneratively was a mark of either the very rich or the socially incompetent, and to "waste time" was downright sinful.

In commercial architecture, the criterion Convenience was equated with a demand for rapid and efficient circulation—of people, of goods, of information, of anything and everything. It required the optimization of space and the mechanization of services. This desire to reduce space-time in order to increase money-value produced the elevator, the telephone, and in time the skyscraper. In the private dwelling, Convenience was linked with physical comfort, as Downing had decreed: "Nothing could be in worse taste than to embellish or decorate a dwelling-house which is wanting in comfort." This forced American architects to consider the problems of storage, private hygiene, and food preparation in all types of residences, even the most modest, fifty years before the majority of their European counterparts. Along with convenient circulation, Americans demanded warmth, light, ventilation, services, and safety.

There was, however, another and equally important kind of "comfort," social comfort, the comfort of knowing that one's style of living was "fitting" to one's station in life. Thus, the comfort of what was comfortable might be determined by the "fitness" of what was fitting. By the 1850s, Downing's second criterion, "Purpose, *the beauty of propriety*" had been subdivided into Comfort and Fitness, and each of these two had absorbed a part of his third criterion,

"Style, *the beauty of form and sentiment*." This new definition of Comfort was highly personal, almost psychological, involving the way that an owner felt about the way the rest of society felt about his lifestyle, as exemplified by the architecture of his place of business and his dwelling. Fitness, however, was determined not by the owner but by the criteria of his society, and Comfort was in part dependent on that society's judgment as to the Fitness of his choice of architectural style. Hence, both Comfort and Fitness were dependent on that exercise of "judgement in decoration," which Sloan gave as the second factor in design consistency. "Decoration" meant the entire visual aspect of the building—its architectural details and their associated values, as well as furnishings and landscaping. In choosing that decoration, one had to balance a desire for convenience and comfort against the strict rules of fitness. Another passage from Sloan's *The Model Architect* gave warning of the risk one ran:

> A man's dwelling, at the present day, is not only an index of his wealth, but also of his character. The moment he begins to build his adopted style of living, the refinement of his taste, and the peculiarities of his judgement, are all laid bare for public inspection and criticism. And the public makes free use of this prerogative.[9]

The criterion of Fitness, as a judgment on the relation of lifestyle to socioeconomic status, is as old as human society, and in any relatively stable environment its tenets are seldom consciously thought about but are instinctively followed. When such an environment begins to change, however, what is "fitting" and what is "not fitting"— so comfortingly understood by everyone only a short time before— becomes disturbingly uncertain. There are no longer dependable signposts, visual ways of telling who is who, and until some new social arbiter redefines Fitness, it is determined by that factor in the environment which most directly confers status. After 1815 that factor in the United States was increasingly money. Almost any lifestyle and its architectural setting was fitting if one had the money to back it up; however, society demanded that the visual symbols accurately reflect the economic substance. Ostentatious simplicity was as much a violation of Fitness as spurious ostentation. The clerk should live in a Cottage, and for a manager a small Villa was proper, but the owner should own nothing less than a Mansion. Scale rather than decoration was the dominant factor, for the oldest of all symbolic equations, Size = Importance, was and still is the most universally understood. The new critical triad—*Convenience, Comfort,* and *Fitness*—had begun to replace the older Vitruvian triad, *Commodity*, *Firmness*, and *Delight*, at the time of Samuel Sloan's birth. By the time he entered practice, it was dominant. That the definitions of this new triad were ambiguous and conflicting bothered no one, for they exactly suited an environment whose values were ambiguous and conflicting. Eclecticism was the only possible approach to architecture in a society that demanded every modern convenience and comfort but was frightened of visible innovations that might overstep the bounds of fitness. Hence, Sloan was an eclectic, but a "creative eclectic"; his stylistic vocabulary was derivative, but his solutions to functional problems were often inventive and original. This was due not only to the accident of his birth and training, both of which inculcated a pragmatic approach to work and clients, but also to his talent for combining in his designs unusual Convenience with acceptable Comfort and Fitness.

CHAPTER II

1815–1850
Background and Training

Sloan, Samuel (T.)
  Born: March 7, 1815, Beaver Dam, Honeybrook Township, Chester
  County, Pennsylvania
  Died: July 19, 1884, Raleigh, Wake County, North Carolina

Samuel Sloan was born into an exciting time, just three months after the Battle of New Orleans. Andrew Jackson's triumphant ending to the long struggle for American independence raised the groundswell of national pride, which had been building since 1783, into a wave of expansive self-confidence that did not break until the financial crisis of 1857. Sloan was born on the front of that wave, and its crest in the decade of the 1850s was his crest. Its rush and turbulence, raw power, and noisy advance became his way of life.

He was born into an exciting place. Beaver Dam, midway between Philadelphia and Lancaster, lay alongside the Conestoga branch of the great turnpike, where westward traffic grew heavier every year after 1815. The wheelwrights and carpenters had more work than they could do building or repairing wagons for people heading to the Ohio. Up along Conestoga Creek they had already made a name that would outlast their wagons by a hundred years. There was a mood of high expectation and optimism. If a man was clever with his hands and his head, he could get on.

Samuel's grandfather, another Samuel, had come to Chester County from Worcester, Massachusetts, before 1760, to be near relatives and friends. These were Protestant Irish from Antrim and Londonderry who had been settling in the southeastern counties of Pennsylvania since the early eighteenth century. By the time Samuel's father, William, married there was a loose network of Sloan relatives and in-laws stretching from Philadelphia to Harrisburg. William married into another widespread clan, the Kirkwoods, who were thickly settled in the Susquehanna Valley on both sides of the Pennsylvania-Maryland line. His bride, Mary Kirkwood, bore William Sloan four children, of which Samuel was the next to last.[1]

Many members of the dispersed Sloan clan were carpenters and cabinetmakers skilled in almost every aspect of the building trades. They were what the nineteenth century called "mechanics"—clever, inventive workmen who could turn their hands to any kind of construction. The Sloans followed in the apprentice-journeyman tradition of craft training, and their formal education was limited. The Kirkwoods, however, had a strong tradition of schooling, but Mary Sloan was not able to oversee the education of Samuel, for she died when he was no more than two or three years old.

William Sloan remarried immediately. His wife, Keziah Diffidiffy (or Diffenderffer), was a descendant of early German settlers in Lancaster County. It is recorded that the last of her four sons, Fletcher Sloan, was born in Lancaster in 1826 but raised in Hamilton Village, just west of Philadelphia. It is also recorded that Samuel was sent at an early age to his schooling and carpenter's apprenticeship in Lancaster. Since it is unlikely that he was sent back to Lancaster from Philadelphia, or that he left home before his sixth year, this move was probably made around 1821. That was the year in which William Sloan resettled his family in Hamilton Village, just west across the Schuylkill River from Penn's Great Town.[2]

The next certain record of Samuel Sloan is for the year 1833. He was then a journeyman carpenter of eighteen working on his first job in Philadelphia, the construction of new cell-blocks (Numbers 4, 5, and 6) at Eastern State Penitentiary. It was not steady work, for the supervising architect, John Haviland, had repeated disagreements with the commissioners, and when Haviland finally resigned in 1834, all construction at the penitentiary was suspended. Work was then in progress on additions to the hospital at the Philadelphia Almshouse, already called "Blockley," and Sloan hired on there until the job was completed in March 1835.[3]

In view of Sloan's later prominence as a designer of institutional buildings, this early experience with the construction of a prison and a hospital—and the opportunity to study firsthand the methods of John Haviland—may have been of major importance to his architec-

tural career. In any event, his experience at Eastern State and Blockley proved beneficial almost at once, for he was employed on the
construction for the new Department for the Insane of the Pennsylvania Hospital from the laying of its cornerstone on June 22, 1836,
until its completion on January 1, 1841. As the new Department
rose, so did Samuel Sloan's position of authority and professional
reputation.

In 1752 the Pennsylvania Hospital had been the first in America
to receive insane patients, and by 1830 overcrowding at the original
Insane Department in downtown Philadelphia had become a serious
problem. A new facility outside the city was proposed, and in 1832
the managers of the hospital purchased for its site a farm of 101 acres
lying between the West Chester and Haverford roads in Blockley
Township. Isaac Holden, a native of Manchester, England, who had
practiced as an architect and builder in Philadelphia since 1826, was
chosen Architect for the new building after a limited competition in
which both John Haviland and William Strickland participated. The
reason for Holden's choice remains a mystery; he was not well known
for institutional design, as was Haviland, nor was he so prominent an
architect as Strickland. His son, John Holden of Manchester, wrote
in 1895, "I do not remember ever hearing what model or systems he
studied, but I should hardly think he had any information beyond
what he could gather in America."[4]

When Holden returned to England in 1838, before the Department for the Insane was half completed, Samuel Sloan was made
"superintendent of work" and was responsible for the building's
completion. This was a position of unusual responsibility for a
twenty-three-year-old carpenter, and it is unlikely that he received it
without recommendations to which the Building Committee of the
Managers listened with respect. It is possible that Sloan was appointed by Holden himself, but it is more probable that he was recommended to the managers by the young alienist, Dr. Thomas S.
Kirkbride, who came to know Sloan over the five years that the department was in construction and who became his lifelong advocate,
patron, and friend.

Thomas Story Kirkbride, member of an old Quaker family whose
founder had come to America with William Penn, was only twenty-
nine years old in 1838, but he was already an acknowledged authority
on the care and treatment of the insane. After receiving his medical degree from the University of Pennsylvania in 1832, he had been resi-

dent physician first at the Friends Asylum for the insane and then the Insane Department of the Pennsylvania Hospital; in 1838 he had been in private practice for about a year. Kirkbride became acquainted with Sloan before the young carpenter was made superintendent of work at the rising new department. The background, training, and social position of the two men were so contrasting that it is difficult to explain the relationship which grew up between them. Their straightforward professional association is amply documented; Kirkbride was the principal source of the many hospital commissions that made Sloan an authority in hospital architecture. But the long and fulsome eulogies of Sloan which Kirkbride included in many of his books have a tone of personal pride, as if the doctor felt a sense of accomplishment in the architect's success. This may indeed have been the case, for the carpenter was not transformed into an architect without help. Sloan undoubtedly cultivated Kirkbride, for to step up quickly from craftsman to professional required support from someone of position and influence in Philadelphia. Kirkbride was most likely that someone.

The advantages were not all one-sided, however, for the young doctor also needed "someone," someone skilled in the building trades whose thinking had not been conditioned by traditional attitudes toward architectural design, someone young, bright, and trainable. Dr. Kirkbride had very decided, and radical, opinions about how hospitals for the insane should be built, and he wanted to see those ideas take physical form. The established architects of Philadelphia would be apt to smile at a young alienist who, stepping out of his own field, had ideas about buildings, but if Sloan—who obviously knew the practical side of his business—were encouraged to study, even supplied with the necessary funds, then in a short time he might be just the man.

Admittedly, this explanation of the Sloan-Kirkbride relationship is largely conjectural, but it is in character with the men and the succeeding events of their lives. From the thirty years of their professional collaboration, which began in 1851, came thirty-two hospitals for the insane, designed on the "Kirkbride system" of care and treatment. These earned for both men an international reputation. If Kirkbride looked on Sloan as, in part, his own creation, then his defensive pride in the architect's accomplishments is understandable. If Sloan appreciated that his rapid climb to success was due in large part to Kirkbride's help, then his loyalty to the "Kirkbride system," long after it had been attacked and partially discredited, is explainable. The two men were so entirely opposite in most of their attitudes and interests that it must have been a matter of strong mutual respect and self-interest that made it possible for them to collaborate for thirty years.

In the early 1840s, Samuel Sloan married Mary Pennell, the daughter of James Pennell, whose big yellow house stood just across the West Chester road from the rising Department for the Insane.[5] Two of her brothers, Nathan and Jonathan, worked as carpenters, first with and then under Sloan, on its construction. Pennells had lived just west of Philadelphia, along the creeks that ran down the Schuylkill, since the days of William Penn. As the city expanded around their holdings, the family turned from farming and milling to carpentering, building, and the development of their property. It is likely that the land in West Hamiltonville, upon which William Sloan settled in 1821, was a part of James Pennell's holdings, for it was in sight of his homestead and only a short distance from the site of the new Department for the Insane.[6] It is also very likely, both families being in the building trades, that mutual interests and neighborliness had made for friendly relations between the Sloans and the Pennells by the time Samuel came from Lancaster to join his family.

The exact date of Mary Pennell's marriage to Samuel Sloan is uncertain; however, its general date can be inferred from other evidence. He was first listed by *McElroy's Philadelphia Directory* in 1844:

"Sloan, Samuel. Carp., George ab 10th Sch 8 ab Cherry"
Sloan, Samuel, carpenter, George [Sansom] above [West of] 10th Street, home Schuylkill 8th [15th] Street, above [North of] Cherry Street

Sloan must have moved into center-city Philadelphia in late 1843 or early 1844 for the *Directory* to give these addresses. The listing "Carp." was the equivalent of today's contractor or builder, and as this was not accompanied by a listing of "cabinetmaker" we can assume that the business address was for an office rather than a shop. Thus, in the two years between the completion of the Department for the Insane and *McElroy's* first listing, Sloan had moved across the line from hired craftsman to hiring contractor. Throughout his early career, Sloan celebrated each improvement in his professional status or private fortune with a change of address. He moved his residence three times between 1844 and 1850, each time to a more fashionable location. Directory listings, census records, and real-estate transactions are almost the only sure documentation of Sloan between 1841 and 1849. It must be assumed that their dates correlate with events for which no other records have yet been found. Thus, his marriage seems to have occurred in late 1842 or early 1843, and his first child, a son, Ellwood Pennell Sloan, was born in 1846.[7]

It is regrettable that these eight years of Samuel Sloan's life are so sparsely documented, for they are the years when he evolved from builder into architect. There is not even a hint in Sloan's own writing, or the reports of others about him, as to the stages of this professional evolution. He retained the *Directory* listing "Carp." until 1851, by which time he had been in full architectural practice for two years. He could have apprenticed himself to an established architect, but no record of such an apprenticeship has been found, and it was not consistent with Sloan's character to have done so after having been in full charge of construction—effectively Isaac Holden's associate—at the Department for the Insane. The more likely assumption is that he was self-taught, with the help and direction of Thomas Kirkbride.

Sloan's mature attitude toward the practice of architecture was greatly influenced by his association, as a young journeyman carpenter, with John Haviland and Isaac Holden, both of whom had received their professional training in England. His observation of and experience with these men—particularly his advantageous relationship with Holden—initiated in him a high regard for English practices and a corresponding suspicion of American architects.[8] This incipient prejudice was reinforced by the taste of his patron, Thomas S. Kirkbride, who supported Sloan's metamorphosis from carpenter into architect. Dr. Kirkbride's library, from which Sloan probably self-educated himself, contained works on architecture and architectural engineering by both English and American authors, but it would seem, from the evidence of Sloan's own publications, that Kirkbride directed his protégé's attentions primarily to the English examples. In his first book, *The Model Architect* (1852), Sloan referred exclusively, with one exception, to English sources.[9] The exception was Robert Dale Owen's *Hints on Public Architecture* (1849).[10]

Throughout *The Model Architect* there are overtones of contempt for the work of American architects, together with a strong, emotional conviction as to the uniqueness of the United States. In the "Preface to the First Volume" of *The Model Architect*, Sloan dismissed earlier publications by American architects:

> It is true that much has been written and read on the subject, and a great number of handsomely engraved designs on fine paper have been presented to the public, threatening annihilation to the architect's bill, but no one knows so well as he who has trusted these promises, the difference between a beautiful picture and a comfortable dwelling. In short such works as have come under notice are quite inadequate to the end proposed. They inculcate very false ideas in the general reader, and give to the builder no new or valuable information. They are much better ornaments for the centre table, than as guides to a practical man.[11]

And in "Concluding Remarks" of Volume 2, he wrote:

> A difficulty encountered during the entire progress of the work has been the fact that the author was without precedents to guide him. American works on architecture are few in number, and no works on American architecture have yet been written—we have been, and still are dependent upon foreign publications for hints and suggestions upon the subject. As works of art, and literature, many of these are perfect in themselves, but are not adapted to American taste and American habits. Our buildings are necessarily, and, in some respects to our loss, unlike those erected in European countries. We are unwilling to expend either the time or the money required to erect similar edifices. The American architect therefore, often to his regret, is compelled to arrange his plans and project his designs accordingly. By the circulation of works upon the subject adapted to our tastes and wants, this spirit must inevitably undergo a change, and every architect owes it to himself and his profession to hasten such a time by every means in his power. It was to supply, in some measure, this deficiency in our national literature, as well as to lend his influence to correcting the prevailing abuses in the noble art, that the author has ventured to turn aside from the daily routine of his profession. It may be that others will follow the example, and we shall soon possess valuable American works on the art of building in our own country.[12]

It would seem that Sloan felt himself to be unique in both his championship of an "American architecture" and his presentation of an "American work." Such was not, in fact, the case. Owen Biddle, in

The Young Carpenter's Assistant (1805), had advertised his book as "especially suited for American use" because there was "a style of building in the United States." The 1833 edition of Biddle's work, expanded with a new introduction and designs by John Haviland, was issued in Philadelphia, as was Haviland's own *The Builder's Assistant* (1818, 1819, 1821), Thomas U. Walter and John Jay Smith's *Two Hundred Designs for Cottages and Villas* (1846), and the 1848 edition of John Hall's book of designs "adapted to the style of building in the United States." Sloan cannot have been ignorant of these "precedents," because Kirkbride's library contained a number of them, and *The Model Architect* evidences dependence on such works. All of Sloan's books elaborated on, but did not change, the format and organization of the American pattern-book as it had developed from Asher Benjamin to John Warren Rich, and his first essays on historic styles derive from the writing of Minard Lefever and particularly Louisa C. Tuthill, whose *History of Architecture* was published by Lindsay & Blakiston of Philadelphia in 1848.[13] Sloan needed little or no instruction in construction techniques, but all of his early works—both buildings and writing—depended for their visual style and historical symbols on existing sources. This was particularly true of his first architectural commission, the public buildings of Delaware County, Pennsylvania.

On May 14, 1849, the Commissioners of Delaware County advertised a competition for the design of public buildings at the new county seat of Media, offering a premium of fifty dollars for "suitable plans" of a "Court House" and giving a program for its design.[14] The premium and the contract for the job were awarded on June 18 to Samuel Sloan; later the design for a prison (or jail) was added to the contract. This first commission was by no means a trivial one, for Thomas Ustick Walter had considered it important enough to submit an entry in the competition. If the Commissioners could choose from the work of recognized architects like Walter, why were the designs of an unknown builder selected? Were Sloan's designs so excellent that their choice was obvious? To judge from surviving illustrations and records, this was not the case, for these describe two very commonplace buildings that became obsolete within a decade and had to be remodeled. What recommended such buildings to the Commissioners? To use their own word, they were the most "suitable"; suitable for the urgent needs which the Commissioners did not, indeed could not, express in the advertisement of their competition. Sloan demonstrated with this his first commission a professional characteristic which he was to retain for the remainder of his career: an unusual sensitivity to the unstated, often unrecognized, needs of his clients.

There are in the papers of Thomas U. Walter, at the Philadelphia Athenaeum, nine diary entries and ten letters, covering the period May 26 to July 30, 1849, which deal with the Delaware County buildings.[15] They show that Walter fully expected to receive the commission for the Courthouse and that he had completed a major part of the drawings for it by May 28. However, on June 18 one of Walter's friends in Delaware County, John P. Crozer, wrote to him:

> Much to my surprise our Commissioners have adopted some other plan of a Courthouse, offered them. I know not by whom. I called on them the day after I saw you and fully expected your plan would be adopted. I am mortified at having recommended you to submit drafts etc. I did then suppose I might have some influence with the Commissioners, but it appears I was mistaken.

The reason for the about-face of the Commissioners is partially explained in a letter from one of them, Mark Bartleson, to Walter, July 9:

> At the close of our session held for the purpose of receiving plans of Courthouse (in which I endeavored, but without effect to secure the adoption of yours), a majority of the Board came to the conclusion they would accept the plan of Sloan with certain modifications, and as I was about to pass through the City, on my way home, it was given me in charge, to be returned to Sloan, with directions for the contemplated alterations; which after consideration I declined giving, a question having arisen in my mind, with regard to the propriety of suggesting alterations previous to the final and formal adoption of the plan, I accordingly merely directed that he should complete his plan (it being in an unfinished stage) and present it at our next meeting. Whilst the plans were yet in my possession I called on Mr. Sunderland, as a practical builder, to obtain his opinion on its merits, upon which occasion he informed me he had been watching the papers expecting our advertisement for plans to meet his eye as he had thought of offering one himself. I informed him you had furnished a plan that I preferred, but that it had been rejected by the board and that of Sloan likely to be adopted; upon his enquiring if it would be in order to present his plan at the next meeting of the Board, I referred him to

Caleb I. Cope for information, he being in the majority. My object in
giving him any encouragement was that of introducing him to the
Board in order to secure his services in carrying out your plan of
prison if one should be furnished and adopted, but that unguarded
expression made to my friend Caleb came . . . [illegible] frustrating
my plan and proving as prejudicial to yourself as to him, for there has
been a strong effort made to force Sloan and his plan on us.[16]

Exactly who was "forcing" Sloan on the board cannot be determined; however, of the Commissioners of Delaware County, one was
Edmund Pennell, a relative of Sloan's father-in-law, and another was
Caleb I. Cope, who became one of Sloan's most frequent clients
throughout the decade of the 1850s. Bartleson's reference to Walter's
design for a prison is helpful in clearing up another puzzle regarding
the Media buildings. There was no mention of a prison in the original May 14 advertisement by the Commissioners; a "Court House"
only was required. Walter's diary has entries from June 12 through
July 21 which show that he assumed he would receive the commission for a prison at Media, for he completed the drawings of it and
even wrote construction specifications. Apparently, Bartleson hoped
to divide the project into two parts, giving the prison to Walter.
Among the Walter papers there is a drawing in pencil and watercolor
of his prison's front elevation; however, it is not the elevation of
the first jail at Media, as that is documented elsewhere, so Walter's
friends failed to secure any part of the commission for him.
    In that spring of 1849, Sloan needed work desperately, for his sec-
ond son, Howard, had been born on April 25, and at thirty-four he
was, by the standards of this time, approaching middle age without
having established a recognized practice. He needed not only work,
but work which would command public attention, and his talent for
seeing beyond the wording of a design program to the real reasons
behind a building's commissioning decided the Delaware County
Commissioners. They needed an "official" building, understandable
as such to all the public. They needed it cheaply and they needed it
immediately, not a score of years later, for they had a serious problem
on their hands. Removal of the county seat from Chester to Media
had been strongly opposed; feelings were high, and there was considerable bitterness over the court action that forced approval of the
new site. A fixed investment had to be established at Media before
litigation to reverse the court's decision was begun. Hence the very
short time of one month for the competition. The incumbent admin-

istration, which had initiated the move to Media, had no wish to make the new public buildings a weapon in the hands of their opponents, so any design that would waste either time or money was out of the question. Despite all these reservations, the building had to be a public monument that satisfied the architectural prejudices of the day. Samuel Sloan's resolution of these needs, which his clients could not publicly express, rather than his solution for the stated requirements of the building program, made it possible for him to win out over more distinguished architects. His designs were convenient and based on accepted precedent; they were reasonably comfortable, and entirely fitting in scale, visual style, and associative symbols. (See Catalogue, entry No. 1.)[17]

A question arises, with this first commission, as to Sloan's stature as a designer, which must be answered for any fair evaluation of his contributions to American architecture. It was a question that worried Sloan himself. He was justifiably proud of his skill as a constructor, of his instinct for functional solutions to involved operational problems, of his mechanical inventiveness; but there remained the question "Were these talents called into play by the stimulus of his client's ideas rather than from his own creative resources?" Sloan recognized his dependence on client stimulus, and it was one of the reasons for his conviction—which became increasingly stronger over the years—that there was a basic flaw in the architectural theory of his time and place. Why was there no distinctive "American Style"? Why did American architects, himself included, feel compelled to follow the dictates of European taste? In 1868, Sloan gave voice to his frustration with American architects in the *Architectural Review*, calling them "mere copyists of European models, mere reproducers of other men's ideals, formed for other purposes than those we have to deal with, here in America."[18] He attributed the inability of himself and his peers to create an "American" vocabulary to a lack of education. In the same 1868 article, he referred derisively to "what are called 'American Architects'" thus: "Ignorant of all that is required to enable them to venture boldly on a new path; without the light and experience which education gives; it is not to be wondered at, that their mental faculties are enthralled by the fear of failure."

Sloan recognized from the outset of his career that architectural inventiveness in the United States lagged far behind that in commerce, industry, medicine, and public education. Hence, he turned to the leaders in those fields—actively seeking them out as clients—

and used whatever tools the technology of his time made available to satisfy their building demands. Fortunately, throughout the first decade of his architectural career, Sloan's clients were men of independent, original, and strong ideas—examples of the thrusting, inquiring personalities who were reforming the cultural context of the United States.

CHAPTER III

1850–1851
Early Practice

A forceful and original personality assuredly characterized Andrew McCalla Eastwick, whose commission for a palatial villa founded Sloan's practice in Philadelphia. In the late winter of 1850, Eastwick had just returned from a six-year stay in Russia, where the firm of Harrison, Winans & Eastwick was completing its contract to build locomotives and rolling stock for the Saint Petersburg–Moscow Railway.[1] His partner, Joseph H. Harrison Jr., came home two years later—decorated by the czar with the Order of Saint Anne—to rejoin Eastwick in expanding one of Philadelphia's early heavy industries. The Russian contract had made millionaires of both men.

As was only fitting, Eastwick commemorated his rise in economic estate with the building of a "substantial dwelling." As the site for that dwelling he purchased the property on the west bank of the Schuykill River which had been the farm of the eighteenth-century naturalist John Bartram. This purchase alarmed Philadelphia society, for Bartram's Gardens were closely associated with the city's history, and it was feared that Eastwick would destroy them. He made it known, however, that he would carefully preserve the old Bartram house and what remained of the naturalist's botanical collection. Then he surprised everyone by choosing for his architect an unknown young man, Samuel Sloan.

How and why did Sloan receive the commission, one that all the established architects of Philadelphia were angling for? A partial answer is given by a newspaper article, written after "Bartram Hall" (as Eastwick named his villa) burned in the 1890s:

About a year later Eastwick returned from Russia, and, as it was known that he intended to build a new residence, an architect, then unknown in the city, and ascertaining the spot where he proposed to erect it, drew up, without consulting Mr. Eastwick, a plan and came with it unasked to him, requesting that he examine it. Eastwick, in a pleasant and courteous way, told the architect that it was unnecessary to examine it, as he had in mind several houses he had seen in the old world, after some of which he intended to pattern his own.

He was finally induced, however, to look at the plan, and in an off-hand way indicated his objections to it, giving the architect a sufficient knowledge of his ideas to draw a more satisfactory plan, which came so near Eastwick's ideal that his visitor was engaged as architect of the building destroyed yesterday, which was built by the well-known Philadelphia builder, John Stewart. This building made the architect's reputation. He designed another almost on the same model for the Abbotts, which is still standing near the Queen Lane Reservoir. The Board of Education soon after adopted his plans for several school buildings, which were on lines entirely new at that time.[2]

Like all good salesmen, Sloan first sold himself to Eastwick and then displayed his talent for translating a client's ideas and values into architecture. Although Eastwick was attracted by the young architect's push and ability, he was a practical man and arranged that Sloan be associated in the construction of the house with an older, experienced builder, John S. Stewart. As it happened, this was a great service to Sloan, for Stewart was his ideal complement, so much so that the two men became partners in 1852, setting up the firm of Sloan & Stewart.

As to the why of the commission, there is only assumption. There were similarities in the background of client and architect that could have drawn the two men together. Both Sloan and Eastwick had graduated into professional life from the ranks of skilled craftsmen; Eastwick began as a machinist, Sloan as a carpenter. Both were hard-working, ambitious, largely self-educated, had much the same goals, and so could understand one another. It is noticeable that a majority of Sloan's large commercial and residential commissions were executed for just such men. With them he was very much at home. He understood their pride of achievement, their desire for recognition, and most important, their business methods.

A review of Bartram Hall in *Gleason's Pictorial* for January 7, 1854, estimated its cost at $50,000 and lauded it as "unequaled by any other structure in the country."[3] Surviving photographs and drawings show a building in the general style of an Anglo-Italian villa, but with a greater admixture of medieval detail than was found in similar designs by John Notman or Richard Upjohn. Sloan called it a "Norman Villa" and made it grander in scale than any of its predecessors of the villa type. Its size, the luxury of its appointments, and the beauty of its site were repeatedly commented on in periodicals of the day. However, little mention was made of its plan or its exterior appearance. In the 1850s, this was a compliment, for it indicated how well the design met the criteria of Convenience, Comfort, and Fitness. (Plate 1.)

It was fitting that Eastwick's residence be big, for he was a "big man" in industry and society. Likewise, the comfort suitable for such a client was luxury, so luxurious appointments were necessary. That the plan of the villa was convenient was assumed; Eastwick would not have accepted anything less. The interior circulation of Bartram Hall was clear and logical, the ventilation and exposures of its rooms were well thought out, and its service areas were sensibly located.

PLATE 1. A Norman Villa, *The Model Architect*, Vol. 1, Design X, Plate XXXIX, p. 48 (Reproduced with permission of the Library of Fine Arts, University of Pennsylvania)

The same approach characterized the site plan and the location of outbuildings, particularly the attention to drainage, which was unusual for the times. (See Catalogue, entry No. 2.)

Sloan expended his best efforts on Eastwick's villa, for it was his professional debut in Philadelphia. As such, it was a notable success. The industrial and mercantile aristocracy of the city found Bartram Hall exactly to its taste and at once took up the young architect. He began to receive large residential commissions early in 1851, and these continued to be a major part of his practice until 1862. Bartram Hall also brought him to the attention of Philadelphia's speculative developers, who, finding him just the kind of man with whom they could do business, made him their favored architect. Many of these early clients sat on building committees—for their churches, their charities, their city, and their state—so the way to public and institutional commissions was opened to Sloan. Before either the Delaware County public buildings or Bartram Hall was completed, and before he had changed his directory listing from "carpenter" to "architect," Sloan had a large practice.

The success of Bartram Hall had much to do with this sudden popularity, but simple luck—being in the right place at the right time—gave Sloan a chance to exploit the contacts which that success brought. The executives and entrepreneurs for whom he worked would not have become clients had it not been for a coincident financial boom that had begun with the close of the Mexican War in 1848 and ran until the Panic of 1857. In those nine years, Philadelphia greatly expanded its urban area and largely rebuilt its older sections. Sloan's practice could not have been started at a more opportune time. By the spring of 1851 he had received commissions for forty houses, a commercial block, a church, and seven public schools.

Residential commissions, which were the backbone of his early practice, came from two sources: developers who were building for speculation, and executives who were building for pleasure. By 1850 the steady westward drift of middle- and upper-class residences away from center-city Philadelphia had jumped the Schuylkill River, and speculative builders were hurrying to develop the open land around suburban communities such as Blockley and Hamilton Village. Two of the more forward-looking of these developers were Nathaniel B. Browne and Samuel A. Harrison, whose aim it was to create an upper-class residential suburb in "West Philadelphia."[4] Both men chose Sloan as their principal architect. The scores of houses they personally commissioned and the many clients they directed to him—for churches and commercial and public buildings, as well as residences—made him responsible for a large part of West Philadelphia's townscape, which rapidly became one of large suburban mansions sprinkled among terraces and rows of less pretentious houses. As Browne and Harrison hoped, the section did attract Philadelphia's commercial aristocracy, and it remained a fashionable address until the middle of the 1870s, when an increase of cheaper houses, incident to the Centennial of 1876, caused the more prominent families to take up their westward trek along the "Main Line" of the Pennsylvania Railroad. (See Catalogue, entries No. 4, 10–15, 48, 49, 63, 66.)

The same families who commissioned suburban mansions west across the Schuylkill River also built country villas east across the Delaware River in New Jersey. This fashion created whole communities at one time, their sites determined either by the route of the Camden & Amboy Railroad or by docking facilities along the river. Biddles, Waltons, and Clothiers built "cottages" into which they moved their entire households for the summer months, boated on the Delaware, bred racehorses, and played at gentleman farming. Sloan was a favored architect of this migration, and until 1857 it brought him a steady stream of clients. He began in 1851 with the design of "Riverton," a summer colony on the Jersey riverbank just north of Camden for which he did a town plan, a pier, and a line of large residences fronting the water. (Plate 2.)

A large plan of Riverton issued by its developers in the mid-1850s shows a gridiron system of streets inland from a curving riverfront drive. The nine riverfront lots are already occupied by villas of the development's financial backers. The remainder of the town, extending eastward to the line of the Camden & Amboy Railroad, is laid off in residential blocks, each divided into six lots. Two blocks, in the southeastern section near the railroad station, are intended as a commercial center. The properties already sold are identified with the name of the owner, and the riverfront villas are shown in small elevation drawings.[5]

An 1890 plan of Riverton, in bird's-eye perspective, shows the riverfront villas in more detail and documents the success of the development, for the town is almost completely built up and has doubled in size after forty years.[6] Of the original riverfront villas designed by Sloan, five were essentially identical—large, square build-

PLATE 2. Riverton, New Jersey, 1890. Lithograph by Otto Koehler
(Reproduced with permission of the Riverton Library, Riverton, New Jersey)

ings of two stories, in no particular style, with many windows and deep front porches stretching across their entire river elevations. Two residences, those of W. C. Biddle and Rodman Wharton, were more pretentious, Wharton's being the only one of brick and brownstone, and Biddle's being the largest.[7] One villa (No. 207 Bank Avenue) showed distinct reflections of Bartram Hall, which is not surprising because many of Sloan's early clients specifically requested designs like Eastwick's villa. The Abbott family asked for, and got, an outright copy, which was built near the Queen Lane Reservoir in Germantown. (See Catalogue, Division II, No. 3.)

In the city itself, Sloan's commissions for 1851 began with nine town dwellings on Logan Square and a commercial block of four stores for Samuel A. Harrison. The townhouse in all of its forms (rows, double villas, or detached mansions) and the mercantile store, or "loft," were building types to which Sloan made significant contributions. The reason was characteristic: their building programs were highly restricted by site or budget or both. Sloan thrived on restrictions and was at his most inventive when trying to overcome them or turn them to advantage. The restriction common to a majority of both townhouses and loft buildings was their site. This was usually a deep, narrow lot with only front and rear exposures. Such a site engendered problems of internal lighting, ventilation, circulation of people and/or goods, and rapid evacuation in the event of a fire. Sloan's general solution for all these problems was the elimination of all but the most necessary internal partitions, replacing them with sliding doors that retracted into stub walls (for the house) or sliding partitions running in metal tracks (for stores). Both doors and partitions were extensively glazed whenever possible. He also increased the window area of both front and rear elevations to the maximum possible limit within a given structural system, often doing violence to the purported "style" of the exterior unless restrained by the client. (Plate 3A & B.)

This concept appeared, tentatively, with his first commissions, but it developed rapidly, and within a few years his plans for townhouses were so flexible that the entire first floor could be thrown open from front to back. In commercial buildings, his sliding, glazed partitions made for easy rearrangement of interior spaces, borrowed light deep into the building, and reduced the hazard of entrapment by fire in interior halls or rooms. The cast-iron elevations of his stores often became that "cage of metal and glass" which was expanded into three dimensions by the later Chicago School. An application of his inte-

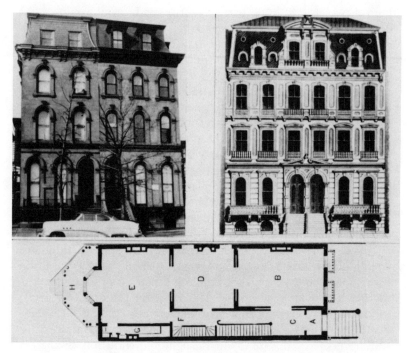

PLATE 3 A & B. Facade treatments and plan for rowhouse design.
Engravings from "Two Adjoining City Residences,"
The Architectural Review, October 1868
(Reproduced with permission of the Library of Fine Arts,
University of Pennsylvania)

rior partition system to the design of school buildings won for Sloan a long series of public school commissions, first in Philadelphia, then throughout the state of Pennsylvania and eventually the United States.

Once again he was in the right place at the right time. In the autumn of 1850, Philadelphia needed a new, safe design for public school buildings, standardized so that it could be repeated frequently. It needed that design right away (in essence, the unexpressed requirements were identical with those of the Delaware County Commissioners in 1849). The city had been made sharply aware of its overcrowded and substandard schools by a disastrous fire that destroyed the North-Eastern Grammar School on July 8, 1850. For two years preceding this fire, the Controllers of the Public Schools for the City and County of Philadelphia had warned of dangerous conditions, but their requests for new buildings had been repeatedly turned down. In 1849 the president of the Controllers, George M. Wharton, resigned in protest, and as a private citizen he brought such pressure to bear on the City Council that an appropriation for new construction was passed. Nine new school houses were hastily commissioned, their contracts awarded to supporters of the incumbent administration.

Wharton felt that such patronage, in this instance, was criminal. He turned for support to the newly formed Friends of Public Education, of which he was a charter member and whose First National Convention had been held in Philadelphia (October 17–19, 1845). The convention had been called by a group of dedicated teachers and school administrators who were alarmed at the disorganized growth of public school systems and the lack of national standards for their buildings and equipment. Although thirty-one states had been represented, 97 of the 202 delegates were from Philadelphia.

Wharton was reelected President of the Controllers on June 30, 1850. Less than a week later, the North-Eastern fire made school houses a major political issue, and he was able to form a committee to examine the standards of design and construction for Philadelphia's schools. As a result of his committee's work, "Samuel Sloan, a well known and efficient architect, was sent to other cities to study school architecture, and many of the buildings erected from 1850 to 1854 were probably from his designs."[8] Once again, the question arises, "Why was Sloan chosen?" He had no experience in the design of schoolhouses; there is no record that even as a carpenter he was ever employed in their construction. However, it was not by chance that the adjective "efficient" was applied to him. He had demonstrated to his early clients a talent for efficient and rapid production, which was important under the circumstances. This reputation may have given him the opportunity to sell himself to the Controllers, but having done that, he then sold them on a design concept which was entirely original and considerably in advance of most contemporary thinking about school buildings.

On Sloan's inspection trips to other cities, it is unlikely that he saw anything similar to the plans he submitted to the Controllers in the early spring of 1851. There was, in fact, no need for him to be "sent to other cities to study school architecture," for the outstanding authorities in that field came to Philadelphia in August 1850 to attend the Second National Convention of the Friends of Public Education. Two papers read before the convention dealt with school architecture. The most important of these, Henry Barnard's 175-page essay, "Practical Illustrations of the Principles of School Architecture," was

included, fully illustrated, as Appendix III of the convention's published *Proceedings*.[9] Sloan need only have attended the convention or
read its proceedings to be as fully informed on schoolhouse design as
was then possible. He probably did study Barnard's essay, but his
own design had little or no relation to the examples used to illustrate
it. Sloan's concept of school design, while it met or exceeded Barnard's requirements (which immediately became the unofficial national standard), was entirely new. He proposed school buildings
made up of modular units containing four rooms divided from one
another by the system of sliding (or folding) glazed partitions with
which he had been experimenting in his commercial designs. Such
units could be stacked vertically (with two stair towers, one serving
each pair of rooms) or adjoined laterally (with connecting halls or
loggias), and so could be used for schools of any size or site. In
school houses made up of such units, interior circulation was greatly
reduced and outside exits were immediately available to every room;
hence, they were safer. They were also less expensive to construct, for
once the unit combinations were worked out they could be repeated
without the need for new details for each building. Moreover, the
problems and dangers of heating, lighting, and ventilation were reduced.[10] Last, and most important at that time, plans for the erection
of these buildings could be made available almost at once. (Plates 4A
& B.)

It is unlikely that the Controllers recognized the revolutionary
nature of this design proposal or foresaw the difficulties which would
arise when traditional systems of teaching were housed in buildings
based on it. At the time, however, it seemed to answer all their requirements, and on March 20, 1851, the Philadelphia *Public Ledger*
announced the commissioning of a new schoolhouse, "on Mr. Sloan's
improved plan, adopted by the Board of Controllers for Public
Schools," to replace the North-Eastern Grammar School, whose destruction by fire less than a year before had set off Philadelphia's
school reform movement. This was the first of seven schoolhouse
commissions received by Sloan before the closing of the fiscal year on
June 30. The *Annual Report* of the Controllers for the year 1851
gave the official reasons:

> Considerable attention has been directed to the construction of
> School Houses, with respect as well to their form as to their proper
> warming and ventilation. Instead of the two or three large rooms,
> with small class rooms adjoining, a preference is now given to rooms

on the same floor of equal size, and separated by moveable glazed partitions so as to allow, at will, the whole space to be thrown into one apartment. By this means, the injurious effects of crowded classrooms has been avoided, and at the same time, the advantage of one large room for the occasional assemblage of the entire school, has been secured.[11]

Almost the same report was given by Wharton to the Third National Convention of the Friends of Public Education (reconstituted as the American Association for the Advancement of Education) in Cleveland, Ohio, August 19–22, 1851.[12] This was the introduction to a national audience of what came to be widely known as the "Philadelphia Plan," which was praised by educational theorists both at home and abroad. Regrettably, the gap between educational theory and traditional teaching practice was too wide for Sloan's innovations to be generally used or accepted. The concept of flexible teaching space was too advanced—almost a hundred years too advanced—for teachers of the 1850s to utilize effectively, and Sloan's system of movable, glazed partitions was the first feature of the "Philadelphia Plan" to be abandoned. The plan was also criticized, by those who could not understand Sloan's modular system, for overemphasis on circulation and the "excessive use of stairways and halls."[13] This was unreasonable, for greater safety in circulation had been one of the demands of the Controllers after the North-Eastern School fire, where poor circulation and inadequate exits precipitated a disaster.

Henry Barnard seems to have felt that his primacy was threatened by Sloan's emergence as an unorthodox school architect. He gave only grudging notice to the "Philadelphia Plan" and avoided using Sloan's name in the *American Journal of Education*, which he edited. Barnard's adherents criticized the new schools on any pretext, and over the next decade they gradually eroded Sloan's reputation in the field of school design and finally succeeded in completely obscuring his contributions to it. From 1851 to 1859, however, Sloan was the principal school architect of Philadelphia, and for the last four of these years he was also the unofficial "official" school architect of Pennsylvania.

The originality and inventiveness which Sloan displayed in the design of school buildings also characterized his early designs for churches, and for twenty years he was a very successful church architect. Denominations whose requirements for space were not deter-

PLATE 4A. School House, *The Model Architect*, Vol. 2, Plate XLIV, p. 46
(Reproduced with permission of the Library of Fine Arts,
University of Pennsylvania)

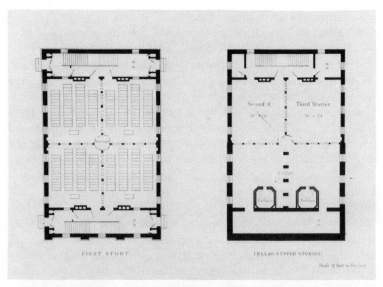

PLATE 4B. Ground plan of the School House, *The Model Architect*,
Vol. 2, Plate XLVI, p. 48 (Reproduced with permission of the
Library of Fine Arts, University of Pennsylvania)

mined by liturgy particularly appreciated the Convenience of his
plans; hence a majority of his early churches were commissioned by
Baptist, Methodist, and Reformed Presbyterian congregations. The
first church erected from his designs was the Ebenezer Methodist
Episcopal Church of Philadelphia, the commission for which he received on May 30, 1851. Before the end of the decade, Sloan had
executed fifteen churches for congregations in Pennsylvania, Virginia, and North and South Carolina. As was always the case, his response to the demands of clients stimulated his talent, and when,
after 1855, he began to receive commissions for Episcopal churches,
their liturgical requirements were met without any sacrifice of Convenience, while his study of visual detail and symbolic decoration
necessary to Episcopal Church ritual enriched his later work for Baptist and Presbyterian congregations.

To mark the significance of the year 1851 in both his personal and professional life, Sloan moved to a new house, opened a new office, and changed his listing in *McElroy's Philadelphia Directory* from "carpenter" to "architect." His new office had a fashionable address, 146 Walnut Street, and his succession of home addresses began to follow those of his clients in their drift westward until, in 1856, he returned to West Philadelphia, which he had left in 1844. The Philadelphia directories also document the emergence of his brothers and brothers-in-law as contractors and builders. Before the end of the 1850s, four of Samuel's brothers and two of his brothers-in-law were associated with the architectural profession, as contractors, dealers in building supplies, or specialists in mechanical equipment. Of these, Fletcher Sloan became an architect in his own right; Charles Sloan became an authority on heating and ventilating; and John Sloan became one of the principal contractor-developers of Philadelphia's westward growth. It is interesting to speculate on the total influence of the Sloan family on American architecture in the mid-nineteenth century, initiated by Samuel's ambition to get on in the world.

CHAPTER IV

1851–1852
The Model Architect

By January 1851, only a year after starting practice, Sloan was, at age thirty-five, one of Philadelphia's best-known architects. This early success was due in part to the social influence of his first clients and in part to the publicity given his work. Sloan sought publicity and repeatedly urged his fellow practitioners to do likewise, for he recognized the need for a more general understanding of the architect's professional role. Philadelphia in the 1850s was a center of architectural book publishing, and its newspapers and periodicals devoted considerable space to the national building boom. The Philadelphia *Public Ledger*, in a daily column entitled "Local Affairs," reported new building projects within its area of circulation, listing their owners, architects, and sites together with a brief description of their designs. If the owner was prominent, or the project imposing, further comments on style, cost, and plan would appear in the column throughout construction. Sloan's choice as architect for the Eastwick villa was reported in "Local Affairs" on January 24, 1851, and thereafter his Philadelphia commissions were regularly announced in the column until 1858. Over the same period his larger commissions were given national publicity by illustrated weeklies, published both in Philadelphia and in Boston, and he became known to a widespread female audience through a series of residential designs executed for *Godey's Lady's Book*.[1]

In 1851 the Philadelphia publishing house of E. G. Jones & Co. contracted with Sloan to issue twenty-four paperback folios of designs. The first of the twenty-four appeared in August 1851 and was so well received that E. G. Jones decided to issue them as a book at once. The book was not just another pattern book hastily compiled and cheaply printed but a superior example of its kind in every way—format, coverage, and presentation. *The Model Architect*, as the book was entitled, was an immediate and continuing success. The first of its two volumes went on sale late in the summer of 1852 and had sold out before the second volume was issued in 1853. E. G. Jones & Co. ran two printings of this first edition; a second edition was brought out in 1860 by E. H. Butler & Co.; a third in 1868 and a fourth in 1873, both by J. B. Lippincott & Co.; and at least two pirated editions were printed. *The Model Architect* was among the most durable works of its kind to be published in the United States.

What kind of a book was it to have such a long-lasting market? It was both traditional and original, familiar and new, an eclectic book that dressed its novelty in conformity. Its layout was traditional: plates of designs, together with their printed descriptions, interspersed with essays on construction, site-planning, service equipment, and the history of architectural styles. However, it was larger and richer in format than any of its predecessors: there were two folio volumes, printed on heavy paper, with many lithographed illustrations. In addition, its coverage was wider and more complete, with a range of building types from cottages to courthouses. The presentation of these designs was unusually thorough; there were many scaled details, complete lists of quantities, specifications for materials, and cost estimations. The book's rich format was for snob appeal, but its thorough design presentations reflected Sloan's carpenter background and his recognition that many potential clients were, like Eastwick, former mechanics who would recognize, and reject, shoddy. (Plate 5.)

Considering that it was the work of a young architect with limited education and brief experience, *The Model Architect* was remarkable. Although many of its designs were similar to those of George Wightwick, J. W. Rich, and A. J. Downing—whose books were a part of Dr. Kirkbride's library—they all contained elements of Sloan's pragmatic approach to design problems. His experience as a builder was most evident in the technical essays, on materials, drainage, construction methods, and service equipment. Most of the essays on historical style were exegesis, but Sloan's own convictions dictated his borrowing, and it was in these discussions of historical styles that his personal approach to design was expressed. Although he presented the historical background of the various revival styles in an orthodox way, including their associated values, he implied that modern Americans need not be restricted in their own lifestyle by either the

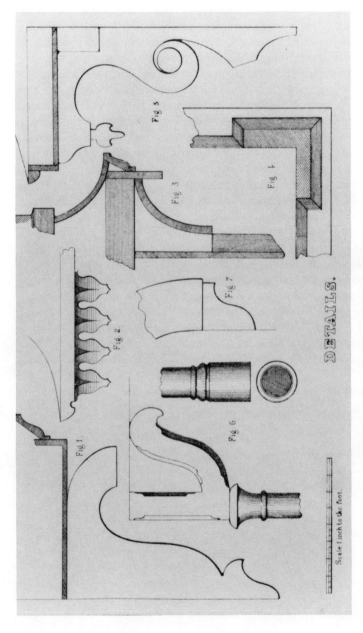

DETAILS.

Fig 5

Fig 3

Fig 4

Fig 2

Fig 7

Fig 1

Fig 6

Scale 1 inch to the foot.

PLATE 5. Details, *The Model Architect*, Vol. 1, Plate XX, p. 28

examples of history or the fashion of Europe. Nor was there any reason for Americans to be apologetic about their desire for convenience and comfort. Sloan's essays, like his architectural designs,
were works of creative eclecticism that offered the public new ideas in
familiar language. Their tone was particularly congenial to the "new
men" of commerce and industry, at whom the book was aimed.
However, Sloan was sincere in these opinions. He believed what he
wrote. Despite elements of snob appeal and self-advertisement in
The Model Architect, the book did present a case for American architecture—a familiar case, it is true, for Sloan had not yet hardened his
own convictions and was following the tradition of "Americanism"
initiated by Downing and Emerson.

   The Model Architect brought Sloan commissions from all over the
United States—for residences, schools, churches, and public buildings. Its designs were also widely copied by contractors and speculative builders. This did not disturb Sloan, for those who copied
would not have become clients in any case. It does, however, make
the identification of his personal work very difficult. The number of
buildings erected as a result of the publication of *The Model Architect*
is impossible to estimate, but it must have been in the thousands, for
few works of its type reached so wide a public. Copies of the book
have been found in public libraries in most of the eastern and midwestern states, in Texas, in California, and in many private collections.[2] That it was pirated is the weightiest evidence of its popularity.

CHAPTER V

1852–1858
The Firm of Sloan & Stewart

To produce the drawings and text of *The Model Architect* while giving the necessary attention to an increasing volume of commissions was more than one man could do. Before August 1852, Sloan formed a partnership with John S. Stewart, the builder with whom he had been teamed by Eastwick.[1] The role of each partner in the firm of Sloan & Stewart is not clear. A large number of its commissions came through Sloan, but Stewart had been operating as a de facto architect for some years before Sloan entered practice, and he brought along many clients. Stewart assumed the formal title "Architect" upon the formation of Sloan & Stewart. He seems to have given a majority of his time to field supervision but not all of it, for "Local Affairs" reported designs under his name.

A second major reason for the formation of Sloan & Stewart was a commission offered Sloan by the Committee for the Alabama Insane Hospital. The committee came to Philadelphia in midsummer 1852 seeking Dr. Thomas Kirkbride's advice on the building of a new facility at Tuscaloosa, Alabama. Kirkbride outlined a schematic plan for the institution and recommended that Sloan carry out the finished design. To fulfill the commission, Sloan needed an office staff and an associate who could make frequent supervisory trips to Alabama, or to whom he could entrust the office when he went himself. Kirkbride was to direct five such commissions to Sloan & Stewart within the following five years. Because of him, both partners gained an international reputation as hospital specialists, Sloan for design and Stewart for construction. The Sloan-Kirkbride collaboration was active for exactly thirty years (1852–1882), and all of the thirty-two hospitals for the insane with which Sloan was credited were designed

on the "Kirkbride System" of organization and treatment.[2] Kirkbride concluded the 1880 edition of his *Hospitals for the Insane*
(which had become almost an official manual since it first appeared in
1854) with this testimonial:

> I cannot close these remarks on the construction of buildings for the
> insane, without acknowledging my obligation to Samuel Sloan, Esq.,
> the distinguished hospital architect—examples of whose taste and
> ability are to be seen in so many sections of the country—for his sug-
> gestions and assistance in the long period during which I have so
> often had occasion to avail myself of his professional services. No one
> of his profession in this country, or elsewhere, has had equal oppor-
> tunities for a practical knowledge of every detail of hospital archi-
> tecture, or has done more to elevate its style and to promote the
> convenient arrangement of buildings.[3]

Thomas S. Kirkbride had been appointed Superintendent and
Physician-in-Chief of the Pennsylvania Hospital for the Insane in
January 1841, taking over the new building, quite literally, from
Sloan, who had been the supervisor of its construction. In the course
of the next ten years, Kirkbride became convinced that many serious
problems in the regimen of hospitals for the insane stemmed from
deficiencies in their physical plants. Existing facilities had been built
with little consideration for the special requirements of insane patients, and their design made improved methods of treatment and
care extremely difficult to implement. His opinions were supported
by Dorothea Lynde Dix, who since 1830 had devoted her life to
arousing both social and political support for the reform of public
institutions for the insane and indigent. The effectiveness of her fifty
years of tireless appeals to state legislatures is evidenced by a score or
more of hospitals for the insane which attribute their founding directly to her influence.[4] On her recommendation, Dr. Kirkbride was
retained as a professional consultant for the New Jersey State Lunatic
Asylum at Trenton, commissioned in 1845 from John Notman; however, Kirkbride contributed very little to the design of the building,
for his theories were as yet untested.

Experiments that Kirkbride conducted at the Department for the
Insane between 1845 and 1847 resulted in concrete evidence supporting his theories on the interrelation of physical plant and treatment. In 1847 he published, at his own expense, a pamphlet entitled
"Remarks on the Construction and Arrangement of Hospitals for
the Insane," in which he reported this evidence and the conclusions

he had drawn from it. These conclusions were presented to the 1851 meeting of the Association of Medical Superintendents of American Institutions for the Insane (Philadelphia, May 20–27) in twenty-six propositions, which suggested minimum standards for every hospital function and facility from dishwashing to fire escapes. Kirkbride concluded his presentation by describing his concept of an ideal hospital for the insane, which he illustrated with architectural drawings. His propositions were endorsed by the meeting as the "acceptable standards of the Association," and the physical organization of his ideal hospital was thereafter referred to as the "Kirkbride System."

It seems probable that the drawings Kirkbride used to illustrate his ideal hospital were executed by Sloan. When an expanded version of Kirkbride's proposals to the Association was published in 1854 as *Hospitals for the Insane*, it was illustrated with plans and elevations of the Alabama Insane Hospital at Tuscaloosa, the commission for which Sloan had received through Kirkbride in 1852.[5] The Alabama committee had been particularly impressed by the quickness with which Sloan was able to produce a schematic design for their consideration. They did not even have to go home and come back. He did it while they were still in Philadelphia, and it met all of Dr. Kirkbride's requirements. From the evidence of *Hospitals of the Insane*, the design Sloan offered the Alabama committee was the same scheme—possibly even the same drawings—that Kirkbride had used to illustrate his system the previous year. (Plate 6.)

The Alabama Insane Hospital was the first of the Kirkbride-Sloan collaborative projects to be realized. The thirty-one that followed it were so similar in design that, except for the various sprinklings of stylistic detail frosting their exteriors, they differed only in size. So basically sound were their solutions to the problems of circulation, security, and maintenance that some were still in use a hundred years after the "Kirkbride System" had been superseded.[6] They were also remarkable for innovations in mechanical equipment and fixtures, most of which were invented by Kirkbride and Sloan. To deal with the problems of confined or violent patients, a restudy of even the most commonplace elements, such as windows and doors, was made. This led to the development of specialized types, some of which are still in use: adjustable louvers to replace window bars, and sliding doors with no exposed hardware. Kirkbride also experimented with remote-control plumbing and even a form of air conditioning.[7]

He was particularly troubled by the problems of heating and its concurrent danger, fire. Even a minor fire in a hospital for the insane

PLATE 6. Alabama State Hospital for the Insane, *History of Education in Alabama,* 1889 engraving opp. p. 156 (Government Printing Office)

was usually tragic. Sloan turned to his clients, Eastwick & Harrison, builders of locomotives, for help in developing a safe central-heating system. The boiler invented by Harrison—and installed in his house as a demonstration of its safety—was one of the best central-heating units available until the late nineteenth century. Sloan also asked the ceramics industry in Philadelphia to provide a method of fireproofing exposed metal construction, and although none of the systems that were suggested—some even patented—were truly fireproof, they initiated research in this field which was to be of great value thirty years later in Chicago.[8]

The most lasting contribution of the Sloan-Kirkbride hospitals was the architectural symbol these buildings became. The public found their appearance particularly right and proper. Huge, rambling structures of heavy masonry sited in extensive grounds landscaped after the Downing tradition, they were objects of great civic pride, something to show the visitor and to be eulogized in guidebooks and local histories. They were Fitting. As a group they were impressive, creating a symbol which the public appreciated and was reluctant to give up. The picture the average American conjures up, even today, from the words "insane asylum" is their legacy. (Plate 7.)

The Alabama Insane Hospital was only the largest in a considerable backlog of commissions with which Sloan & Stewart began practice. Sloan brought a dozen or more jobs into the firm, among them the courthouses for Lancaster County, Pennsylvania, and Camden County, New Jersey. These two buildings, both commissioned in May 1852, became steps in Sloan's development of a standard courthouse design. He had learned the program requirements for county courthouses with his first commission, the Delaware County Courthouse at Media. In Lancaster and Camden he was not faced with Media's highly restrictive budget, and he worked out a design in the visual tradition of the national Capitol building which was both flattering and functional. The final version of his standard courthouse was executed in 1853 at Greensburg, Pennsylvania, for Westmoreland County. It was completed—from commissioning to occupancy—in less than two years and came within $386 of the estimated cost.[9] The Greensburg Courthouse was published—with all details and specifications—in Sloan's *City and Suburban Architecture* (1859), thus complicating the question of how many times the design was reproduced by his office and how often it was copied from his book. There are occasional references to "another courthouse" in the letters

PLATE 7. Male Department for the Insane of Pennsylvania Hospital, *The Architectural Review*, Vol. 1 (April 1869), p. 626
(Reproduced with permission of the Library of Fine Arts, University of Pennsylvania)

of Sloan's draftsman and future partner, Addison Hutton, but no indication of the buildings' locations.[10] (Plate 8.)

This standardized approach also became Sloan's method with the church commissions, which formed a considerable part of his practice between 1852 and 1857. Once the general problem "church" had been solved, he was content for the office to ring the changes on it. This is certainly true of the long series of Baptist churches which came from his office. For them Sloan developed a standard design in the general tradition of James Gibbs which was suited to the particular needs of that denomination. First used in 1852 for the First Baptist Church of Germantown, Pennsylvania, this design was immediately published as "The Church: Design Thirty-Fifth" in volume 2 of *The Model Architect* (1853), and it was the basis for five of the seven Baptist churches Sloan is known to have executed. (Plate 9.) Why Sloan was favored by the Baptists is a puzzle. The Sloans were "old church" Presbyterians, but Samuel's mother had been Methodist, and until his marriage he had followed that denomination. The Pennells were Quakers of long history, their ancestors having come to America with William Penn. Samuel and Mary avoided denominational family problems by becoming Presbyterians. However, Baptist churches were among Sloan's earliest out-of-state commissions, first bringing him to North and South Carolina, where so much of his later practice was to be.

In work for other denominations, Sloan & Stewart followed the tradition of the Medieval Revival as it had been established in the United States by Renwick and Upjohn. *Hints on Public Architecture* by Robert Dale Owen also seems to have had considerable influence on Sloan, for he referred to it more than once in his own publications and turned to its categories of Medieval style for precedent in the design of Presbyterian and Episcopal churches.[11] There was no standard form established for these, but one version of parish Gothic— first executed in 1854 for the Episcopal Church of St. James the Greater at Bristol, Pennsylvania—became popular, was repeated several times, and was published as "Design IV: A Church" in Sloan's *City and Suburban Architecture*.

The nine Philadelphia schoolhouses which the firm had in hand at its formation were increased to seventeen before the end of 1852. Fifteen of these were specified to be on "Mr. Sloan's improved plan" and were routine office work. Two, however, were of greater importance, the new buildings for the Central High School and the Normal School. The Central High School was Philadelphia's pride.

PLATE 8. Westmoreland County Court House, Greensburg, Pennsylvania, *History of the County of Westmoreland, Pennsylvania*, George Dallas Albert, ed. (Philadelphia: L. H. Everts and Co., 1882), 426

Established in 1837, it had soon become one of the most highly respected secondary schools in the nation and "assumed in public estimation, the rank, and received from the Legislature of Pennsylvania, the distinctive attributes of, a college."[12] Its graduates included leaders in the sciences and the professions, in state and national politics, in commerce and in industry. Only slightly below it in public esteem was the Normal School, established in 1848, which had been Philadelphia's response to the need for trained teachers in the Common Schools. (See Catalogue, entries No. 53, 55.) For a single firm to be given both buildings was a high compliment, and also an open invitation to accusations of corrupt patronage.

The city's older practitioners were bitter over Sloan's domination of public school work, and the state's leading educators were adherents, to a man, of Henry Barnard, who was jealously opposed to "Mr. Sloan's improved plan" for schoolhouses. Sloan seems to have

PLATE 9. The Church, *The Model Architect*, Vol. 2, Design XXXV, Plate XXV, p. 33 (Reproduced with permission of the Library of Fine Arts, University of Pennsylvania)

been too self-confident to take warning from the hostility which began to be expressed over his virtual monopoly of school commissions
after 1853. For example, the *American Journal of Education* (edited
by Barnard and the most influential of educational periodicals),
while it could not ignore the extraordinary growth of Philadelphia's
school program, was careful not to mention the architects involved
except when it was unavoidable.[13] In like manner, the *Pennsylvania
School Journal* (edited by Thomas H. Borrowes, a man of national re-
pute in public education) went to absurd lengths to avoid mentioning
Sloan's name. The enmity of Borrowes was to prove most damaging,
for he and Sloan were thrown into forced collaboration.

In December 1854, Superintendent Black implemented Section
XLV of the Common School Law of Pennsylvania, which had been
passed on May 8 of that year. Section XLV read:

> The Superintendent of Common Schools shall be authorized to em-
> ploy a competent person or persons to submit and propose Plans and
> Drawings for School House Architecture, for different Grades and
> Classes of School Buildings, that shall be adapted for furnishing good
> light and helpful ventilation; and if such Plans and Drawings are ap-
> proved by the Superintendent of Common Schools he is hereby di-
> rected to have them engraved and printed, with full Specifications and
> Estimates for building in accordance therewith; and shall furnish a
> copy of the same to each School District.

Acting on this authorization, Black chose Sloan & Stewart as the
"competent person or persons" and asked Borrowes to act as general
editor. The result was *Common Schools of Pennsylvania or Pennsylvania
School Architecture: A Manual of Directions and Plans for Grading,
Locating, Constructing, Heating, Ventilating, and Furnishing Common School Houses*, published and distributed by the state in 1855.
(Plate 10.)

This book was ill-fated before it was even published. Black's
choice of an editor could not have been worse. In 1859, Borrowes
publicly admitted to having sabotaged the work and feeling justified
in doing so:

> A year before the passage of the law authorizing this work, Mr. Bor-
> rowes had attempted to secure passage of an act providing for the pur-
> chase of Barnard's *School Architecture* for the use of the districts; but
> having failed, he felt himself at liberty to perform the duty, assigned

PLATE 10. From *Common Schools of Pennsylvania*, Thomas H. Borrowes, editor, State of Pennsylvania, 1855 (Reproduced with permission of the Gunnin Library of the College of Architecture, Clemson University)

without any solicitation on his part; and in the discharge of it adopted a plan quite different from that of the larger and more valuable work just named, or any other then in existence.[14]

This kind of sanctimonious washing of hands had also been used by Borrowes in a postscript at the end of *Pennsylvania School Architecture*:

These drawings and plans had been selected by the proper State authority and the Editor did not feel at liberty to have them altered to suit his own views, but contented himself with suggesting a few improvements they seem to admit of, and of adding such remarks as were deemed proper.[15]

However, the editor did feel at liberty to make disadvantageous comparisons between Sloan & Stewart's designs and those of architects approved by Barnard. These were the remarks that he apparently "deemed proper." Black and Sloan were powerless to prevent this deliberate undermining of the book, for Borrowes delayed its publication until the Superintendent was out of office and the architect was out of favor with the new administration. Despite Borrowes, *Common Schools of Pennsylvania* was widely influential on school-building in the state. A majority of Pennsylvania city and county histories published before 1880 refer to the book's use as a guide in the expansion programs which the Common School Law of 1854 made necessary. The period of its influence was limited, not by Sloan's detractors but by national events. The Panic of 1857, the depression of 1858, and the shadow of approaching civil war effectively halted new school construction, and *Common Schools of Pennsylvania* was never reissued.

Of the twelve commercial buildings in Philadelphia which were designed by Sloan & Stewart, two were so greatly admired that large colored lithographs of them were issued for general purchase. These were the mercantile stores of Hoskins, Hieskel & Company and of Bennett & Company, which stood, directly across from each other, in the 500 block of Market Street. They exemplified opposite extremes in the firm's approach to commercial buildings. Hoskins, Hieskel & Company, at 513 Market, was classically severe. Bennett & Company, at 518 Market, was theatrically picturesque. (Plate 11.)

Bennett & Company was an exception to Sloan's normal approach in designs for loft buildings and, as is so often the case with exceptions, "Tower Hall," as Mr. Bennett called his emporium, remained a prominent feature of Philadelphia's townscape longer than any of Sloan & Stewart's other center-city buildings.[16] Colonel Joseph M. Bennett was one of Philadelphia's more flamboyant self-made millionaires. Born in 1816, and so almost exactly contemporary with Sloan, he paralleled the architect's career in rising from tailor's apprentice to the largest manufacturer and retailer of ready-made clothing in the city. Having arrived on the mercantile Acropolis of Market Street, Bennett was determined that his store should be a fitting monument to his success. Its name, "Tower Hall," was a Bennett trademark which had been carried by all of his earlier stores. He was determined that his final Tower Hall be a striking architectural symbol of its name.

When he commissioned the building in May 1855, Bennett demanded an efficient plan, in which the circulation of customers and goods was optimum and the interior lighting was maximum, and a street front which was a translation of the store's name, "Tower Hall." In short, he wanted both Convenience and Fitness. Sloan was able to give him both. There were no interior columns or fixed partitions in

PLATE 11. A Mercantile Building in the Norman Style, *City and Suburban Architecture*, Design XII, Plate LVI, p. 57

the plan of Tower Hall, and despite the collection of battlements, tourelles, and crenelations that decorated its facade, a very high ratio of window to wall was retained. There was also a clear expression of vertical support in its metal skeleton which was more characteristic of Sloan's commercial work than florid decoration. (See Catalogue, entry No. 96.)

The *Public Ledger* in "Local Affairs" for December 14, 1852, announced that Hoskins, Hieskel & Company was "the most ornamental iron front yet projected in our city" and called it "Norman-Italian" in style. However, further description of the building (no interior brick lining of the iron front, no interior columns, floors supported by trussed girders, movable glazed partitions) indicates that whereas the ornament may have been "Norman-Italian" the design was American Commercial. A contemporary lithograph of "Hoskins, Hieskel & Co." shows a facade in which three-quarter columns and thin, recessed spandrels bracket windows that fill almost the entire wall surface. The "ornamental iron front" was in reality a prefabricated window-wall. (Plate 12.) Sloan always used extensive glazing in his commercial buildings if his clients would let him. As early as September 1851, "Local Affairs" reported that he was installing "the largest plate glass windows yet seen in our city" for Simes Block. Interior flexibility was almost an obsession with Sloan, and he finally carried it to an extreme in the Washington Building of 1856, each floor of which was divided internally "with folding doors, so that a person may occupy from one to eight rooms." [17]

It is fruitless to argue the ancestry of the skyscraper, for the social context which demanded its appearance was national rather than local. However, it seems repeatedly necessary to bring the myth of its revolutionary creation in Chicago nearer the more modest evolutionary truth. Boston, New York, and Philadelphia can all claim major places in its family tree, but Philadelphia has perhaps the strongest claim, for there was a direct line of descent from its creative eclectics of the 1850s, 1860s, and 1870s to the Chicago School of the 1880s and 1890s. [18] Sloan has not been considered a figure in this evolutionary chain, but he deserves to be included, for Philadelphia architects of the late 1860s and 1870s did not hesitate to copy his commercial designs and take credit for his innovations.

PLATE 12. Hoskins, Hieskel & Co. Lithograph by Inger & Haugg, printed
by P. D. Duval, 1854 (Reproduced with permission of
the Library Company of Philadelphia)

CHAPTER VI

The Second Masonic Temple and the Harrison Commissions

The largest, and some feel the most significant, of Sloan & Stewart's five civic buildings was the Second Masonic Temple (or Masonic Hall; the names are variously used). Professor Winston Weisman has made the following critique of the building.

> Related to the Jayne [building] by virtue of its skeletal and vertical emphasis is the Masonic Temple erected between 1852 and 1855 by Sloan and Stewart. In some respects the Masonic Temple is even a better example of structural design than the Jayne. In this case it would seem that an attempt is made to show the part being played by the various perpendicular supports. Those piers that appear to the eye to do the most work are the broadest, highest, and have the greatest projection. Those that support only the windows and walls in each section of the facade are made smaller and thinner. Thinnest and smallest of all are the colonettes which only hold in place the windows.
>
> The fact that the architectural language of the Jayne and the Masonic Temple comes out of the Medieval past should not be interpreted as vitiating the argument being developed here. On the contrary, it strengthens it, for it must be remembered that where Gothic forms were more often than not employed picturesquely, as is the case of the Grover, Baker Sewing Machine Company Building, erected in New York between 1857 and 1858 by George H. Johnson. In other words, the preference of Sloan and Stewart for a structural interpretation of Gothic, rather than a picturesque one, is significant.[1]

Structural emphasis was the general rule in Sloan's use of Gothic style for public, civic, and commercial buildings, and in the Second Masonic Temple this was reinforced by an emphasis on iron as the structural material. A large part of its principal elevation was iron, while internal support was provided by a modular spacing of "52 iron posts."[2]

The preference of Pennsylvania Masons for Gothic surroundings in their Grand Lodge has been consistent. The First Temple—erected in 1809–1810 from the designs of William Strickland—was in this style, as was Sloan's Second Temple on the same site (Chestnut Street, between 7th and 8th Streets). Strickland's building was more "Gothick" than Gothic, and the interior of Sloan's was somewhat more Moorish than Medieval; however, Joseph Windrim's Third Temple at the corner of Broad and Filbert Streets, which has been the home of the Grand Lodge since 1873, is standard Victorian Gothic after the manner of William Butterfield. (Plate 13.)

Exactly why and how Sloan received the commission for Masonic Hall is unclear. He was one of three finalists in a competition for its design advertised by the Committee on Plans of the Grand Lodge of Pennsylvania in the fall of 1852, but his entry was not the first choice of either the committee, which recommended that of Edward Collins, or of the Grand Lodge, which awarded the commission to John Notman. The acrimonious controversy which developed between the Building Committee and Notman when the lowest bid for the erection of his design exceeded the committee's estimate by more than 50 percent, and the reopening of the competition, has been documented by Constance Greiff in *John Notman, Architect*.[3] What her exhaustive research could not show, for there is no evidence in the records of the Grand Lodge, is why the commission was finally given to Samuel Sloan.

There were two very good reasons for *not* giving Sloan the commission. The Committee on Plans had unanimously recommended the design of Edward Collins because of "the splendour and beauty of Mr. Collins' plan, combined with its economy." Sloan's design was estimated by the committee to cost some $8,000 more than that of Collins if executed in stone; however, the cost of the two would be identical if carried out in iron. The Masons had originally wanted stone, hence Collins' submission was the logical second choice. In addition, unlike Collins, Sloan was a Mason of very recent initiation, having been taken into Lodge 52, "Harmony," on January 7, 1852, barely nine months before the competition.[4]

The report of the Building Committee on April 18, 1853, discontinued any further relations with Notman. After acceptance of that

PLATE 13. Masonic Hall (Temple), Chestnut Street, Philadelphia in
James D. McCabe, *Illustrated History of the Centennial Exhibition*
(Philadelphia: Jones Brother Co., Printers, 1876)

report by the Grand Lodge, there is no mention of any further discussion regarding the choice of an architect for the new building in the *Minutes* of the Grand Lodge. There is only a single sentence report by the Building Committee, in April, that Samuel Sloan had been selected as Architect.[5] That Sloan, acting for the firm of Sloan & Stewart, was the designer of the building is firmly documented by a series of reports in Philadelphia's newspapers. These are consistent until the dedication ceremonies of the building. Then there is an unexplained change in attribution. At the laying of the cornerstone on September 29, 1853, Sloan was addressed as follows:

> Brother Samuel Sloan—I now deliver to you, the Architect of this Masonic Temple, the implements of architecture and the symbols of our craft. May the Great Architect on High speed you and the craftsmen under you; and may He prosper the work that it may prove the *beauty*, *strength*, and *wisdom* of our art, and lend to his everlasting glory.[6]

However, in the program for the dedication of the new Temple on September 26, 1855, and on the tickets for admission to those ceremonies, there was printed "Architect, Bro. Jas. B. Sloan."[7] It has been impossible to determine what relationship James B. Sloan had to Samuel Sloan, or why he was suddenly elevated to the position of Architect for the dedication ceremonies.

Of the fifty-one residential commissions received by Sloan & Stewart, those executed for Joseph Harrison Jr. and Samuel Aden Harrison show the range of their work in private housing. Joseph Harrison Jr. returned from Russia in 1852 a richer and more famous man than his partner, Andrew M. Eastwick. Like Eastwick, Harrison built an architectural symbol of his success, but it was very unlike that of Eastwick. His long stay in Russia had somewhat de-Americanized Harrison, and he returned with a high regard for the manner and style in which Russian aristocrats lived. Harrison determined to build two residences—a town mansion and a country estate, after the Russian fashion—having in mind specific prototypes which he had known in Saint Petersburg. Eastwick recommended Sloan, who is credited with the design of both buildings. It is more accurate to say, however, that Harrison and Sloan collaborated on the Rittenhouse Square mansion and the country estate of "Riverdale." (Plate 14.)

The great townhouse for Harrison was Sloan's first attempt at a Baroque Revival ensemble, for the fashions of Napoleon III had not

PLATE 14. Joseph Harrison Mansion, Rittenhouse Square, Philadelphia,
Philadelphia and Notable Philadelphians, Moses King, editor
(New York, 1901–1902)

yet become popular in Philadelphia. However, what he was asked to
simulate was not an academic French design but an exotic Franco-
Russian hybrid. The imitation of French taste by Russian aristocrats
had spawned a strange version of Baroque Revival in Saint Petersburg during the second quarter of the nineteenth century. It was this
manner—heavy, formal, and rigidly symmetrical—that Harrison admired. He had not, however, admired the lack of conveniences with
which his Russian friends had been willing to live. Harrison was, at
base, an American mechanic and saw no reason why grandeur could
not also be comfortable and efficient. As a result, his Rittenhouse
Square mansion was supplied with central heating, excellent plumbing, and all the mechanical equipment then available for American
Comfort. It also included some features that were decidedly un-
American at the time: a private gallery for his collection of paintings
and sculpture, bedrooms *en suite*, and a formal garden that stretched
a full city block from his residence to the back of Harrison Row, a
group of ten rowhouses that protected his grounds from Locust
Street. Harrison Row was radical in both social and design concept,
being planned as a "community" which shared many services as well
as the open space of its owner's garden. In this community Harrison

proposed to house his dependents, a manorial attitude that seemed strange and disturbing to Philadelphians of the time.[8] Neither Harrison nor his family were comfortable in the American mid-century environment, and shortly after the town mansion and country house were built, they returned to Europe for three years before settling permanently in Philadelphia.[9]

Sloan probably began to work on the designs for both Harrison residences in 1853, but public announcement of the Rittenhouse Square commission was not made until July 1856, when the house was almost ready to be occupied. Only one announcement of the "Riverdale" commission was ever made, and information about the building is scarce.[10] The first edition of Sloan's *City and Suburban Architecture* contained a lavish presentation of the townhouse (Design XXIV: "A Suburban Mansion") with a special section devoted to the "Heating Apparatus," a feature of which Harrison was very proud as he had designed, built, and installed it himself. The *City and Suburban Architecture* presentation does not include a complete site plan or any drawings of the houses in Harrison Row. That experiment in communal housing was the most innovative element of the entire project and could have been very influential had Philadelphians been able to consider it without bias.[11]

Working together with Sloan, Harrison made two other experiments in public housing, both of which were viewed with distrust. Harrison was misunderstood. His projects were not a *noblesse oblige* gesture, as Philadelphians suspected, but an expression of real concern for the improvement of living conditions among craftsmen and mechanics in the city. Having experienced those conditions, Sloan was in complete sympathy with Harrison's aims and was just at the height of his inventive powers. In 1853 they erected two rowhouse developments, which because of their design could be rented for a very low figure. Instead of being acclaimed for this, Harrison was accused of ulterior motives. Disgusted by Philadelphia's provincialism and suspicions, Harrison took his family back to Europe. Sloan continued to investigate low-cost housing, publishing his results in *Sloan's Homestead Architecture* (1861), but he never found another patron with enough interest and resources, so his later designs were never built.

If the architectural projects of Joseph Harrison Jr. were an uneasy mixture of grand-seigneurism and social reform, those of Samuel Aden Harrison had but one simple aim—profit. This is not to say that his developments in West Philadelphia were cheapjack or shoddy.

Quite the contrary. Over the course of a long career as entrepreneur and speculator, he had discovered that, in the end, quality made money. Hamilton Terrace—five urban villas occupying the entire west side of Hamilton Street (41st Street) between Becket Street (Chester Avenue) and the Baltimore Pike—was the largest unified housing group designed for him by Sloan & Stewart. Commissioned in 1856, it was the climax of Harrison's promotional building in West Philadelphia, for panic, depression, and war effectively halted the growth of that area for a decade thereafter. The five buildings of Hamilton Terrace ran the gamut of mid-century residential taste, both in style and in scale. At each corner was an "Elizabethan Cottage," next were "double villas" in the Classic manner, and in the center a "Norman Villa in stone" which was occupied by Harrison himself.[12] All were surrounded by ample grounds, the back gardens and service areas being fenced and the group of front yards landscaped as a unit. The graduated scale of the buildings produced a triangular massing profile whose apex was the entrance tower of the Norman villa. The dwellings were so well built that most of them were in good repair a hundred years later.[13]

The year 1856 was the last one of Philadelphia's building boom, and the last of full employment in Sloan's office. Like the majority of Philadelphia's business and professional firms, Sloan & Stewart was hurt by the failure of the city's banks in the Panic of 1857. Many of its commissions still in the design stage were canceled, and work on some of those already under construction was halted. There was not enough work to support a firm, so in the autumn of 1857 the partnership of Sloan & Stewart was amicably dissolved.

CHAPTER VII

From the Panic of 1857 to the Outbreak of the Civil War

For four decades prior to the Civil War, the fiscal stability of the United States was disturbed by a nationwide optimism among its citizens which manifested itself in increasingly reckless speculation. The effect of this attitude on the nation's social values was not generally recognized in the euphoria of the time, and those few who had fears did not voice them publicly until shortly before the Panic of 1857 brought the period to a disastrous close. Despite warnings that financial crises in 1836 and 1847 had given, the speculative mania continued to grow, until by 1850 it influenced every economic class, even planters and farmers in the agricultural backwaters of the South and West.[1] It was encouraged and sustained by a rapidly changing economy. Between 1817 and 1857, the United States underwent "the greatest economic transformation in its history."[2] Its agriculture shifted from self-sustaining household production to commercial production, it became one of the leading manufacturing nations in the world, and its export-import trade increased sevenfold.

Despite constant increases in general production, the country could not supply the demands of its expanding population, and foreign imports rose steadily throughout the period. A major part of the import trade was financed by European investors, who by 1851 held over $250 million in American long-term securities. Capital was increasingly concentrated at a few centers, such as Philadelphia and New York, whose banks were deeply involved in the speculative financing of commerce, industry, agriculture, land development, and especially the railroads, which tied all these sectors of the American economy together.[3] Mutual indebtedness among these banks became

dangerous in a crisis, as the panics of 1836 and 1847 had demonstrated, and conditions in 1857 were more extreme than ever before.
The *New York Herald* for June 27, 1857, acidly portrayed the social
environment of the nation:

> The same premonitory symptoms that prevailed in 1835–36 prevail
> in 1857 in a tenfold degree. Government spoliation, public defaulters,
> paper bubbles of all descriptions, a general scramble for western lands
> and town and city sites, millions of dollars, made or borrowed, ex-
> pended in fine houses and gaudy furniture; hundreds of thousands in
> the silly rivalries of fashionable parvenues, in silks, laces, diamonds
> and every variety of costly frippery are only a few among the many
> crying evils of the day. The worst of all these evils is the moral pesti-
> lence of luxurious exemption from honest labor, which is infecting all
> classes of society. The country merchant is becoming a city stock-
> jobber, and the honest country farmer has gone off among the gam-
> blers in western land. Thus, as this general scramble among all classes
> to be rich at once, and by the shortest possible cut, extends and in-
> creases, our rogues, defaulters and forgers are multiplied. The epi-
> demic and its attending evils must run their course.

Architects of the Jacksonian generation, like Samuel Sloan, knew
no other conditions. Their business methods had been learned in the
1840s and practiced in the 1850s, and it took a man of unusually
strong character and sound background to resist the euphoric mate-
rialism of the time. From the opening of his practice most of Sloan's
clients had been, in greater or lesser degree, speculators, and the wave
of seeming prosperity which supported his practice was founded on
thirty years of speculation. He did not, therefore, recognize the panic
and depression of 1857–1858 as the end of an era, but saw it as only
another temporary setback. However, Philadelphia was at the center
of a major financial storm. In 1859, English economist D. Morier
Evans published a study of the 1857 panic in which he described the
Philadelphia situation:

> Then commenced a scene of failure and fraud, and sacrifice of prop-
> erty, of blasted hopes and family distress, of national embarrassment
> and stagnation of business, which almost defies description. The evil
> was radical in the system of basing prosperity on artificial credit. So
> far as respected the outstanding circulation of unredeemed and unre-
> deemable bank notes at the time of the crisis, Philadelphia and Penn-

sylvania generally had a full share of suffering; and as the city largely depends for prosperity on the transit of business . . . it could not be otherwise than that the effects of the collapse as it affected her were far and widely felt. It was in Philadelphia that the way in which the inducements of those banks were the means of increasing disasters and hastening crisis was most apparent. . . . The banking system of Pennsylvania has been regarded by Pennsylvanians themselves as less secure than any other State of the Union.[4]

Evans' tabulation of bankrupt businesses and bank failures from October through December 1857 runs into the hundreds; among them were many of Sloan's clients.

The Panic of 1857 had profound effects on the people of Philadelphia. It forced them to reconsider the careless opportunism which had brought them almost to ruin, and by the end of 1858 there was general rejection of speculator values and a distrust of those adroit speculators who only a year before had been admired and imitated. This more sober attitude was short-lived, for the Civil War offered too many opportunities to the speculator, but he did not reappear in the wide-open, freewheeling, obvious form of the mid-1850s. The war speculator may have been just as crass, but his operations were less public, for there had been a genuine change of popular attitude, not just in Philadelphia but in the nation as a whole. An element of what has been labeled "Victorian morality" became a part of the American social environment in reaction to the Panic of 1857. Samuel Sloan had no experience of this value change, for he was absent from Philadelphia when it took place. His reaction to the halting of virtually all business in Philadelphia in 1858 had been to take a five-month European vacation with his family. Nor did he fully recognize the change for many years after his return to the city.

In the spring of 1857, Sloan had hired a young draftsman, Addison Hutton, who remained in his employ—except for four months in 1859—until the autumn of 1861. It is through the letters of Hutton, and the "Memoir" written by his brother, Finley Hutton, that we have the only direct, intimate view of Samuel Sloan and his reaction to what proved to be the turning point in his life and career.[5] On May 24, 1857, Hutton wrote to his mother:

Sloan and I have got along quite satisfactorily, I think, tho' he is rather of an exciteable turn, and gives the whole crew a swipe sometimes, but soon gets over it. There is a good deal of excuse for him tho; the press

of business which I take to be enough for any two men, and not being
by any means a healthy man, tho a very quick active one, and these
combined with the disappointments and mistakes incident to the business when there is so much hurry, are enough to set any man in fits,
once in a while. He has never scolded me any yet personally, but is in
the main very pleasant and rather inclined to be talkative.[6]

From this letter one gets a picture of Sloan as an intense, short-
tempered man who, because of the number of commissions which he
accepted, worked under constant pressure. Hutton's mention of
Sloan's quickness and talkativeness is consistent with such a personality, as is the reference to his health, for Sloan probably suffered
from the usual companions of tension—stomach trouble and high
blood pressure. This is partially borne out by the stroke which ended
his life. He was a compulsive worker, and from the opening of his
practice had accepted far more work than any small office could have
been expected to turn out; however, it was accomplished, if not always on time. The "disappointments and mistakes incident to the
business when there is so much hurry" of which Hutton writes were
the inevitable results of an overworked staff under pressure to get out
the jobs.

Hutton's aside that the press of business was "enough for any two
men" is strange, for there were two men. In May 1857 the partnership between Samuel Sloan and John S. Stewart had not yet been
dissolved; the firm of Sloan & Stewart was still a firm, and the commissions which Hutton listed in a subsequent letter were reported in
the *Public Ledger* under the firm name. However, there is no mention
of Stewart in the Hutton letters, nor any reference to Hutton's working for the firm, but only for Sloan. There had been an estrangement
between the two partners, about a year earlier, when Stewart brought
his younger brother, Thomas S. Stewart, into the office. This may, in
part, explain the move of the firm from their original location at 80
South 4th Street (renumbered 152 South 4th Street in 1858) to
much larger offices at 274 South 3rd Street, where each man could
have his personal suite and staff.

This move was made early in the summer of 1857 and suggests
that Sloan had no suspicion of the panic to come in October, as the
rent at the new office was twice that he had been paying. By summer
there was some nervousness and hesitation in the business world of
Philadelphia, but not enough for Sloan to anticipate more than a

brief recession, as there were fifteen large commissions in the office. Hutton wrote to his sister, Mary, on June 6, 1857:

> We have a great deal to do. I will name some of the buildings—Harrison's dwelling 18th St., Harrison's Row, Locust St.—Pennsylvania Hospital for the Insane, West Phila., Episcopalian Church, West Phila., Presbyterian Church, Kensington; church at Holmesburg—at Bristol on German St.,—at West Chester—and I cannot remember how many more—New Castle, Delaware Prison,—college in Delaware County, Pa.—Church, Greenville, South Carolina—besides stores and dwellings, too tedious to enumerate. We expect to do some drawings for Nashville, Tenn., some of these days. I say *we* although I may have nothing to do with it.[7]

Some of Sloan's most important buildings are included in Hutton's list, which also documents his expanding involvement in the South. In the same letter there is the first mention of Sloan's second book, *City and Suburban Architecture*:

> Sloan intends publishing a work on City Buildings shortly, he asked me yesterday evening if I thought I could compile the written matter, if he would rough it out for me, I told him I did not know; I think he was hardly in earnest to suppose that a boy like me could stick a book together, even if the material was *delivered* in the rough. At any rate, I don't care much about it as I would be obliged to devote my whole attention to that alone, in order to make it come out correct.

It is obvious that Sloan anticipated no serious interruption of business; however, the buildings which Hutton listed on June 6 were to be the last commissions to come into the office for the rest of 1857. After the October climax of the panic virtually halted all business in Philadelphia, the firm of Sloan & Stewart was dissolved for lack of work. The former partners continued to occupy the office jointly until its lease expired in September 1858, when Sloan removed to the firm's old quarters on 4th Street.[8]

Sloan tried to keep his office open, if only with a token staff, throughout 1858 and 1859, although no record of any architectural commission to him has been found for those years. To occupy Hutton's time, Sloan put him to work on the illustrations for *City and Suburban Architecture*, which J. B. Lippincott & Co. was willing to publish despite the depressed state of business.[9] It is not clear if Hutton was roughing out *Sloan's Constructive Architecture* as well. The book was issued by Lippincott in August 1859, at the same time as *City and Suburban Architecture*, and although Hutton does not mention the work by name, after June 1858 he refers to "books," in the plural, so he may have been working on it.[10]

On May 26, 1858, Samuel Sloan and his family sailed from New York on the *Persia* and remained in Europe until October, making a grand tour of the major capitals and watering places. He returned to Philadelphia to find the city still in the grip of depression and no new work in the office, so he turned to completion of the two books. It is clear from the letters of Addison Hutton that he contributed a great deal to *City and Suburban Architecture*, both in the drawing of its illustrations and the layout of the book. It seems that Sloan gave his full, personal attention to the work on architectural construction, in which he had far greater experience than Hutton and about which he had very decided opinions. Both books were a financial success as they, fortunately, appeared while Philadelphia was experiencing a brief recovery in the fall of 1859. Their popularity was not a thing of the moment, however, for they were reissued many times, and *Sloan's Constructive Architecture* was considered the definitive work on its subject for another decade.

City and Suburban Architecture was more polished and sophisticated in its presentations than *The Model Architect* had been, but it lacked much of the spontaneity and enthusiasm of the earlier work. Many of its designs—presented in meticulous drawings, a number rendered in four colors—were very similar to those recently published by other architects—such as Minard Lefever, W. H. Ranlett, J. W. Rich, and Calvert Vaux—while others evidenced that Sloan had been much taken with the French Baroque Revival during his European trip.[11] However, there was no lack of originality or force in the presentation of those building types with which Sloan felt himself to be a master—schools, public buildings, and city mansions. *City and Suburban Architecture* was richer in its format—the quality of its paper, lithography, and binding—than *The Model Architect* and considerably more expensive. It was aimed at the successful commercial class, and once again Sloan correctly judged his public, for despite the recent depression the book sold well.

After compilation of the two books was finished, there was no work in Sloan's office for Addison Hutton. He was not dismissed, but being discouraged by his poor salary, and with no prospects of its improving, Hutton left Sloan's employ in April 1859 to try his hand at gold prospecting in the West, a venture that did not turn out well. The two men parted amicably, and when Hutton returned to Philadelphia in August, Sloan immediately rehired him. There was new work in the office by the fall of 1859, the result of that brief resurgence of business which made Sloan's new books a success. In hand were two large jobs in the South, the First Presbyterian Church of Wilmington, North Carolina—to which Sloan dispatched Hutton, for supervision, immediately upon his rejoining the office—and "Longwood," the octagonal Oriental villa of Dr. Haller Nutt in Natchez, Mississippi.

"Longwood" is the most widely known of all Sloan's buildings. Although surviving in an unfinished state, it has attracted the interest of both historians and tourists and has become a feature of the yearly "Natchez Pilgrimage." Three books, numerous articles, and countless photographs of "Longwood" have been published. Of greater value to the researcher are the unpublished Haller Nutt Papers, among which is an almost day-by-day account of the building's construction, and the letters of Addison Hutton, who superintended the work at "Longwood" for over a year while living with Dr. and Mrs. Nutt.[12] Revealing as these sources are, they deal with the building after its commissioning, giving no clue to its inception.

The genesis of "Longwood" seems to have been a hypothetical design which Sloan published in Volume 2 of *The Model Architect*. This was "An Oriental Villa: Design Forty-Ninth," presented with an unusually large number of drawings and preceded by an essay on the architecture of Arabia and Constantinople.[13] Sloan was apparently fascinated by the idea of an oriental villa, for he had made an attempt at such a design in volume 1 of the book, "An Oriental Villa: Design Eighteenth," which was little more than a rectangular bracketed villa to which a few vaguely Moorish details had been applied. By the writing of volume 2, however, Sloan had done some research. The introductory essay to "Design Forty-Ninth" referred to the mosques of Damascus, and Baghdad and the Church of Saint Sophia. "Design Forty-Ninth" was an octagonal building with a central multistory space under an "onion" dome, rigidly symmetrical in plan with ornamentation which, while still a pastiche, was theatrically "Oriental." Its plan owed almost nothing to any Oriental prototype—except, perhaps, in the extensive use of balconies—but a great deal to O. S. Fowler's "octagonal mode of building."[14] It was this mixture of octagonal geometry and Islamic frosting that seems to have attracted Haller Nutt.

After having attended lectures at the University of Virginia and graduating in medicine at Louisville, Haller Nutt had returned home to Mississippi to engage in scientific farming. Early in the century, Haller's father, Dr. Rush Nutt, had moved from Virginia to Mississippi, where he introduced a very profitable hybrid of Egyptian long-staple cotton particularly suited to delta cultivation. Dr. Nutt and Haller had successfully improved Whitney's cotton gin so that it would process this cotton, and after Haller returned to Mississippi, he began extensive cotton production. In 1853 Haller purchased the site in Natchez on which "Longwood" was later built.[15] By that time Haller was a wealthy man, widely traveled and with cultivated tastes.

Precisely when Sloan received the commission for "Longwood" is not certain. Two of Haller Nutt's daughters went to a school for young ladies in Philadelphia in the late 1850s, and one or both of their parents traveled to and from the city with them. At any time after 1853 Nutt could have seen Sloan's second "Oriental Villa" in volume 2 of *The Model Architect*, for the book had become a fashionable parlor accessory in Philadelphia. Haller had been attracted to Islamic architecture during an extended tour of Egypt and the Near East which he made with his father in 1849. He would also have been attracted to "Design Forty-Ninth" because of his interest in octagonal residences, which had been stimulated by a summer's trip to the upper Hudson River valley, where he had admired the octagonal houses on bluffs overlooking the river.[16] Sloan's design was the largest, most monumental, and fanciful octagonal house to have been projected, and the earliest correspondence in the Haller Nutt Papers leads to the conclusion that Nutt approached Sloan about its adaptation for "Longwood" in August 1859.[17] (Plates 15, A & B.)

Because Haller Nutt accepted "Design Forty-Ninth" very much as Sloan had published it, the office was able to produce finished studies of "Longwood" for Sloan to take with him on his first trip to Natchez in mid-January 1860. He was back in Philadelphia by the first week in February with all the changes and additions suggested by Haller and Mrs. Nutt. Thereafter, only a few minor alterations were made in the design; working drawings were quickly produced, and Sloan began to send workmen, bulk materials, finished cabinet-work, overmantels, and eventually furniture to Natchez, by coastal shipping for the most part. In the spring of 1860 he sent Addison

Hutton to supervise construction. Sloan himself made at least one additional trip to Natchez and had made plans for another, on which he intended to take his youngest son, Howard, but the Civil War overtook the building of "Longwood."

A detailed history of "Longwood" would take up too much of a general study of Samuel Sloan, although the quantity of primary source material is unique, for Sloan's life is not otherwise well documented. However, the majority of the letters in the Haller Nutt Papers consist of routine notations about materials—their delivery, or nondelivery—the progress and problems of construction, and the cost of all these. The few personal letters between client and architect tell a moving story of the great house being pushed almost to com-

PLATE 15A. Oriental Villa, *The Model Architect*, Vol. 2, Design XLIV, Plate LXIII, opp. p. 73 (Reproduced with permission of the Library of Fine Arts, University of Pennsylvania)

PLATE 15B. Longwood. Wood Engraving from Samuel Sloan,
Homestead Architecture, 1861 (Collection of the author)

pletion despite increasing difficulties, the shadow of approaching civil war, the desertion of workmen, damaged shipments of materials, and local hostility to its antisecessionist owner. Nutt and Sloan wanted desperately to complete "Longwood," for they were very much alike in temperament—stubborn, self-confident, and accustomed to success.

By the autumn of 1860 the Northern workmen began to feel uncomfortable, even unsafe, in Natchez. Hutton slipped away in early winter after having overheard Mrs. Nutt complain that his presence in the house was an embarrassment to the family.[18] As coastal shipping became less and less dependable, Nutt began to receive damaged materials and broken millwork, for which Sloan had already paid and for which he could get no recompense, but Nutt persisted in trying to finish the house, even after Mississippi seceded from the Union on January 9, 1861. The last Philadelphia craftsmen did not leave Natchez until March of that year. With the Union blockade of Confederate ports in late 1861, shipments of materials stopped altogether. Nutt continued the work, as he could, through 1861, but little was accomplished after the Northern workmen had gone. As late as October 1863, both Sloan and Nutt were hopeful that the building might be completed, but Nutt's death in 1864 brought an end to the saga of "Longwood." Dr. Nutt's widow, Julia Nutt, lived in the first floor of the house until she died in 1897, and her daughter, another Julia, continued in residence until her death in 1932. Throughout those sixty-eight years, the building remained essentially as it was in 1864, only the few alterations needed to make private living possible in what had been designed as the public rooms being made. The property was inherited by collateral relatives, who sold it, in 1938, to the Kelly E. McAdams family of Austin, Texas, who preserved the house and made necessary but minimal restorations, having decided to leave the unfinished sections—where workmen's tools, workbenches, and building materials were still where they had been abandoned in 1864—unrestored. In 1970, "Longwood" was given to the Pilgrimage Garden Club of Natchez by the McAdams Foundation. It is now a feature of that organization's yearly "Natchez Pilgrimage," and has been designated a National Historic Landmark.

The commissions Sloan received in late 1859 and early 1860 confirmed his belief that business was getting back to what it had been before the Panic of 1857. Acting on this belief, he committed a professional blunder that shadowed his reputation in Philadelphia for the rest of his life. He maneuvered for the commission of Philadelphia's new City Hall in a way that would not have been looked on with disfavor before October 1857 but which in September of 1860 brought accusations of conspiracy and malpractice. On September 3, 1860, at the close of the competition for the "New Public Buildings of the City of Philadelphia" (City Hall), three Philadelphia architects were among the finalists: John J. McArthur Jr., George S. Bethell, and Samuel Sloan. McArthur's design was the unanimous choice of the Committee on Public Buildings, and he was awarded the commission. Shortly thereafter McArthur was also awarded the contract for erecting the building. Some members of the City Council did not approve of this double award, and some did not agree with the site on Central Square, which had been chosen by the Committee, thus moving City Hall from its traditional home on Independence Square. Both dissident factions joined to provoke a long and acrimonious debate over McArthur's commission and contract.[19]

At a meeting of the Select Council on September 27, Councilman John Ketcham raised strong objections to McArthur's contract for construction, because much lower bids had been submitted by other men. Ketcham all but accused McArthur of collusion with the members of the Committee on Public Buildings.[20] Sloan, speculating that he might be awarded the commission if it were withdrawn from McArthur, allowed his name to figure prominently in the attack made by Ketcham on the Committee on Public Buildings. Following Ketcham, a Mr. Beideman, a member of the Committee on City Property, proposed a resolution to disapprove the contract already approved with John McArthur, citing the authority of the Council to do so as granted by the State Supreme Court. Following Mr. Beideman: "Mr. Neal read a communication from Mr. S. Sloan, a prominent architect, agreeing to erect suitable fire proof Public Buildings, with all necessary accommodations, in Independence Square, for $400,000.00."[21] This cost figure was a telling argument, because the rumored estimate of the accepted bid from McArthur was $1.5 million.

To allow tempers to cool, the question was postponed for a week. However, the Philadelphia newspapers continued to make front-page news of the dispute, reprinting Mr. Neal's speech in full and reporting that Ketcham had filed a "Bill in Equity" asking for an injunction to stop the Council from awarding the contract to McArthur.[22] When the question was reopened, those Council members who supported the Committee on Public Buildings diverted argument from the double contract for the building to the choice of its site. They argued that the difference in cost between the Sloan and McArthur proposals was directly related to the difference in site, and that the real decision before the Council was the location of the building. Initially, Philadelphia's newspapers had strongly supported the site on Independence Square, but as the wrangle in Council dragged on, this attitude began to change. It was noted that Ketcham's objections were by no means disinterested one, since he was the contractor who submitted the lowest bid on the McArthur design. It was also pointed out, by truly disinterested parties, that the city was growing westward and that a centralized location for its administrative center made more sense than a sentimental attachment to Independence Square. In late October a compromise was reached in the Select Council. The construction contract with McArthur was disapproved, no mention being made of the architectural contract, and a resolution to elect a "City Architect," who would supervise all construction of municipal buildings, was resoundingly passed. There the matter rested until after the Civil War.

Samuel Sloan's role in the City Hall dispute cannot be mistaken. He speculated that in providing the Ketcham-Neal faction with support he had an excellent chance of receiving the commission for the buildings. If Ketcham had not been a contractor as well as a member of the Select Council, Sloan's actions would not have seemed like conspiracy; however, by aiding the attack on McArthur in the hope of personal gain, Sloan was guilty of "unprofessional" conduct. In 1860, "unprofessional" was a new word among architects, and it denoted a new attitude toward their vocation and its ethics. This new attitude was the direct result of influence from the newly organized American Institute of Architects.

A case can be made that the American Institute of Architects was a spinoff product of the crisis year 1857. It was chartered in February of that year, and among its organizers were Philadelphians John Notman and Thomas U. Walter. Both Notman and Walter had long believed in more rigorous standards for the business practices of architects and in the greater sense of professional fraternity needed to enforce those standards. Walter had been one of the founders of the short-lived American Institution of Architects, which had attempted to gain acceptance of such aims in the crisis year of 1836, while Notman's refusal to participate in competitions which offered only a premium to finalists, while retaining their designs, sparked his disagreements with the Masons of Philadelphia.

Sloan was well aware of the movement toward "professionalism" among architects, for he was to be one of the nineteen practitioners who applied for the charter of the Pennsylvania Institute of Architects in February 1861.[23] The Pennsylvania Institute was not intended to compete with the American Institute but to supplement it, bringing its national functions to a local level. In the words of its charter, the purpose of the Pennsylvania Institute of Architects was:

> To perfect the knowledge and elaborate the art of architecture and the sciences in connection with it. To elevate the standing of its professors by affording facilities for a free interchange of thought and mutual agreement on the laws and rules necessary to be observed in its practices. And on a combined effort to utilize the art so as the better to adapt it to the general public and private wants upon safe and economical principles.

In subscribing to this charter and becoming a founding member of the Pennsylvania Institute, Sloan was reacting to necessity, for he recognized that changes were taking place in his profession. Those changes had been brought home to him by two serious business reverses. On September 6, 1860, two weeks after arguments over the City Hall commission had made front-page news, the Board of Controllers for the Public Schools suspended all commissions for public school buildings, effectively canceling Sloan's de facto position as "architect to the Board of Controllers of the Public Schools."[24] Three weeks later, on November 16, Sloan was refused payment by the Finance Committee of the Select Council for plans of the Municipal Hospital for Contagious and Infectious Diseases, and action on his commission for the building was tabled until November 1862.[25] There is no firm evidence that these setbacks were the result of Sloan's participation in the City Hall imbroglio; that is, there is no immediate evidence, but a report issued by the Controllers of the Public Schools in 1864, reviewing their actions of the preceding decade, leaves little doubt that they had been anxious to rid themselves of association with Sloan in 1860.[26]

Addison Hutton returned from Natchez in the winter of 1860–1861 to find Sloan's office almost at a standstill. No new commissions were received that spring and summer as the nation came closer and closer to civil war. With Hutton's help, Sloan put together two more books during this period: *Sloan's Homestead Architecture* and *American Houses: A Variety of Designs for Rural Buildings*. There was little original material in either book, the majority of their designs being adapted and redrawn from commissions that the office had already done or projects that had appeared in Sloan's earlier books. However they sold well, running through several editions after the first issue of 1861, because they were small (quarto editions) and inexpensive. Sloan tried to keep his office open even after war broke out in April, but a total paralysis of trade in Philadelphia followed the first Battle of Manassas, and Sloan was forced to dismiss Hutton and suspend practice in the early autumn of 1861.[27]

CHAPTER VIII

1859–1869
The Decade of Transition

The events of 1859–1861 determined the future course of Samuel Sloan's personal and professional life. His failure to recognize, until forced to do so, that there had been changes in America—changes in politics, economy, and attitudes—brought him quickly from the top almost to the bottom of his profession in Philadelphia. Having achieved success so rapidly and so easily, Sloan had a stubborn optimism about his practice that caused him to ignore or dismiss the probable results of local and national events.[1] The panic and depression of 1857–1858 had shaken his confidence somewhat, but the brief resurgence of business in the autumn of 1859 seemed to reconfirm his optimism. Sloan found it hard to concede that there were events which he could not, in some way, control or get around. This attitude embroiled him in the Philadelphia City Hall dispute, whose consequences—cancellation of his city contracts, even the defection of his old allies, the Controllers for the Public Schools—he could not foresee, and once begun, the withdrawal of Philadelphia's esteem was as rapid as its award had been. After 1860, Sloan received almost no new commissions until 1864, when he formed a partnership with his former draftsman, Addison Hutton.

Sloan's contracts made during 1860 were honored until the war made new construction impossible, and it was in the fallow period between 1861 and 1864 that one of his most influential hospital designs was partially realized. This was the Hospital of the Protestant Episcopal Church in Philadelphia, which was considered by medical consultants to be the finest general hospital in the United States until the construction of the hospital of Johns Hopkins University in the late 1870s.[2] The Protestant Episcopal Hospital was widely praised for implementing in full—for the first time in America—the recommendations of the French Academy on the planning and construction of hospitals.[3] Unfortunately, this acclaim did not come in 1861, when

Sloan needed it, but only after the close of the war. It was the emergency use of the partially completed building during the war that convinced physicians and administrators of its excellence. (Plate 16.)

Construction of the hospital was begun in May 1860 and continued until February 1862, by which time the central administration building and the chapel had been fully completed and the west wing partially completed. Beginning in the summer of 1862, the unfinished building was occupied for nine months by war wounded, many of those from the first Battle of Bull Run being accommodated there.[4] Construction began again in 1871 after a nationwide fundraising campaign, which made the building known throughout the country, and the completed facility was dedicated in 1874.[5] The impact of its design on hospital planning in the United States can be judged by the text of *Hospital Construction and Organization*, a collection of recommendations made by consultants to the Committee on Construction for the Johns Hopkins Hospital. It was, in their consensus opinion, "the finest example of the Pavilion System in the United States."[6] This system was first recommended by the French Academy in its report on the improvements of hospitals of 1788, but was generally ignored until the Crimean War, when the writings of

PLATE 16. Hospital of the Protestant Episcopal Church, Philadelphia, Pennsylvania, *The Architectural Review*, vol. 2, March 1820, p. 514 (Reproduced with permission of the Library of Fine Arts, University of Pennsylvania)

Florence Nightingale directed attention to conditions in military hospitals. The schematic plan suggested by the Academy was derived from the traditional pavilion-plus-link system of design common to a majority of large French buildings in the late Middle Ages and early Renaissance. Patients were separated, according to sex and treatment required, into a series of pavilions, which also contained treatment facilities and nurses stations. These pavilions were connected by long wards, the center corridor of which carried the circulation between pavilions, making them the equivalent of a "long gallery." Such an arrangement provided maximum supervision by minimum staff and was easily expandable, because the plan was bilinear, centering on the administrative pavilion. As the Johns Hopkins Hospital, and a host of others that took it as a model, was built on the Pavilion System, the long-range influence of the Protestant Episcopal Hospital was probably greater than any of Sloan's other hospital buildings.

Another of Sloan's innovative hospitals was temporarily shelved in the backwash from the Philadelphia City Hall brouhaha. The Select Council denied Sloan the supervision of the Municipal Hospital for Contagious and Infectious Diseases of the City and County of Philadelphia, but failed in their attempt to deny or reduce his fee for the design that had been accepted in 1856.[7] Arguments in Council blocked erection of the building from November 1860 until November 1862, when a commission of eleven members was appointed to supervise its construction. Progress was slow, and the hospital was not handed over to the Board of Health until April 27, 1865.[8] The Hospital for Contagious and Infectious Diseases followed, once again, the recommendations of the French Academy for the treatment of cholera patients. The scheme was again bilineal, centering on an administration and treatment block which was flanked on each side by long wards opening off a single-loaded "balcony" corridor. It achieved maximum air circulation and sunlight in wards by expanding fenestration to encompass virtually the entire outside wall, raising ceilings to fourteen feet and opening the single-loaded corridors to the exterior so that convalescent patients "could enjoy a sheltered walk in the open air."[9] The hospital continued in use until the first decade of the twentieth century, when it was relocated, not because the building was considered obsolete but because it was deemed too close to the center of the city.[10]

Both of these hospital commissions had been awarded before the rowdy sessions in Philadelphia's Councils over the new City Hall which were so fully reported in Philadelphia's newspapers. That publicity had excited interest in the professional responsibility of architects, and Sloan was shortly thereafter involved in two lawsuits, in one of which he was the defendant, in the other the litigant. At the inquest held on December 10, 1862, upon the death of a workman who fell from a "wall gable" during the construction of Sloan's North Broad Street Presbyterian Church, he had to present the court with evidence of the structural soundness of that detail.[11] This was one of the first instances of an architect's being required to defend his provisions for the safety of workmen engaged in the construction of one of his buildings. Both Sloan and the builder, John Ketcham, were exonerated by the jury, which held that the accident was not the result of any negligence or deficiency on their part but was caused by the absorption of water into the raw masonry over the preceding week of torrential rain. Three years later Sloan was the litigant in a suit upholding the right of an architect to the ownership of his plans. The action arose from the reuse of his drawings for the courthouse of Lycoming County, Pennsylvania, to erect the courthouse of neighboring Northumberland County.

The confused affair of the Northumberland County Court House, Sunbury, is an example of the confused public understanding of the architect's professional role at that time. Sloan had received the commission for the Lycoming County Court House, in Williamsport, in April 1860. He had not produced a reworking of his standard courthouse, but an entirely new design "in the Itallian manner."[12] The citizens of Lycoming County found the building exactly to their taste; it satisfied all the requirements of Convenience, Comfort, and Fitness and was inexpensive, costing only $41,030. The courthouse immediately became—and remained, until its razing in 1969—a source of pride to the county.[13] Its builder was D. S. Rissel, former sheriff of Lycoming County, and he was commemorated for his job—along with Sloan, as architect—on a stone tablet imbedded in the wall of its southwestern tower. The building was occupied in March 1861, less than a year after commissioning, which is evidence of the suitability of Sloan's design and the efficiency of Rissel's construction methods.[14] (Plate 17.)

Three years later, in November 1864, the Commissioners of Northumberland County, having been prodded by a "Presentment" from the grand jury, resolved to build a new courthouse in Sunbury.

To this end arrangements were made to visit the court houses recently erected in adjoining counties, in order that plans and specifications might be prepared before the close of the year. This was accomplished, the court house of Lycoming County being taken as the model. On the 5th of January, 1865, proposals ranging from ninety-seven to one hundred five thousand dollars were received, and the contract was awarded D. S. Rissel at the first amount named.[15]

Rissel could make the lowest bid because he did not have to pay an architect for plans and specifications; he already had them. The Northumberland Commissioners had expressed a wish to make the

PLATE 17. Lycoming County Court House, Williamsport, Pennsylvania
(Photo reproduced with permission of Emerson J. Probst Jr. family)

Williamsport building the "model" for their own; Rissel complied by erecting a mirror image of it in Sunbury. The reversed copy cost $55,970 more than the original. Rissel and the commissioners, in the context of their time and its understanding of architectural services, saw nothing illegal in reusing Sloan's work without his permission and without paying him a fee. Sloan did. He sued. Exactly what party he sued—the former sheriff, the Commissioners, or the County—is not clear, for the court records are unexplainably missing. However, that he did receive a settlement is reasonably verified, although the only published record is a dry summation in a *History of Northumberland County, Pennsylvania*, published in 1891: "The aggregate cost considerably exceeded one hundred thousand dollars." The writer of the history did not itemize what the "aggregate" included.[16]

It is ironic that Samuel Sloan, who only four years before had been criticized for unprofessional conduct, should have been the first Philadelphia architect to follow the precedent of the Hunt *v.* Parmly case of 1861 supporting the right of a practitioner to the ownership of his work. His suit against Northumberland County was a public defense of professional status and is evidence of the change in his approach to practice which the City Hall scandal initiated. By the end of the 1860s Sloan was, in some ways, the most "professional" of professionals, but not in all ways. He had by that time become a charter member of the Pennsylvania Institute of Architects and begun publication of *The Architectural Review and American Builder's Journal*, which for its first two years was virtually the house organ of the reconstituted American Institute of Architects, of which he was made a Fellow in 1869. In the October 1868 issue of *The Architectural Review*, Sloan set forth his personal definition of architectural "professionalism" in a long editorial, "The Progress of Architecture in the United States."[17] His "professionalism" in matters pertaining to the rules of practice such as relations between architect and client, architect and contractor, and architect and employee was identical with that of his peers, and he supported the fight for legal rights and social recognition. However, he could not accept the implied rules of style and taste that were held by the majority of his co-practitioners in Philadelphia. This attitude he documented in the November issue of the *Review* with the first of a series of essays on what can be called Sloan's "philosophy of architecture," "An American Style." In this first essay were the two implied criticisms of the Philadelphia profession which evidence Sloan's opinion of his co-practitioners: "Yes, it is an undeniable fact that the great majority of what are called 'American Architects' are mere constructors whose sole effort is to attain fortune and thus acquire position" and "In fine, let American Architects cease to transfer the designs of Europe, with all their antiquated appliances, once so useful and significant; and *Here so absurd*."[18]

Sloan was uncomfortable in the company of his peers. This stemmed from a feeling that Philadelphia's architects had always condescended to his craftsman origins and his business methods. Sloan had little understanding of or respect for architecture as an accomplishment rather than a trade. At base he was a craftsman, trained to solve problems and proud of being "hired" to do so. His success as an architect had resulted from this ability rather than from any grounding in theory and aesthetics. His attitude toward visual "style" had always been pragmatic. Admitting its usefulness—as a symbol of status, or category, or intent—he had used its visual vocabulary in the same way that he had used the right tool for a particular job when he was a carpenter.

Sloan had never considered "style"—the Comfort and Fitness of the new triad—as a primary criterion of architectural design. It was Convenience, function, that was Sloan's primary criterion. "Let everyone arrange his dwelling so as to secure the greatest amount of convenience, and then exercise his judgement in decoration" appeared in the first edition of *The Model Architect*. The large number of low- and medium-cost dwellings illustrated in this first of Sloan's publications all evidence the clarity, directness, and privacy of circulation, which was the primary ingredient in his definition of Convenience.[19] He also ensures a minimum of two exposures in most of the rooms in these designs, for cross-ventilation, and is generous in his allocation of space to the service rooms. By contrast, his attitude toward visual style is somewhat offhand. In both "Design Eleventh: A Plain and Ornamented Villa" and "Design Twelfth: A Design for a Cottage" of volume 1, "two versions of the entrance elevation are presented; the client can take his choice."[20] All the essays on historical styles in his books were borrowed from other sources; they were correct but superficial. By contrast, his analyses of the functional requirements of building types—schools, hospitals, stores, even dwellings—were penetrating and original. The visual appearance of a building was another one of its necessary functions; yes, of course. What was the visual purpose of this building—to attract, to reassure, to awe, to proclaim status, to manifest service? From the stylistic vocabulary of his time, a visually functional appearance was chosen because it solved a problem, just as the arrangement of spaces or the choice of materials solved problems.

It was this pragmatic approach that attracted Sloan's most important clients and patrons—Kirkbride, Eastwick, Harrison, Browne, Bennett. Out of it came his most significant work, the long shadow of which fell across the design philosophies of later pragmatic eclectics, of Furness, of Sullivan, of Wright. Sloan's conviction, which grew stronger as he grew older, that there should be an *American* way of architecture was founded on his early exposure to the arguments of Downing and Emerson and to his training as a problem-solving craftsman who was expected to understand the needs of his client better than the client himself did and who was hired to satisfy those needs. He believed that American needs could be satisfied by forms and methods derived from the American environment.[21] To those architects of the eastern United States, already bemused by European academicism with its rigid canons and regularized methods, such an attitude was unlettered and crude. They regarded Sloan's arguments as the cries of a "has been" trying to maintain an already lost position. They also objected to his business methods. Sloan sold his services in the most direct, obvious way because, in his opinion, the reason for being in business was to be in business.

So to stay in business Sloan changed his business methods, joined the Pennsylvania Institute, adopted the new code of architectural practice, and became a "professional" rather than a speculator. If the lawsuit he brought over the reuse of his plans by Northumberland County was intended to convince the Philadelphia public that he was a changed man, a reputable member of the fraternity, it was not successful, for his practice did not improve, despite an explosive revival of business in Philadelphia after the Battle of Gettysburg (July 1, 1863). Sloan's reaction to the stagnation of his local practice was a scramble for work outside Pennsylvania, outside the Northeast, even outside the United States. There is in the collection of the Dickinson College Library in Carlisle, Pennsylvania, a series of letters from Sloan to Eli Slifer, Secretary of State for the Commonwealth, for whom he designed a country villa outside Lewisburg, Pennsylvania, in 1860. These letters cover the years 1861–1869, and one of them, dated "Jany 20th, 1864," is a request for a recommendation:

> Allow me the privilege of asking a line or two from you stating my Standing as an Architect. My object is to forward a few testimonials to *Peru South America*, being in treaty with persons there for a matter of

considerable proportions, and I wish to establish myself fairly before
them, although they seem to have some knowledge to warrant their
opening a Correspondence. If you will do me the above favor, I am
sure it will benefit me and shall forever be grateful for the kindness,
and should also be glad to have the *Governor's* signature. He might,
from the knowledge he may have, be willing to sanction your
statement. The influence in a *Foreign Country* would be of much
importance.[22]

There is no evidence that Sloan contemplated emigrating to Peru,
but his solicitation of work from a "Foreign Country" is indicative of
his wide search for jobs. No further reference to the project in Peru
has been found, and his work problem was solved with the formation
of his partnership with Addison Hutton.

Hutton was by no means eager to reaffiliate himself with his former employer. After leaving Sloan's office in the autumn of 1861,
Hutton had tried his hand at storekeeping for a year, but business
was at a standstill in Philadelphia, and in December 1862 he joined
the architectural office of George C. Howard as a draftsman. In
March of the following year he opened his own one-man office. Hutton's close association with the Quaker community in Philadelphia
brought him commissions, and by September he could move into
better quarters and hire an occasional draftsman. It was at this time,
autumn 1863, that Sloan first approached Hutton with the sugges-
tion of a partnership, which the young man declined. Although Hutton felt some obligation to, and a measure of personal affection for,
Sloan, he was aware of Sloan's equivocal reputation in Philadelphia
and had experienced his mercurial temper. However, Sloan still occupied large quarters on 4th Street, and his national reputation, particularly as a hospital architect, was still bright. After Sloan agreed to a
limited association of only three years, Hutton accepted his offer, and
the partnership was formed on January 7, 1864. Later that month the
new firm of Sloan & Hutton opened at Sloan's old office.[23]

Sloan & Hutton continued as a firm until January 1868, the
agreement being extended for one year. In that time it executed over
a dozen major commissions. The hospital work can be assigned to
Sloan. So also can several Presbyterian churches, for Sloan continued
to be favored by the Presbyterians, even in Philadelphia. But it was
Hutton's Quaker connections that brought Sloan & Hutton the
commissions for the first building of Swarthmore College and the
Banking House of the Philadelphia Saving Fund Society (P.S.F.S.).

It was also Hutton's known probity that caused the Controllers for the Public Schools to relent and give the firm three Philadelphia public schools; the buildings were not, however, designed on "Mr. Sloan's improved plan."[24]

There is no ambiguity in the documentation of Swarthmore and the Banking House of the P.S.F.S. Edward Parrish, the "father" of Swarthmore, for whom the building was later named, was a personal friend of Hutton, and letters in the Hutton Papers show that the two men worked closely together on its design.[25] Sloan had withdrawn from the firm of Sloan & Hutton before the commission for the Banking House of the P.S.F.S. was received, and although his name appears on the competition drawings, the Board of Managers of the Society gave Hutton entire credit for the building's final design.[26] The authorship of Horticultural Hall, Philadelphia, and the Seminary of Saint Charles Borromeo at Overbrook is not as clear. Records of the Horticultural Society of Pennsylvania mention Samuel Sloan, only, in connection with the erection of their first hall in 1866; however, when it burned in 1881, Addison Hutton was called on to reconstruct the building, which suggests that he had a larger part in its original design than the records show. With Saint Charles Borromeo, Sloan alone is mentioned in the initial documents, but it was probably Hutton who finished the drawings for the building and supervised its construction.

In every period of Sloan's professional life after 1852, when the first edition of *The Model Architect* appeared, it is difficult to determine which buildings came from his office and which were taken from his publications. A case in point is a group of works in Lock Haven, Pennsylvania, which terminated with the Clinton County Court House. A design for this building, from the office of Sloan & Hutton, was accepted by the Commissioners in July 1867, and the courthouse was completed in the late summer of 1869.[27] The building, still in use, is a variation of the Northumberland–Lycoming County design and closely resembles the former Williamsport and extant Sunbury Courthouses. Seven or eight other buildings in Lock Haven are credited by local historians either to Sloan, directly, or to his influence. Their similarity to designs of Sloan, in one or another of his publications, is striking.[28] One of the group, the Great Island Presbyterian Church, is said to have been designed by Sloan himself "in the early part of 1863" but not erected until 1865–1869. A publication of the Clinton County Historical Society, *Historic Lock Haven: An Architectural Survey*, contains the following passage:

> His [Sloan's] contributions to Lock Haven occurred early in his career
> and had such a profound effect as to make Lock Haven different from
> other small towns built at the same time. Sloan's Norman window and
> arcaded corbel coursing found expression in so many buildings in
> Lock Haven that at one time the whole town may have appeared to
> have been designed by one architect.[29]

If this is indeed the case, then Lock Haven had the largest body of
local works designed by Sloan, either directly or indirectly, outside of
Philadelphia.

Addison Hutton's limitation on the firm life of Sloan & Hutton
was wise, for relations between the partners began to deteriorate as
early as September 1865, when Hutton brought his brothers, Finley
and Harmon, into the office as draftsmen. The partnership became
increasingly uncomfortable thereafter, and on January 7, 1868, the
fourth anniversary of its formation, the firm was dissolved. Sloan resigned to Hutton all unfinished or pending commissions and gave it
as his intention to open a practice in New York. He also agreed not to
practice in Philadelphia for at least two years.[30]

Hutton's professional behavior, after Sloan's departure, was strictly
correct; he issued, or presented, all work remaining in the office
under the firm name, Sloan & Hutton, although much of it was his
alone. Samuel Sloan was not so correct in his behavior. After a few
months' absence he was back in Philadelphia, opening an office in the
late spring of 1868. In violation of his agreement with Hutton,
Sloan began to accept local commissions, but his main efforts for the
remainder of that year were directed to the publication of *The Architectural Review and American Builder's Journal*, the first periodical devoted exclusively to architecture and building to appear in the United
States. Hutton was justifiably annoyed. Not only had Sloan broken
his given word, but his new office was in the same building with
Hutton, which led to confusion among visiting clients. With con-
summate tact, Hutton persuaded Sloan to take back his old rooms,
which the former firm of Sloan & Hutton had used, while he moved
to a small building on the site of the new Banking House for the
P.S.F.S., whose construction he was supervising.[31]

The interlude between the dissolution of Sloan & Hutton in January 1868 and Sloan's reopening of an office in late spring of the same
year is, as yet, without any documentation. Sloan told Hutton that
he was going to New York, and later events seem to bear out that he
did so, for upon his return to Philadelphia, Sloan threw himself into

promoting the newly reconstituted American Institute of Architects, whose national headquarters were then in New York. His first, and most important, service to the institute was publication of *The Architectural Review*, whose prospectus declared: "No Periodical on Architecture and Construction is, or ever has been, issued in the United States." With the *Review* as his national rostrum, and the tacit backing of the American Institute, Sloan could return to Philadelphia and once more be a power in the city. For a time, he was.

CHAPTER IX

The Architectural Review
and the Centennial

Samuel Sloan's association with the American Institute of Architects (AIA) was closely interconnected with his publication of *The Architectural Review and American Builder's Journal*. During the time that the *Review* was issued (July 1868–November 1870), Sloan was a figure of some importance in, and to, the AIA, but his participation in its affairs almost stopped when the periodical failed, and by 1877 he had allowed his membership to lapse.[1] Sloan became a member of the Institute during his absence from Philadelphia in the early spring of 1868 and immediately upon his return began the organization of the *Review*.[2] With the first issue, he assumed the role of publicist for the AIA, reporting its meetings and committee actions and repeatedly calling on practitioners to support the organization. The AIA accepted this gratuitous role, for it needed exposure and did not have the finances to publish an organ of its own. Sloan saw this tacit recognition as an endorsement of his architectural beliefs and within a short time looked on himself as spokesman, rather than just publicist, for the AIA. In the November 1868 issue of the *Review* he began a series of essays on the state of architecture in America which, because of their frequent references to the AIA, seemed to be an expression of its philosophy. This was not the case, but its governing board did not, at first, object; although some members found Sloan's preoccupation with "An American Style" to be "a well worn subject."[3]

"An American Style" was the title of Sloan's first essay; its initial tone was reproving, as evidenced by the previously quoted sentence: "Yes, it is an undeniable fact that the great majority of what are called 'American Architects' are mere constructors whose sole effort is to obtain fortune and acquire position." This, from Sloan, must have sounded laughable to the architects of Philadelphia, but on second thought it was not so amusing, for what "American Architects" other than those of Philadelphia did he know well? Sloan went on to strike at imitative design and to reiterate—though it is doubtful that he remembered the source—the ideals of Emerson. His tone, here, was evangelical:

> Let their [American architects] designs be those drawn from the school of nature, as she abundantly presents them in the peculiarity of flower, shrub and tree; the sky-line of her mountains; the stately taper of her pines; the graceful growth of her palmettos; the pendant beauty of her aspens; and the thousand lessons that she everywhere gives.

He concluded with a plea for professional unity, extolling its good effects as exemplified in the work of the Royal Institute of British Architects, and decrying the timid support of the AIA:

> There are a few architects among us who have shown an inclination to enter on such an enterprise; but unfortunately, they "hide their light under a bushel," and a very limited portion of the community, indeed, is aware that there is in New York an Institute of American Architects.[4]

The opinions Sloan expressed in this first essay were pertinent and in large measure valid, but he was championing a cause that seemed outdated to practitioners on the eastern seaboard. Americanism in architecture had been an ideal of the Jacksonian era; it had appealed to the independent craftsmen and mechanics of the frontier, and in the burgeoning centers of what had been the old frontier—in Saint Louis, Indianapolis, Chicago—it continued to have appeal. The East, exhausted or disillusioned in the aftermath of civil war, had turned for leadership in architectural design to the regularized canons of European theorists, to Ruskin and the academicians of the Ecole de Beaux Arts. This was particularly true in Philadelphia, where the Napoleon III Baroque of John McArthur and the Victorian Gothic of James Windrim were the popular modes.

By the end of 1868 the *Review* had become, to all intents and purposes, the house organ of the AIA, and its service to the Institute was invaluable. It offered the scattered practitioners beyond the eastern seaboard a way to display their work to a national, rather than only a local, audience. For the first time, architects in the midwestern cities could have their designs appraised by their peers in the eastern centers, while keeping abreast of what was being done in New York and Boston. The *Review* associated this service with the AIA, giving to that organization an immediate tradition of service and an aura of prestige which it could not otherwise have obtained for many years.

Samuel Sloan was made a Fellow of the American Institute of Architects on February 8, 1869. In the April 1869 issue of the *Review*, Sloan's second essay, "Architecture in America, Naissant and Renaissant," appeared. Its tone was prophetic rather than evangelical, but it harked *back* to the prophets of the 1830s and 1840s—to Emerson in particular:

> In our *Naissant* style we would be governed altogether by the fitness of the design. Its fitness for the purpose for which it is to be erected. Its fitness for the locality where it is to stand. Its fitness in the material chosen, not alone as the strength and durability, but with respect to color also. The fitness of ornamentation is a feature of our Naissant style, which should be especially attended to. Let us have no leaves, or flowers that belong not to our soil; no animals, that never had existence, such as griffins, dragons and the like. None of these. Let everything be American, in feeling and effect.

This ideal of American architecture was to be realized in the Midwest within a decade. Sloan's presentiment of the future was influenced by the gratifying response of midwestern architects to the *Review*'s call for publishable designs. Eastern response had diminished in 1869, largely because of increasing annoyance at Sloan's use of the *Review* to broadcast his personal views as if they were those of the AIA. Moreover, his continued antagonism toward Philadelphia had become embarrassing, particularly as the leading figure in the AIA's reorganization was a Philadelphian, Thomas Ustick Walter.[5] As a result, the periodical received fewer and fewer submissions from New York and Boston—almost none from Philadelphia that were not self-generated—and its published examples were increasingly midwestern in origin. There is another possibility, and this is admittedly speculation. Sloan may have chosen to present the midwestern work, over that from the East, because he was more in sympathy with its design approach. It is obvious, from the quotation given above, that Sloan's definition of Fitness was almost identical with the terms "functional" or "organic" as they were to be used by later midwestern architects.

Whatever the case, support of the *Review* from eastern centers of the profession declined. Sloan saw this as the result of personal enmity rather than objective judgment and considered it a threat to the future of the AIA. In the October 1869 issue of the *Review*, he pleaded for unity and the putting aside of personalities:

> The Institute of American Architects is the entering wedge in the reform movement so necessary to the welfare of our profession, as well as to the full acknowledgement of its claims to distinction as a higher art. O, that we could see banished the petty, unworthy bitternesses which cause so much contempt in the public mind, and the architects of America rally with one heart to the upholding of our noble profession, thus perfecting an Institute that would be a pride to our own, and a boon to succeeding generations.

Sloan was sincere in this wish, but unfortunately he could not restrain his own "petty, unworthy bitternesses." The Philadelphia Chapter of the AIA was organized on November 11, 1869. This was important Institute news which Sloan should have heralded in the *Review*, but no mention of it was made in any issue. At no time in the remaining life of the *Review* was the slightest reference made in its pages to the Philadelphia Chapter.[6]

Sloan attempted to counteract the resentment his feud with the Philadelphians was generating by giving more and more space in the *Review* to the national activities of the AIA. He published extensive reports of the 1870 national convention, together with digests of the papers read before it, and gave particular attention to new chapters being formed in the Midwest.[7] But because of his intransigent attitude, the *Review* had become a liability to the Institute, and after the 1870 convention it withdrew sanction and support. The periodical's last issue appeared in November 1870, and in it Sloan published the most radical of his essays, "Is Novelty in Architecture Desirable." It began with an analysis of the disruptive and usually transient effect of "Novel" design, but concluded with a wry judgment upon his generation of architects, from which judgment he did not exclude himself:

> Yet it must be confessed that there exists far too much sameness in Architectural design among us in a highly progressive age like the present; and that we build, or seem to build, on borrowed ideas—hints picked up here and there, and associated under one slight covering of "style."

Sloan ended his last essay with a defiant restatement of the principle he had not always followed but had always believed: "Our mission is one of utility founded on progressive civilization, and we must assign a reason for what we do, and be independent in our thoughts and designs."

During the life of the *Review*, Sloan carried out few architectural commissions. Those he did execute between July 1868 and November 1870 came to him because of his long-standing association with the Presbyterian church and his reputation as a school architect. None of the commissions was unusual or demanding in its program, and Sloan was able to produce the construction documents without interrupting his editorship of the *Review*. The church designs were very stereotyped. For example, the front elevations of Trinity Reformed Church and the Chapel of Calvary Presbyterian were so similar that the engravings of them that appeared in the same July 1869 issue of the *Review* are difficult to tell apart.[8]

The Cumberland Valley State Normal School in Shippensburg, Pennsylvania, was commissioned from Sloan just two months before the last issue of the *Review* appeared. The *Shippensburg News* of September 17, 1870, reported, "Sloan, the architect, was in this place last week." The building—which survives almost intact as "Old Main" of Shippensburg State College—was dedicated on April 15, 1873. Of Sloan's many educational buildings, this rather obscure example has had a longer useful life than any, its dormitory pavilions being closed only in May 1976, the interior remodeled in 1981–1982, and today containing the business offices of the college.[9]

Although Sloan did not actively seek building commissions while the *Review* was being published, he did enter two major competitions for large public works. In 1869 he submitted a design, which placed second after that of John J. McArthur Jr., in the second competition for the New Public Buildings of the City and County of Philadelphia (City Hall). This was the last act in the long, drawn-out affair of Philadelphia's new City Hall. McArthur had won the first competition, in which Sloan—the second-place winner—had played a contradictory role. It is not surprising, therefore, that McArthur was chosen the final finalist in 1869. What is surprising is Sloan's second second-place. Perhaps Sloan's reputation in Philadelphia was not as dubious as fragmentary documentation has made it appear. Certainly the firm of Sloan & Hutton had not lacked for important commissions during its lifetime, and in 1869 Sloan's *Review* was still the unofficial house organ of the American Institute of Architects. Three months after the awards, the Philadelphia chapter of the AIA was founded, with McArthur as its first president. Sloan's *Review*, the presumptive spokesman for the AIA, made no mention of the fact.

The second competition Sloan entered in this period was for the New City Hall of San Francisco, California. This was advertised on June 23, 1870, and judged on November 17 of that year. Sloan's entry was not among the first five premiums. However,

> in addition the Commissioners decided that three other sets of designs and plans were of such merit that the sum of $500 was awarded the author of each—*viz.* to Messrs. Laugerfeldt and Attwood of Boston, Messrs. Patton & Jordan of San Francisco, and Mr. Samuel Sloan of Philadelphia.[10]

All of the designs were exhibited "for public inspection" over a period of some weeks. This was Sloan's introduction to possible clients in California, and it may have resulted in a commission. Kirkbride, in the second edition of *Hospitals for the Insane* (1880), credits Sloan with having designed, or been consulted on, a hospital of the insane "in every State of the Union." The Napa State Hospital was the only such hospital built in California after the San Francisco competition. It was designed on a compromise system in which the Kirkbride element was dominant.[11] The Napa State Hospital was begun in 1872, and although no documentation connecting Sloan with the Napa Hospital has been found, his award in the San Francisco competition, his reputation as a hospital architect, and his close association with Kirkbride all lend weight to the possibility of his association with the design of the building.

For the lifetime of the *Review*, Sloan accepted almost no residential or commercial commissions. Indeed, from 1861 to 1871 only three residences and one commercial building can be credited to him.[12] To bring himself before such clients again after the *Review* failed, Sloan turned to his books. In the summer of 1868, Lippincott reissued *The Model Architect* (3rd ed.) and Henry C. Baird brought out the second edition of *American Houses*. The expensive, two-volume *Model Architect* sold well, but the cheaper *American Houses* did not. Baird had been persuaded to reissue *American Houses* because of Lippincott's modest success with the second edition of Sloan's *Homestead Architecture* (1867). However, when Lippincott issued the third edition of *Homestead Architecture* in 1870, it did not sell. Sloan's long and profitable career as an author of architectural books virtually came to an end in 1870. Lippincott, which owned the rights to both books, issued a fourth edition of *The Model Architect* and a third of Sloan's *Constructive Architecture* in 1873, but after that no further editions of his earlier books, and no new work by him in book form, was published. Considering the quantity of Sloan's publications—their many editions and wide circulation—it is astonishing that they were forgotten within a decade. Sloan's obituaries in the architectural periodicals that succeeded, and copied, *The Architectural Review*, and the brief notices about him that appeared in biographical "cyclopaedias" for a few years after his death, made mistakes in the listing of his book titles as well as in the names and locations of his buildings.[13]

Finding the residential and commercial fields virtually closed to him in Philadelphia, Sloan turned to those building types in which he still had a national reputation—public buildings, schools, and hospitals—and turned away, almost completely, from eastern Pennsylvania as an area of practice. His gradual withdrawal from Pennsylvania—from the North-Central States as a whole—can be said to begin in 1870. In 1871 he was asked to make modifications and additions to the New Jersey State House at Trenton. Because of piecemeal appropriations by the New Jersey Assembly, this commission, which expanded into one of considerable magnitude, was not completed until 1875. His first additions initiated a chain reaction of modification which eventually altered the appearance and use of the entire building. In her definitive study of the State House, Professor Zara Cohan, of Kean College, gives the following sequence of building programs: 1871–1872, New Legislative Chambers, Governor's Suite, Library, and Executive Offices; 1872–1873, refurbishing of the Reception, Chancery, and Supreme Court rooms; 1873–1876, additions to the Facade ("an additional story upon the main portion and two stories upon the wings"). She adds, "By the time this project was completed, John Notman's 1846 State House had all but disappeared." The major fire that the building suffered in March 1885 destroyed a majority of Sloan's work, and the present Statehouse, other than some alterations and an office building added in the twentieth century, follows the outcome of the 1885–1895 rebuilding.[14]

Before work on the New Jersey State House was completed, Sloan received a nostalgic commission. The old Presbyterian church at the forks of the Brandywine River near Glen Moore, Pennsylvania, had fallen into disrepair. On March 14, 1874, the Board of Trustees asked Sloan to examine the building to see if it could be saved. This was home territory, Glen Moore being only a few miles from Honeybrook, where Samuel was born, and the graveyard of the church was full of Sloan headstones. There was even a Sloan from Honeybrook on the Board of Trustees of the church. Samuel reported that the building was beyond repair and recommended "the erection of new church edifice." He was offered the commission, accepted, and the cornerstone of the new building was laid on August 7, 1875. A history of the church published in 1885 describes a single nave plan, in the "American Gothic" style, without a corner tower, and a "galilee porch" entrance. Sloan may have reused the plan for "A Country Church," which he had published in the January 1870 issue of *The Architectural Review*. The building survives, with the addition of a tower that was not a part of Sloan's original design.[15]

Between the New Jersey State House and the Brandywine church came the two competitions for the proposed buildings of the Centennial Exhibition of 1875. Sloan recognized the Centennial commissions as a sure way of reestablishing himself, both professionally and personally, and he made a supreme effort in his submissions to the Committee on Plans and Architecture. His entry in the first competition (announced on April 1 and judged on August 8, 1873) was entitled "Americanus" and was a terminal statement of Sloan's critical triad, Convenience, Comfort, and Fitness.[16]

"Americanus" proposed a monumental central building of permanent construction, flanked by two wings of temporary construction; each wing contained ten identical pavilions, five to each side. It was in these temporary wings—intended for the displays of the exhibitors—that Sloan's talent for Convenience in design was most evident. They were of modular, cast-iron construction, easily prefabricated, erected, and taken down. Each pavilion was lighted by a central lantern, and the center promenade was roofed with glazed skylights. The wide side aisles that separated the pavilions, and the doubly wide center promenade, made "Americanus" the safest and most Convenient design submitted in the first competition, and because of Sloan's attention to lighting and the inclusion of regular "rest points" along the length of the center promenade, it provided an unusual amount of Comfort for both exhibitors and visitors.[17] (Plate 18.)

In the permanent, central building of "Americanus," Sloan put forward his concept of American Fitness, those forms and symbols that were fitting expressions of American culture and the American way of life. It was an eclectic design, a strange mixture of historic elements used and joined in nonhistoric ways, but in that it was a true expression of American culture, which was still, in 1873, an un-

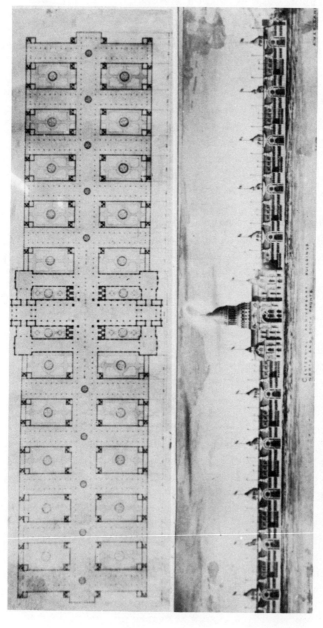

PLATE 18. Elevation and plan of "Americanus," Samuel Sloan's first entry in the Centennial Competition (Reproduced from *Scrapbook of T. U. Walter* with permission of the Library of Fine Arts, University of Pennsylvania)

homogenized collection of historic elements adapted, modified, and ingenuously joined in unhistoric ways. The building's central dome, surmounted by a statue of "America," closely resembled that of the Maryland Statehouse at Annapolis.

Forty-three entries in the competition were received by the Committee on Plans and Buildings on July 15, 1873. Sloan's "Americanus," Number 9 on the roster of entries, was first in the list of ten finalists released by the Committee on Plans and Architecture of the United States Centennial Commission on August 8, 1873.[18] John J. McArthur Jr., in collaboration with Joseph M. Wilson, was second on the list with Number 11, "Lexington-Yorktown." Each of the ten winning entries received a premium of $1,000 and the right to enter the second, and final, competition, from which the Architect of the Centennial was to be selected. As it happened, no entrant in either competition was selected. Many problems and pressures beset the Committee on Plans and Architecture, and their final choice was H. J. Schwarzmann.[19]

In the same announcement that listed the ten finalists of the first competition, the submission date for entries in the second competition was given: September 20, 1873. For so short a time to be allowed before the second submission, the Committee must have assumed that second entries would require only some refinements and minor alterations necessary to comply with a few new requirements set forth in their August 8 announcement. However, the submission date had to be moved forward to October 10, for most of the competitors—Sloan in particular—reworked their entire schemes. Sloan abandoned "Americanus" and all it represented to him, symbolically and architecturally, for a French Baroque Revival scheme. That this Frenchified entry received second prize in the final competition does throw light on the architectural prejudices of the jury and explains, in part, Sloan's drastic change in design approach. He wanted, very badly, to win that competition, and if pandering to the taste of the judges might get him the prize, he would pander.

Sloan's design for the second competition was based on the Paris Exhibition of 1867. He proposed an enormous permanent building in florid Baroque Revival, subtended in the rear by a huge semicircular display shed, its narrow aisles roofed with skylights. This permanent building was a mixture of the Napoleon III Louvre, Versailles, and the Arc de Triomphe de l'Étoile crowned with the dome of the Invalides. (Plate 19.) The perspective of its interior rivaled Piranesi's more imaginative visions.[20] It would have cost far more

PLATE 19. Perspective of the permanent building. From Samuel Sloan, *Description and Design and Drawings for the Proposed Centennial Buildings* (Philadelphia: King & Baird, 1873)

PLATE 20. Interior perspective of permanent building. Second
Competition for the Centennial Buildings
(Reproduced from *Scrapbook of T. U. Walter* with
permission of the Library of Fine Arts, University of Pennsylvania)

than the Commission had to spend, and have been, when the Centennial was over, the most conspicuous white elephant in Philadelphia's townscape. Yet this pretentious, extravagant building inConvenient, unComfortable, and most unFitting as a memorial to America's independence—won second prize. One would like to think that Sloan meant it as a joke, but he was undoubtedly dead serious. The admiration of the Philadelphia public for McArthur's French Baroque design for City Hall seems to have convinced Sloan that the only way to win was to out-Baroque McArthur, and this he did. (Plate 20.)

The second-place award of $3,000 would barely have covered Sloan's expenses for his entry. He submitted twenty-two drawings— some as much as five feet long—and two printed pamphlets containing descriptions of the drawings and a bill of quantities for the proposed buildings.[21] Being second place, again, must have been bitter; he had been second place in Philadelphia competitions so often. He was not offered—or did not choose to accept—a commission for one of the subsidiary buildings of the Exhibition after its final plan was decided on. Sloan's failure with the Centennial Exhibition was a major factor in his eventual decision to remove from Philadelphia entirely. That he delayed for another seven years before doing so was a measure of the hold the city had on him.

CHAPTER X

1874–1884
The Final Decade

For over a year after the close of the Centennial competition, Sloan was without work. In the late autumn of 1874 he wrote two articles, "Heat and Ventilation" and "Our Designs," for the *Church Extension Annual* of the Methodist Episcopal Church. In a preamble to the first of these articles, the board advised:

> We invite special attention to this article by Mr. Sloan, and earnestly commend it to the careful study of all who propose to build. Indeed it would be a most wise expenditure of money to overhaul hundreds of our old churches and provide for warming and ventilating them in harmony with the simple laws of nature, here so clearly presented.[1]

"Heat and Ventilation" reads as rationally and as technically correct today as it did in 1874. Sloan's understanding of mechanical equipment, and his appreciation of its importance in American architecture, increased steadily throughout his career. His attention to this factor in design was initiated by Thomas Kirkbride, who insisted on maximum Comfort for the patients in his hospitals for the insane. Kirkbride had already published *Notice of Some Experiments in Heating and Ventilating Hospitals and Other Buildings by Steam and Hot Water* before he began to collaborate with Sloan, and their long association produced numerous improvements and innovations. Sloan's knowledge of heating systems also benefited from his association with Joseph Harrison, who designed the safe heating system for Kirkbride's hospitals. In the late 1850s, when he had a large practice, Sloan turned over this subdivision of the business, as a specialty, to his brother, Charles Sloan, who became an authority in the field before his death.[2]

The second article, entitled "Our Designs," presented plans, perspectives, and bills of quantities for nine church buildings ranging in estimated cost from $19,780.50 to $1,500. All were in the "Gothic Style," in the manner of Gilbert Scott and William Butterfield. Sloan was trying to conform to the new tide in taste, for he needed work badly, as the preamble to "Our Designs" gives evidence.

> He [Sloan] is one of the best practical Architects in the country, and parties from a distance can, by giving the needful information—description of site, cost of material, labor, &c.,—obtain plans, specifications, detailed drawings, estimated cost, &c., of Mr. Sloan, on reasonable terms.[3]

This mail-order approach to practice evidently brought in inquiries, for in 1877 he contributed another article, also entitled "Our Designs," to the published *Minutes* of the General Assembly of the Presbyterian Church, in which it was included as an appendix.[4] It consisted of plans and elevations for two modestly priced churches in wood construction, in what has been called "stick style." Sloan had first tried his hand at this manner two years before, when he contributed three designs (Nos. 17, 18, and 19) to the 1875 edition of Bicknell's *Wooden and Brick Buildings with Details*.[5]

Between November 1875 and February 1876 there occurred the last, and strangest, episode in Sloan's ambivalent relationship with the American Institute of Architects. Sloan had been a member of the national organization since 1868, and a Fellow since 1869, but he had never been listed on the roster of the Philadelphia Chapter. Thomas U. Walter, president of the Philadelphia Chapter in 1875, had been one of the founders of the original AIA (1857), was the prime mover in its refounding on the base of the chapter system (1867), and was to become its second president, holding office from 1877 to 1887. That there were, in 1875, architects of national reputation in Philadelphia—for example, Samuel Sloan—who were Fellows of the AIA but not members of the Philadelphia Chapter must have been a source of embarrassment to Walter.

Sloan's relations with the Philadelphia Chapter had been anything but happy. He had studiously ignored its existence in the pages of the *Architectural Review*, and the chapter had retaliated with a vituperative condemnation of Sloan's Horticultural Hall. However, Walter was determined that his chapter present a unified face at the ninth Annual Convention of the American Institute of Architects, to be held in Baltimore from November 17 through 19, 1875. He persuaded Sloan to join the chapter, and on November 15—just two days before the convention—called a special chapter meeting at which he himself proposed both Samuel Sloan and Addison Hutton for membership. Only four professional members and one junior member were present to vote. Noticeably absent were Henry Sims, author of the scurrilous paper on Horticultural Hall, and Messrs. Burns and Clark, who had moved that the article be engrossed on the minutes of the chapter. The vote was in favor, and Walter could report at the Convention, "The Chapter takes this occasion to say that all the prominent architects of Philadelphia are now included on its roll of membership."[6] Sloan's attitude toward this maneuver can be judged from the later *Proceedings* of the annual conventions of the AIA, which list him as "Lapsed, Feb '76"; nor is he listed on the roster of the Philadelphia Chapter after 1876.[7]

The last period of Samuel Sloan's professional life began in May 1875, when he was offered two hospital commissions in North Carolina. A delegation from the Insane Asylum of North Carolina to the annual convention of the American Association of Medical Superintendents of Hospitals of the Insane, held that year at Auburn, New York, stopped in Philadelphia on its way home to consult with Dr. Kirkbride. The General Assembly of North Carolina had just passed appropriations for enlarging the existing State Asylum in Raleigh and construction of a new insane hospital in the western part of the state. Kirkbride sent the delegation to Sloan, with his strongest recommendation, and Sloan was offered, and accepted, both commissions.[8]

These two large commissions turned Sloan's attention more and more to the South and were major factors in his eventual decision to move his office from Philadelphia to North Carolina. He was well known in the Carolinas, where he had executed several commissions before the Civil War, and he discovered on his first trip to Raleigh that there were many opportunities for further work in the Southeast as that section of the nation began to rebuild its institutions destroyed or delayed by the war.[9] Moreover, there was in Raleigh a spirit of rebuilding, of enthusiasm and hope for the future, that reminded Sloan of Philadelphia in the 1850s. The people seemed ready to gamble on that future being a good one and to take risks on its expectations. This attitude was the result of adroit and hardheaded leadership by such men as Governor Zebulon Vance, who saw no reason in looking back to what was and what might have been, but very strong reasons for looking forward to what could be.

Sloan went to Raleigh in the early summer of 1875 to confer with the Commissioners to Build the Western Insane Asylum about the site for that facility. Agreement was quickly reached on a location specified as "250 acres of land, one half mile south of the depot of the W.N.C.R.R. [Western North Carolina Rail Road] at Morganton."[10] Agreement was also reached as to the size and character of the building, for Sloan was able to issue printed specifications for its construction (and presumably foundation plans) before the end of the year.[11] On the same trip he met with the board of directors of the asylum at Raleigh to determine what additions were needed at that institution.[12] Thereafter, work on both projects proceeded haltingly because of minimal appropriations made by the North Carolina legislature.

Although North Carolina had been the least ravaged of all the southeastern states in the Civil War, and the first to reestablish its sovereignty and regain a measure of prosperity, it could not support the additions at "Dix Hill," as the Raleigh asylum was known, and the uninterrupted completion of the Morganton facility. The Assembly, in an act of March 7, 1877, had to restrict the commissioners of the Morganton asylum to completion of the main "centre" building and the south wing.[13] (Plate 21.)

Despite the attractions and opportunities in the South, and his pressing need for work, Sloan was reluctant to give up his old home base in Philadelphia. Occasional jobs still came into the office, and he continued to hope, for another six years, that he could rebuild his practice in the city. One of Sloan's last Pennsylvania commissions came in 1876: "Rocklynne," a suburban villa for Theophilus D. Rand, located along the line of the Pennsylvania Railroad in Radnor. It was one of the first examples of what westward migration of well-to-do Philadelphians out of the city which was to rechristen the commuter line of the Pennsylvania Railroad between Philadelphia and Paoli the "Main Line."[14] A number of those who followed in Rand's path had been residents of West Philadelphia, which was no longer the fashionable district that it had been in the 1850s, when Sloan was the principal architect of its developers. The number of cheap dwellings thrown up during the Centennial years caused its earlier residents to look for more spacious residential sites, and the dependable service of the railroad made it possible for them to move farther away from their banks and businesses without any great loss of Convenience.

PLATE 21. State Hospital—Morganton. From *North Carolina/and Its/ Resources* (Raleigh: North Carolina State Board of Resources, 1896)

To maintain the Philadelphia office during his frequent and length-
ening trips to North Carolina, Sloan formed his last partnership. He
took as partners Charles Balderston and Isaiah B. Young, the new
firm of Sloan, Balderston & Young being first listed by the Philadelphia business directories in 1877. Charles Balderston, a friend of the
Hutton family, had worked as a draftsman in Sloan's office for a brief
period in 1874.[15] Isaiah Young is a mystery. Aside from his name in
the business directories as a partner of the firm, no other documentation of him has been found. He withdrew from the partnership in
1878, the firm being listed in 1879 as "Sloan & Balderston." Charles
Balderston remained Sloan's partner, and the firm continued to list a
Philadelphia office through 1883, when Sloan moved permanently
to Raleigh. Two North Carolina buildings are credited to the firm
rather than to Sloan alone. They are the Craven County Jail and the
Craven County Courthouse at New Bern. The jail was demolished in
1907, but the courthouse is extant and contains a commemorative
plaque bearing the names of the County Commissioners, "Sloan &
Balderston, Architects," and the year 1883.[16]

Samuel Sloan made his last bid for a major public commission in
Pennsylvania with the competition for the Pennsylvania Lunatic Asylum (later the State Hospital for the Insane) at Norristown. This
competition was announced on July 21–25, 1877, and was vigor-
ously opposed by the Philadelphia Chapter of the American Instiute
of Architects because its conditions did not conform to the rules for
competitions recently adopted by the Institute. Despite this, twenty-
five submissions were made, among them ones from Addison Hutton (Hutton & Ord), Wilson Brothers, J. F. Stuckert, and Samuel
Sloan, all of Philadelphia. Entries were received on August 4, but because of the continued opposition of the AIA, the Committee on
Buildings of the Insane Hospital Commission did not announce its
choice of Wilson Brothers for the commission until November 23.
Sloan, together with Hutton, Stuckert, and Perry & Sedgwick of
New York, received an award of $500.[17]

Sloan's failure to receive the commission for the Norristown hospital was indicative of the waning influence of Dr. Kirkbride. Sloan's
submission to the competition was based, as always, on the "Kirkbride System," which had been challenged in 1866 by Dr. George
Cook of the Asylum for the Chronic Insane at Ovid, New York. Dr.
Cook maintained that the huge, monolithic buildings which Kirkbride's system engendered were detrimental to patient recovery and
insupportably expensive to staff and maintain. He proposed a hospi-

tal composed of small dispersed buildings, residential in scale, containing only that number of patients whose needs could be met by one or two staff members, one of whom would be in residence. This arrangement came to be known as the "Cottage System."[18] It was acclaimed by many alienists in the Northeast, and a number of institutions built from 1870 were designed on it. In the South, however, those states which had partially completed facilities based on the "Kirkbride System," such as the Alabama Insane Hospital or the South Carolina Hospital for the Insane, could not—during the Reconstruction—afford to change their building plans and treatment methods. So they turned to Sloan, Kirkbride's accredited architect, not only for the completion of old buildings, but for the design of new facilities as well.

After 1877 it was necessary for Sloan to be in Raleigh for longer and more frequent periods, because appropriations by the General Assembly of North Carolina for the Morganton asylum were barely enough to keep work in progress, and he needed to be on the site, or in the capital, to assure even that level of support.[19] The expense of travel, and of maintaining himself while in Raleigh, made retrenchments in Philadelphia necessary. He maintained the office of Sloan & Balderston at 152 South 4th Street, but moved in 1878 from the residence in West Philadelphia, which he had occupied for twelve years, to smaller quarters in North Philadelphia, which he shared with his son, Ellwood P. Sloan. By 1881 further economies were needed; Ellwood and his mother, Mary Sloan, moved to an even less fashionable section of town, and Samuel did not list any home address in the Philadelphia directories.[20]

It was in that year, 1881, that Sloan met and hired his last draftsman/associate, Adolphus Gustavus Bauer. Bauer, a student at the Philadelphia Academy of Fine Arts, was introduced to Sloan by George W. Childs, editor of the *Public Ledger*. Sloan employed Bauer exclusively on the southern commissions, at first in the Philadelphia office and later at his field offices in both North and South Carolina. Bauer's "memoir," written many years later and the only primary document that deals with the events of Sloan's last years, devotes only one short passage to his time with Sloan.

> The expenses of my college career were paid by my earnings saved while I was at the Tinners trade. I graduated in June 1879. Then took a 3 months course at the Iron City Business College, Pittsburg, Pa. I there wove carpets for 2 years, studying hard in the meantime, & saved

enough to enable me to enter the Phila. Academy of Fine Art in 1881.
While in Phila. was introduced to Samuel Sloan, Architect, by George
W. Childs, Editor, & remained with him until June 1883, when we
came South together & remained several months at Columbia, S.C.
Thence we came to Raleigh, N.C. where Mr. Sloan died after a few
months. I, having been his only draftsman toward the close of his life,
succeeded him in his business. I made the best portion of the drawings
for the Western N.C. Insane Asylum, all the drawings for the Swain
Memorial Hall at Chapel Hill & additions to the Insane Asylum at
Columbia, S.C. besides a great number of others, while with him.[21]

Most of the drawings for the Morganton Asylum must have been
done in Sloan's Philadelphia office before Bauer was hired, for the
News & Observer, a Raleigh newspaper, reported on September 26,
1880, that the building was almost half finished, adding, "The cost of
the work thus far, strange to say, has fallen below the original estimate of the architect."[22] Bauer's claim to have done "the best portion
of the drawings for the Western N.C. Insane Asylum" must refer,
then, to those of the north wing of the building, which was not begun until after Sloan's death.

Sloan's commission for the new Governor's Mansion of North
Carolina seems to have been another factor in his final move to
Raleigh. The *News & Observer* for April 27, 1883, reported, "Yesterday Mr. Samuel Sloan, the well known architect of Philadelphia, arrived in the city bringing with him the designs for the Governor's
residence."[23] (Plate 22.) A new, "decent" residence for the governor
was a project of T. J. Jarvis, who after fulfilling the unexpired term of
Zebulon Vance when Vance was elected to the United States Senate
in 1879, had been elected to a full term as governor in 1881. Largely
due to the persistence and determination of Mrs. Jarvis, the project
for a new mansion was reluctantly approved by the legislature. The
News & Observer for April 13, 1883, reported its decision "that the
Governor be directed to employ an architect to submit to the council
a sketch of a plan for the house, but that the drawings and specifications of no plan be made until it is adopted by the council."[24] Only
two weeks later, Sloan arrived in Raleigh with the "designs," so he
and Mrs. Jarvis must have been discussing the building for some time
before the legislature gave them official permission to do so.

Sloan remained in Raleigh for almost a month, not returning to
Philadelphia until the North Carolina legislature granted him the
commission for the Mansion. The *News & Observer* for May 8 reported the legislature's decision: "It is understood that the design for

PLATE 22. Governor's residence in Raleigh
(Photo in the collection of the author)

the Governor's Mansion which was submitted by Mr. Sloan will be
adopted, with modifications agreed upon by some able builders of
this city."[25] The legislators apparently tried to impose some restraints
on Mrs. Jarvis and Sloan, but they were not very successful, for the
large and elaborate building in a modified Queen Anne Style came to
be known as "Jarvis's Folly." Unable to affect the design of the building, the legislature retaliated with niggardly appropriations, which
delayed its completion until 1889. Mrs. Jarvis never got to live in her
house; the first governor to occupy the new Mansion was Daniel G.
Fowle, and he had to bring his own furniture.[26] The building has
been renovated several times, but it retains most of Sloan's original
design and continues as the official residence of the governor of
North Carolina. It is the only one of Sloan's large residences to have
survived intact.

From the evidence of Bauer's memoir, it would seem that Sloan
closed his Philadelphia office in June 1883, by which time he had

received at least eight commissions in North and South Carolina. Bauer states that he and Sloan went directly to Columbia, South Carolina, and remained there for several months.[27] Sometime in 1882, Sloan had been asked by the General Assembly of the state of South Carolina to submit proposals for the completion of the State Hospital for the Insane at Columbia, which lacked a "centre" building to join the two wings already erected. These had been designed upon the "Kirkbride System," and a letter of 1854 from Dr. Kirkbride to "The Commissioners of the South Carolina Hospital for the Insane" had recommended Sloan, although he had not received the commission.[28] Construction was begun in 1857 from the design of George E. Walker, but the war interrupted work, and only the two lateral wings containing the men's and women's wards had been completed by 1882. A central treatment and administration pavilion was needed to connect them. As Sloan was then in Raleigh more often than in Philadelphia, and so his travel expenses for supervision would be correspondingly less, it was decided to apply to the architect of Kirkbride's first choice. The design of the Centre Building (now the Babcock Building) was agreed upon during Sloan's first trip to Columbia in December 1882, and the working drawings were executed by Bauer either there or in Sloan's new Raleigh office. The building, which is still extant, was not accepted until August 1885, so Bauer was in charge of its completion after Sloan's death in July 1884.

Approval of the design for the Centre Building at Columbia was not given by the General Assembly until November 27, 1883. By that time Sloan had made at least four trips to Columbia and one protracted stay, from late June until early September 1883, over which time he is also credited—without firm documentation—with the design of the Central National Bank (now Sylvan's Jewelers) in downtown Columbia. This handsome little building in French Baroque Revival is extant, only slightly modified, and may be the only example of Sloan's commercial buildings surviving. It was characteristic of Sloan's practice that wherever he executed public commissions he was also offered commercial and residential work. Many of these tributary buildings cannot be firmly documented or unquestionably attributed to him, but the Central National Bank at Columbia and two villas in North Carolina—"Dunlieth," formerly in Greensboro, and "Mistletoe Villa," in Henderson—were probably from his office.

Shortly after Sloan returned to Raleigh in November 1883, he was offered the commission for the State Exposition Buildings of North Carolina at the Raleigh fairgrounds. The annual state agricultural exposition had been revived after the Civil War by Governor Vance as one of his many projects to stimulate the state's economy. Vance had spent the state's small revenues so wisely that North Carolina was in advance of the other southeastern states in its recovery, and Vance's successor, T. J. Jarvis, successfully attracted northern capital and investors to the state by advertising its advantages. He sent to the Boston Exposition of 1883 a large exhibit of the state's products and natural resources which received very complimentary reviews in northern newspapers when the Exposition opened on September 3. The success of the exhibit elicited an unexpected response from the citizens of Raleigh. The *News & Observers* for November 3 printed the following:

> We, the business men of Raleigh, representing all the trades and professions here, viz; banking, mercantile, mechanical and professional would respectfully memorialize you, the Governor, and the Board of Agriculture of North Carolina, to have the State's exhibit, now in Boston, which has deservedly attracted so much attention in New England, exhibited as a whole at the State Agricultural Exposition at Raleigh in October, 1884.[29]

The next day a Citizens Meeting assembled and passed a resolution calling for "a grand exposition in the city of Raleigh next fall" which should include the Boston exhibit, as very few North Carolinians would otherwise have an opportunity to see it. Neither Governor Jarvis nor the legislature was prepared for this reaction, and in an attempt to dampen enthusiasm the Honorable Monfort McGehee, Commissioner of Agriculture, addressed the steering committee of the Citizens Meeting on November 5 and stated that "The buildings of the fair, he did not think, were large enough to hold the Boston exhibit."[30] The committee suggested that a new building was in order, and because agitation for this action continued, Samuel Sloan was offered the commission in early December. His design for it was published in the *News & Observer* on March 25, 1884, and on June 11 the paper could report that the new building was already completed, that the Boston exhibit would be installed, and that the Exposition would run from October 1 to October 28.[31]

By a chain of coincidences, the State Exposition Building at Raleigh, one of Sloan's least important commissions, became widely publicized. His first obituary, in the *News & Observer* of July 20, 1884, which listed only Sloan's North Carolina works, was used by

Philadelphia's newspapers for their own notices of Sloan's death. Although they deleted most of the North Carolina buildings, replacing them with Pennsylvania examples, they retained the Exposition
Building, probably because it sounded like a major commission in
the light of Sloan's association with the Centennial competition.
Somewhat later, architectural periodicals used Philadelphia newspapers as the source for their memorials of Sloan, again substituting
some examples of this work but retaining the Exposition Building.
The final step was the Biographical Cyclopaedias published after
Sloan's death, which used the periodicals for their information and
so listed the Exposition Building as one of his major works. This is
ironic, for it had been designed and erected in five months and was
not to be compared with the hospitals, schools, and churches of his
earlier practice. However, there is a fitting aspect to the coincidence,
for the Exposition Building was the only one of Sloan's late commissions in the South that he saw completed.

The remainder of the North Carolina work—the Centennial
Graded School (also called the White Graded School), St. Mary's
School, St. Augustin Normal School, and additions to Peace Institute (all in Raleigh); the New Bern Graded School (also called the
Second Academy Building); and Swain Memorial Hall and a ball-
room/gymnasium on the campus of the University of North Carolina at Chapel Hill—was unfinished at the time of his death. Of
these, only the New Bern Graded School was given any mention in
his Philadelphia obituaries, which is strange because it was in no way
unusual. The building that was unusual, Swain Memorial Hall, received no notice outside North Carolina, where it was at first praised
and then execrated. Swain Hall, intended as an auditorium for the
commencement exercises of the university, was commissioned from
Sloan in June 1883, the only requirement being that it seat at least
two thousand people. He designed a hexagonal building, 154 by
128 feet, whose roof was supported by wooden arches, spanning
from outside wall to outside wall, which rose to a height of 52 feet.
Unfortunately, his estimation of the building's cost fell so far short of
reality that construction had to be suspended in November 1883 for
lack of funds. Although described in 1889 as "one of the handsomest
college buildings in the Union," it was later called a "fat coffin" and
a "Spooky Architectural Monstrosity."[32] Swain Memorial Hall was
dedicated on June 3, 1885, almost a year after Sloan's death. It survived until 1930, when it was demolished to make room for newer
buildings.

Samuel Sloan's life and career ended in the same obscurity with which it began. At this writing, no firm date can be given for the closing of his Philadelphia office—and hence the dissolution of the firm of Sloan & Balderston—nor the opening, or address, of his office in Raleigh. A great many legal records are missing; neither his will nor any notice of administration is deposited in the files of the City and County of Philadelphia or those of Raleigh, Wake County, North Carolina. The disposition of the unfinished commissions in Sloan's Raleigh office is uncertain; the larger ones were completed by Bauer, but the smaller school and residential commissions cannot be assigned to him with certainty. It is perhaps Fitting, in Sloan's own understanding of the word, that he should have exited from the architectural stage as suddenly and unconventionally as he appeared upon it.

The notices of Samuel Sloan's illness and death are themselves confused. The first report of his terminal illness was in the *News & Observer* of Friday, July 18, 1884, and was mistaken both in his name and in the nature of that illness. "The condition of Mr. William Sloan, who has been quite ill at the Branson house with typhoid feaver for several days, is no better." The next day the newspaper had to print a correction. "The types made us say yesterday morning that Mr. Sloan, at the Branson house had the typhoid feaver. Such is not the case, so we are informed." On Sunday, July 20, the same paper printed "Death of Mr. Samuel Sloan," a notice and obituary which reported his death on early Saturday morning, giving his age as 67, which was incorrect, Sloan being almost 70. The notice continued: "Mr. Sloan has been sick about a fortnight. His body will be placed in a vault here and later will be taken to Philadelphia. His family was with him in his last moments. His daughter is completely prostrated and is very sick." At the end of this report was an announcement of funeral services to be held from the Branson house at 9:30 A.M., Sunday morning. On Monday, July 21, a report of the funeral listed the minister and pallbearers by name but did not give the names of any family members present. It concluded: "The body was taken to the cemetery and there deposited in a vault until the autumn, when it will be taken to Philadelphia."[33]

None of this would appear unusual except for some curious omissions and absences in the records. Although the names of the attending physician and male nurse, during his illness, are known, no official notice of Sloan's death has been found in the archives of Raleigh or Wake County. Despite a firsthand report of his body's placement in a Raleigh cemetery, no record has been found of such an interment. Sloan's body was not finally interred in Mount Moriah Cemetery, Kingsessing, Philadelphia, until February 4, 1885, more than six months after his death.[34] The large plot in Mount Moriah Cemetery is identified on the entrance step of the granite-curb surround as "SLOAN-LOFLIN": however, there are no Loflins buried there. The plot is relatively empty, containing only five Sloan graves along its eastern limit: Samuel; Mary, his wife; Ellwood, his older son; Laura, Ellwood's wife; Helen, Ellwood's daughter; and Howard, Samuel's younger son.

The published notices of Sloan's death are also confused. Those appearing in Philadelphia newspapers are filled with mistakes. The *North American* for July 23, 1884, after a brief, inaccurate precis of his career, concluded with: "Mr. Sloan leaves a widow and two daughters, one of whom is living in this city and is dangerously ill. Pending her sickness, the remains will be interred at Raleigh and will be brought to this city for burial in the near future." Sloan did not have two daughters, but one daughter and two sons, and as he had been a fairly prominent citizen of Philadelphia for forty years and his family was still resident there, this seems a strange mistake.

The *Public Ledger*, also for July 23, 1884, printed the most accurate of all Sloan's obituaries, with his age and surviving family correctly given; but even the *Ledger*, which had been Sloan's most faithful publicist throughout his career, had a lapse of memory. "He was for a time in partnership with Mr. Addison Hutton, but up to about eight years ago, he practiced his profession chiefly on his own account." This ignores Charles Balderston, his most recent partner, who was alive and practicing in Philadelphia, and overlooks John S. Stewart, with whom he had executed the majority of his major commissions. The *Ledger* also made one embarrassing *faux pas*: "Under the joint supervision of himself and Mr. Balderston the new Swarthmore College was built." This mistake must have tried Addison Hutton's Quaker forbearance. The *Philadelphia Press* for July 23, 1884, simply reprinted the Raleigh *News & Observer* notice verbatim, appending an expression of thanks from the Sloan family to the people of Raleigh for their kindness and support.[35] Later obituaries, which appeared in professional journals such as *Building* and the *American Architect and Building News*, were brief and obtained their information from the Philadelphia newspapers, including the mistakes.[36]

Although the Philadelphia Chapter of the American Institute of Architecture took no notice of Sloan's death, the *American Architect*

and Building News, which had succeeded Sloan's *Architectural Review*
as the unofficial house organ of the national AIA, paid him a two-
edged compliment in its obituary:

> Although belonging, like other architects who began business fifty
> years ago, to a school which has ceased to excite commotion in the
> artistic world, Mr. Sloan was one of the most distinguished of that
> school, and his career, in activity and usefulness, was one which the
> ablest of the younger generation might be glad to emulate.[37]

The telling phrase "has ceased to excite commotion in the artistic
world" would have amused Sloan. He had never confused architecture with art and had very little patience with those who did. He saw
the profession as one that supplied a service, and the architect as an
educated version of the old Jacksonian "mechanic." His major contributions to the evolution of American architecture were functional
rather than aesthetic: clarification of circulation in hospitals, schools,
and commercial buildings; flexible space in all building types that
would accept it; modular, repetitive construction; particular attention to fire safety; improvement of mechanical equipment; and a
pragmatic view of visual style. Sloan was a creative eclectic, an inven-
tor, a natural politician, persuasive, conceited, hungry for acclaim,
but also talented, perceptive, and so understanding of the needs and
dreams of his fellow men that he could give them architectural form.

Notes

CHAPTER I: THE SOCIAL CONTEXT

1. John Taylor, in his *An Enquiry into the Principles and Policy of the Government of the United States* (1814), clearly, if bitterly, contrasted the "fictitious" property of the new era with the "real property of the Jeffersonian dream."
2. Henry Van Dyke, "Emerson," Encyclopaedia Britannica, 14th ed. (New York, 1929), vol. 8, p. 393.
3. "Notes on Domestic Architecture," *Atlantic Monthly* vol. 1, no. 111, Jan. 1858, pp. 161–162.
4. A. W. Colgate, "The Development of American Architecture," *Continental Monthly* (New York), vol. 5, June 1864, p. 472.
5. Samuel Sloan, *The Model Architect* (Philadelphia: E. S. Jones & Co., 1852), vol. 2, pp. 71–73.
6. A. J. Downing, *Cottage Residences* (New York and London: Wiley & Putnam, 1842; Dover edition, ed., Adolf K. Placzek, New York, 1981), p. 2.
7. Ibid., p. 5.
8. D. Morier Evans, *The History of the Commercial Crisis, 1857–58* (London, 1859), pp. 98–99.
9. Sloan, *The Model Architect*, vol. 1, p. 10.

CHAPTER II: 1815–1850: BACKGROUND AND TRAINING

1. See the Appendix, "Ancestors, Family, and Descendants of Samuel (T.) Sloan," to the present work. Mary Kirkwood seems to have married "beneath her station," for her children had no later contact with their Kirkwood relatives, some of whom became prominent men. Mary's nephew, Daniel Kirkwood (1814–1895), was principal of the Lancaster (Pa.) High School in 1854 and a well-known mathematician and astronomer. Another nephew, Samuel Jordan Kirkwood (1813–1882), was Secretary of the Interior under President Garfield and twice governor of Iowa.
2. The year 1821 has been adduced from the following facts. Fletcher

Sloan (b. Apr. 8, 1826), the last of Keziah Sloan's children, although he was probably born at Keziah's family home in Lancaster, Pa., considered West Philadephia his home town, as did his older full-brother, Wesley Sloan, who is known to have been born in Lancaster in 1821. Samuel was six years old in 1821, at which age he could begin formal schooling and apprenticeship. William Sloan is not listed in the tax records of Lancaster in 1822. See the Appendix of the present work and Harry Rush Kervey, "Notes on Chester County Authors," manuscript in the collection of the Chester County Historical Society, West Chester, Pa.

3. Sloan's employment at Eastern State and the Philadelphia Almshouse is given in Kervey's "Notes on Chester County Authors." To have worked at both sites, he cannot have come to Philadelphia later than 1833. The cross-comparison that gives this year was made from (a) Norman Johnson, "John Haviland's Prisons and Their Relation to the Development of Prison Architecture" (manuscript kindly lent by its author), and (b) Roland B. Curtin, "The Philadelphia General Hospital," *Founder's Week Memorial Volume* (Philadelphia, 1909), pp. 443–446.

4. The property on which the Department for the Insane was built had once been the estate of Paul Busti, whose Palladian mansion was still standing; see Francis R. Packard, *Some Account of the Pennsylvania Hospital* (Philadelphia, 1938), pp. 119–120. The same source gives the members of the Building Committee of the Managers. The letter of John Holden, which documents the "limited competition," is reproduced in Thomas G. Morton, *The History of the Pennsylvania Hospital, 1751–1895* (Philadelphia, 1895), p. 165, n. 1. Isaac Holden submitted an entry in the competition for the Preston Retreat, the only other design for a medical institution which he is known to have executed.

5. There is a discrepancy in the records of Mary Pennell as to her first name. The greater majority, including her gravestone, give it as "Mary"; however, both the Session Book and the Record of Communicants of Calvary Presbyterian Church, Philadelphia, list her on June 16, 1854, as "Mara Sloan." The baptismal records of Calvary Presbyterian Church document the baptism of "Ada, daughter of Samuel Sloan of the City of Philadelphia, Architect, and of Mara, his wife," on April 7, 1858. Because all other sources call her "Mary," she will be so designated hereafter.

6. The locale (and incidently the color) of the Pennell homestead is given in "Old West Philadelphia," *West Philadelphia Telephone* (newspaper), November 24, 1894. William Sloan's house at Till (40th St.) above (North of) Washington (Market St.), where he is last listed by *McElroy's Philadelphia Directory* for 1854, would have been no more than two blocks away and in the direction of Pennell's Mill (later the site of the Good Intent Mills).

7. Ellwood Pennell Sloan's gravestone in Mount Moriah Cemetery, Kingsessing, Pa., shows the dates 1846–1912 (no months given). The Phila-

delphia census for 1850 gives his age as four, which substantiates the 1846 date. The gravestone for Mary Sloan, wife of Samuel, in the same location, shows the dates October 3, 1820–November 16, 1891, the 1820 date also being confirmed by the census of 1850, which gives her age as twenty-nine. Hence, Mary would have been twenty-four at the time of Ellwood's conception, so that the latest year for her marriage to Samuel Sloan would be 1844. The year 1844 corresponds to the first directory listing of Samuel Sloan as an independent craftsman and householder. It is unlikely that Mary's father, James Pennell, would have agreed to her marriage to Samuel Sloan until after 1841, when Samuel had received the support of Kirkbride, for the Pennells were also Quakers, and Kirkbride's favor would have carried weight with them. The year of the marriage is therefore assumed to be late 1842 or early 1843.

8. This opinion hardened with the years and became, in time, almost an obsession. In the November 1868 issue of Sloan's periodical, *The Architectural Review*, in an essay entitled "An American Style," Sloan wrote: "Our Architects are, at best, but mere copyists of European models, mere reproducers of other men's ideals, formed for other purposes than those we have to deal with, here in America."

9. These were the works of the engineer John Smeaton, the carpenter-builder Peter Nicholson, the architectural essayist Edmund Aiken, and the antiquary Francis Grose. Aside from the recommendation of several Philadelphia dealers in building supplies—who incidently were also his clients—Sloan mentions Americans only in connection with construction techniques or the installation of mechanical equipment: John Basehore and Robert Riddell of Philadelphia for the erection of circular stairs, and a Mr. Chilson of Boston for the problems with warming and ventilation equipment.

10. C. L. V. Meeks, "Picturesque Eclecticism," *Art Bulletin* (New York: Garland Publishing, 1950), vol. 32, pp. 226–235.

11. Sloan, *Model Architect*, vol. 1, p. 7, "Preface to the First Volume."

12. Ibid., vol. 2, pp. 99–100.

13. The portion of Dr. Kirkbride's library bequeathed to the Fine Arts Library of the University of Pennsylvania in 1933 by Miss Elizabeth Kirkbride contained the following:

   a. George Wightwick, *Hints to Young Architects . . . with additional notes and hints to persons about building in this country by A. J. Downing*, 1st American ed. (New York and London: Wiley & Putnam, 1847). (Signed on the title page "Thomas S. Kirkbride.")

   b. Andrew Jackson Downing, *A Treatise on the Theory and Practice of Landscape Gardening Adapted to North America*, 2nd ed. (New York and London: Wiley & Putnam, 1844).

   c. Andrew Jackson Downing, *The Architecture of Country Houses* (New York: D. Appleton & Co.; Philadelphia: G. S. Appleton, 1850).

   d. Louisa C. Tuthill, *History of Architecture* (Philadelphia: Lindsay &

Blakiston, 1848). (Signed on the title page "Thomas S. Kirkbride, 1848.")

e. All of Samuel Sloan's publications, including bound volumes of *The Architectural Review*. (Vol. 1 signed on the first page of text "Thomas S. Kirkbride.")

f. The second edition of Dr. Kirkbride's own book, *Hospitals for the Insane* (Philadelphia: Lindsay & Blakiston, 1880).

g. The portion of the Kirkbride bequest left to the Library Company of Philadelphia (Ridgway Branch) is documented only by a fragmentary, handwritten list formerly in the Scrapbooks of the Ridgway Library, vol. 2, p. 9, Item 23. This includes Peter Nicholson, *The Student Instructor* (New York: Offices of the *Railroad Journal*, 1837). Richard Brown, *Domestic Architecture* (London: George Virtue, 1841). John W. Ritch, *The American Architect* (New York: C. M. Saxton, 1847). Robert Dale Owen, *Hints on Public Architecture* (New York and London: George P. Putnam, 1849).

14. A copy of this advertisement is among the papers of Thomas U. Walter. (The Walter papers have been kindly made available by Robert B. Ennis, Walter's biographer, and the Philadelphia Athenaeum. All references to or quotations from those papers are by their kind permission.) The advertisement reads as follows:

CIRCULAR

The Commissioners of Delaware County will give a premium of Fifty Dollars for the best plan offered to be adopted by them for a new Court House about to be erected. The base to contain thirty-two hundred square feet, the lower story of which to be adapted to and appropriated to the different offices of the County, and to be fire proof. The second story for Court and Jury rooms, finished with a cupulo or belfry. The said plan and draft to be sent to the Commissioners at Chester, on or before Tuesday, the 29th inst.

> Edmund Pennell
> Mark Bartleson (Commissioners)
> Caleb J. Hoopes
> Commissioners Office, Chester,
> May 14, 1849

15. The diary entries are: 1849, vol. 8, May 26, May 29, June 12, June 13, June 16, June 18, July 13, July 21, July 23. The letters are: two drafts of letters to the Commissioners of Delaware County dated May 28 and June 16, 1849; two drafts of letters to Mark Bartleson dated July 5 and July 30, 1849; four letters from Mark Bartleson, these dated July 3, July 9, and July 14, 1849, and one undated; two letters from John P. Crozer, dated May 17 and June 18, 1849.

16. When this letter was found by Robert B. Ennis, Walter's biographer (see n. 14), it was torn to pieces and had to be reassembled. Ennis conjectures that Walter intended at first to destroy it, but changed his mind.

17. The best condensed report of the removal dispute and its consequences is found in George Smith, *History of Delaware County Pennsylvania* (Philadelphia, 1862), pp. 368 ff. It is interesting that a Mr. Abram Pennell, representative of Middletown Township, voted for the removal and the new buildings.

18. "An American Style," *The Architectural Review*, vol. 1, Nov. 1868, p. 334.

CHAPTER III: 1850–1851: EARLY PRACTICE

1. The firm of Eastwick & Harrison was recommended to the Czar by Major G. W. Whistler (father of the painter), who was consulting engineer for the Saint Petersburg–Moscow Railway. The contract was considered too large for one firm, so they were associated with Thomas and William Winans of Baltimore, and the combined firm of Harrison, Winans & Eastwick operated in Russia from 1844 to 1856. I am indebted to Mr. Richard Haywood for this documentation.

2. This passage is part of an article entitled "A Noted House Burned," a clipping from an unnamed newspaper, in vol. 99 of the Campbell Collection, Historical Society of Pennsylvania.

3. The review in *Gleason's Pictorial Drawing Room Comparison*, vol. 6 (Boston, 1854), p. 328, is unusually fulsome for *Gleason's*, which was very biased when it came to New England. Sloan's own presentation of the "Norman Villa" in *The Model Architect* (vol. 1, pp. 49–52) was written with an eye to further clients, so his cost figures are considerably less than "fifty thousand." The most personal description of the building is a paper, "Bartram Hall," given by Mrs. Andrew M. Eastwick to the City Historical Society of Philadelphia on Dec. 14, 1910 (*Publications of the City Historical Society of Philadelphia* [Philadelphia, 1930], pp. 207–213).

4. The best collective source that documents Nathaniel Borrodail Browne's primary role in the development of West Philadelphia is the *Biographical Encyclopaedia of Pennsylvania* (Philadelphia, 1874), pp. 355–356. Samuel A. Harrison is less easy to summarize; however, he was involved in so many enterprises (heating and ventilating, terra cotta and tile products, real estate, etc.) that brief references in newspapers and directories piece together a picture of the archetypal Jacksonian speculator who began as a "conveyencer" (hauling and draying) and ended up a rich man. Harrison's listings in *McElroy's* and *Gopsill's* directories from 1850 until 1876, and in such other commercial listings as Chapman's *Philadelphia Wholesale Merchants and Artisans Business Directory*, together with the

notices in the *Public Ledger* from the beginning of his patronage of Sloan in 1852, are the sources from which his life can be reconstructed.

5. This lithographed plan, entitled "Plan of the New Town of Riverton, N.J., beautifully situated on the Cinnaminson Shore, on the River Delaware, eight miles about Philadelphia," is in the collection of the Riverton Library. It was presented to the library by William Rodman Wharton, son of Rodman Wharton, one of the original backers of the Riverton development, for whom Sloan designed villas. A more accurate plan, with the same title, slightly later in date, is in the collection of the Porch Club in Riverton, N.J. Both these documents were brought to the author's attention by Mrs. J. W. Hahle of Riverton, who has done all the primary research in the documentation of Riverton's founding and development. The writer is greatly indebted to Mrs. Hahle for the use of her work.

6. "Riverton, N.J., 1890, Des. Lith. & Publ., by Otto Koehler, Riverton, N.J.," isometric plan, collection of the Riverton Library, Riverton, N.J.

7. A survey of Riverton was carried out in the spring of 1977 by students from the College of Architecture, Clemson University. At that time, eleven original riverfront villas were extant and comprised a State Historical District. These included nine Sloan buildings and two designed by John Frazier. They were in good condition, although there had been alterations made to all of them, and the owners permitted extensive photographic documentation. These photographs, together with others of the town, are in the collection of the College of Architecture, Clemson University. Mrs. J. W. Hahle of Riverton has also photographically documented all the extant Sloan buildings and has made her work available to the author.

8. This passage from J. R. Sypher's *School History of Pennsylvania* (1868) is the earliest source that specifies that Sloan himself was sent "to other cities." The visitations are confirmed, but as made by "suitable persons," in "A School House: Design Forty-Third," in Sloan's *The Model Architect*, vol. 2, pp. 48–49.

9. This essay was the fruit of a twelve-year struggle by Barnard to improve the public schools of Connecticut (for details, see Joseph Henry, "Report on the History and Study of School Architecture," *Proceedings of the Second Session of the National Convention on the Friends of Public Education*, Philadelphia, 1850, Appendix 3). It was the most comprehensive and authoritative treatment of school architecture in English, and its long-range effect on school-building in the United States was enormous. Reprinted innumerable times, it served as a pattern book in rural and frontier areas long after its illustrated examples had been condemned as obsolete by Barnard himself. (Henry Barnard, *Practical Illustrations of the Principles of School Architecture* [Hartford: Tiffany & Co., 1850, 1851], thereafter incorporated into Barnard's *School Architecture* [New York: A. S. Barnes & Co., editions until 1860].)

10. Sloan presented this system, both principles and applications, to the general public with a long essay and two designs in *The Model Architect*, "School Houses," vol. 1, pp. 69–73; "A School House: Design Seventeenth," vol. 1, pp. 73–76; and "A School House: Design Forty-Third," vol. 2, pp. 48–49.

11. *Thirty-Third Annual Report of the Controllers for the Public Schools of the City and County of Philadelphia* (1851), pp. 11–12.

12. *Proceedings of the First Session of the American Association for the Advancement of Education* (Philadelphia, 1852), Appendix F, p. 106.

13. A summation of all the objections to Sloan's school designs is found, surprisingly, in a work by the Architect to the School Board of London, Edward Robert Robinson: *School Architecture*, 2nd edition (London, 1877), pp. 27–45. Robinson is very pro-Barnard and concludes with "A study of trans-Atlantic schoolhouses, as set forth in numerous published reports, leads generally to the conclusion that those of New England are the best."

CHAPTER IV: 1851–1852: *THE MODEL ARCHITECT*

1. *Gleason's Pictorial Drawing Room Companion*, a Boston weekly, whose illustrated reviews of contemporary architecture were one of its major attractions, was particularly generous in its praise of the Eastwick villa (vol. 6, Jan. 7, 1854, p. 328). Sloan's series of designs in *Godey's* begins with vol. 45 (July–Dec. 1852) and runs until vol. 66 (Jan.–June 1863). See also George Hersey, "Godey's Choice," *Journal of the Society of Architectural Historians* vol. 18, Oct. 1959, pp. 104–111.

2. Mr. Louis Reed, a Chicago architect, now deceased, told the writer that he remembered leafing through a copy of *The Model Architect* in the office of Adler & Sullivan while waiting for an appointment. This cannot be authenticated, of course, but the writer would like to believe it is true. A copy of the book formerly in the Ridgway Branch of the Library Company of Philadelphia had come to the Company from the collection of Frank Furness.

CHAPTER V: 1852–1858: THE FIRM OF SLOAN & STEWART

1. The first reference to the firm of Sloan & Stewart is in the *Public Ledger* for Aug. 11, 1852 (vol. 33, no. 119), under "Local Affairs." It is first listed in *McElroy's Philadelphia Directory* for 1853, with the address "SE 6th and Walnut" (also given as "154 Walnut" in the individual listings of the partners), where it continues to be listed until 1856. In that year Sloan's business address is given as "80 S 4th," but the *Merchants & Manufacturers Business Directory* (Philadelphia: Griswold & Co.) for 1856–1857 lists the firm at the old address, and the last reference to the firm as a firm is the *Public Ledger* for Nov. 2, 1857 (vol. 46, no. 37).

John Stewart is continuously listed by all sources at "SE 6th and Walnut" (or "154 Walnut") from 1853 through 1860. Beginning in 1854, Thomas S. Stewart is listed at the same address as "civil engineer"; beginning in 1857, he is listed as "architect and engineer."

2. Both Sloan's obituary in the *News and Observer* (Raleigh, N.C.), vol. 23, no. 56, July 20, 1884, and Kervey's "Notes on Chester County Authors" give his hospital commissions as thirty-two. Although Kirkbride died in 1882, Sloan continued to represent him on unfinished work designed by the team until his own death in 1884.

3. Thomas S. Kirkbride, *Hospitals for the Insane*, 2nd ed. (Philadelphia: Lindsay & Blakiston, 1880), p. 152.

4. Francis Tiffany, *Life of Dorothea Lynde Dix* (Boston, 1892).

5. *Public Ledger*, vol. 34, no. 58, Nov. 30, 1852, "Local Affairs."

6. These include, in part, the Alabama Insane Hospital (now Bryce Hospital), Morris Plains Division of the New Jersey State Hospital for the Insane, Insane Asylum of North Carolina (both Raleigh and Morgantown divisions), and the General Hospital for the Insane of the State of Connecticut. The Department for Males of the Pennsylvania Hospital for the Insane and the Kalamazoo State Hospital, Kalamazoo, Mich., were demolished only recently.

7. Kirkbride, *Hospitals for the Insane*, 2nd ed., pp. 108–152, and *Notice of Some Experiments in Heating and Ventilating Hospitals and Other Buildings by Steam and Hot Water* (Philadelphia, n.d.) (the only copy of the latter work known to the writer is in the collection of the Library Company of Philadelphia, Cat. No. 21116, O.D.). See also Samuel Sloan, "Hospital Construction," *The Architectural Review*, vol. 1, Apr. 1869, pp. 626–642.

8. The "Harrison Steam Boiler," patented in 1859, was the final result of Joseph Harrison's efforts to produce a safe heating plant for residences and hospitals. It was awarded the first-class medal at the London World's Fair in 1862, the American Institute Medal in New York in 1869, and the Rumford Medal from the American Academy of Arts and Sciences at Harvard University in 1872. For the progress of experiments in fireproof construction, see *The Architectural Review* 1, Mar. 1869, p. 537, and Samuel Sloan, *City and Suburban Architecture* (1st ed., Philadelphia, J. B. Lippincott & Co., 1859), Designs III and XIII.

9. Sloan apparently aimed at, and achieved, not only a standard design but one whose cost he could estimate very closely no matter where the building was erected. The Camden, N.J., courthouse came in at $40,870.79, and the Greensburg, Pa., edition at $39,614 (although it was somewhat larger).

10. A compilation of Pennsylvania county histories published in 1883 contains illustrations of at least four courthouses erected before 1860 that are redactions of Sloan's standard design. See William H. Engle, *History*

of the Commonwealth of Pennsylvania, 3rd ed. (Philadelphia: E. M. Gardner, 1883). The four buildings are the courthouses for Clarion County at Clarion (p. 547), Columbia County at Bloomsburg (p. 584), Jefferson County at Brookville (p. 798), and Montour County at Danville (p. 961).

11. Sloan, *The Model Architect*, vol. 1, pp. 45–58.
12. John S. Hart, "Description of Public High School in Philadelphia," *American Journal of Education*, vol. 1, 1855, p. 93.
13. The prime example of this is found in "School Architecture: Plans of Public School Houses in Pennsylvania," *American Journal of Education* vol. 13 (n.s. 3), 1864, pp. 817–835. Of the six buildings discussed in this article, five are by Sloan, but his name appears only once, in connection with the North-East Grammar School House (the first that he did), and not at all in the discussions of the High School or the Normal School.
14. "Thomas H. Burrowes. With a Sketch of the History of Common Schools in Pennsylvania," *American Journal of Education*, vol. 6, no. 17, June 1859, p. 567.
15. *Common Schools of Pennsylvania*, ed. Thomas H. Burrowes (Harrisburg: A. Boyd Hamilton, 1855), p. 158.
16. The building was still standing in 1926. See Joseph Jackson, *America's Most Historic Highway* (Philadelphia: John Wanamaker, 1926), p. 158, 172.
17. Both these quotations are from "Local Affairs" in the *Public Ledger*; the first from vol. 21, no. 145, Sept. 12, 1851, the second from vol. 41, no. 70, Dec. 11, 1856.
18. That Sullivan did a portion of his apprenticeship in Philadelphia is established, and the lasting effect of the Jayne Building on his design vocabulary is evident in the terminus of the Guaranty Building in Buffalo, N.Y. The author is indebted to Mr. Louis Reed of Chicago (who knew Sullivan personally) for information relative to the inviting of ceramic craftsmen from Philadelphia to Chicago to produce the cast terra cotta panels that Sullivan used for decorative revetment.

CHAPTER VI: THE SECOND MASONIC TEMPLE AND
THE HARRISON COMMISSIONS

1. Winston Weisman, excerpt from a paper delivered at the Annual Meeting of the Society of Architectural Historians, Detroit, Michigan, 1957; by kind permission of Professor Weisman.
2. *Public Ledger* (Philadelphia), vol. 36, no. 83, Dec. 29, 1853, "Local Affairs."
3. Constance M. Greiff, *John Notman, Architect* (Philadelphia: The Athenaeum of Philadelphia, 1979), pp. 181–185.

4. Secretary of the Grand Chapter, "Record Book," 1852, n.p.
5. *Minutes of the Right Worshipful Grand Lodge*, vol. 8: 1849–1884 (published by the Grand Lodge, 1905), p. 350.
6. Ibid., Appendix B, p. 496. See also Julius F. Suchse, *Freemasonry in Pennsylvania* (Philadelphia, 1919), vol. 3, p. 419.
7. *Minutes of the Right Worshipful Grand Lodge*, vol. 9: 1855–1858, (published by the Grand Lodge, 1905), Appendix A, p. 348. In 1955 there were in the scrapbooks of the Ridgway Branch of the Library Company of Philadelphia (vol. 1) a ticket to the cornerstone-laying ceremony and a ticket to the dedication ceremony.
8. Charles J. Cohen, *Rittenhouse Square, Past and Present* (Philadelphia, 1922), p. 261.
9. A. T. Baker, *Time*, vol. 118, no. 7, Aug. 17, 1891, p. 73. While in England in 1852, Harrison purchased a large part of the exhibition of George Catlin's paintings of American Indians. These Harrison brought back to Philadelphia on his return but did not hang in his gallery. He stored them in a basement at his boiler factory, from where they were recovered in 1879. It would seem he bought them to help out a fellow American rather than as paintings he admired.
10. One of the few descriptions of "Riverdale" is found in S. F. Hotchkin, *The Bristol Pike* (Philadelphia: George W. Jacobs & Co., 1893), p. 213. It is here quoted in full: "A long white fence on the State Road marks the estate of Joseph Harrison, now rented to the city for the use of the House of Correction, and tilled by the inmates. Here is the Russian mansion with its dome built by Mr. Harrison, who was engaged in railway work in Russia with Messrs. Eastwick (of Gray's Ferry, Philadelphia), and Winans (of Baltimore)."
11. There were community laundries on the fourth floor with roof decks for "drying the wash" (George B. Tatum, *Philadelphia Architecture in the Nineteenth Century* [Philadelphia: University of Pennsylvania Press, 1953], p. 36, plate 95).
12. A photostat in the print collection of the Historical Society of Pennsylvania reproduces a large watercolor of Hamilton Terrace as originally designed. The descriptions in quotes are from the *Public Ledger*, vol. 41, no. 110, July 30, 1856, "Local Affairs."
13. One of the cottages, one double villa, and Harrison's house (much altered and chopped up into flats) survived until 1955 but are not listed in Richard J. Webster, *Philadelphia Preserved* (Philadelphia: Temple University Press, 1976), and are presumed demolished.

CHAPTER VII: FROM THE PANIC OF 1857 TO THE OUTBREAK
OF THE CIVIL WAR

1. Two detailed studies of the Panic of 1857, separated in time by over one hundred years, are invaluable in understanding the influence of the specu-

lative attitude on American culture. A great deal of the material in this chapter has been derived from these studies. They are: D. Morier Evans, *The History of the Commercial Crisis, 1857–58, and the Stock Exchange Panic of 1859* (London, 1859; reprint, New York: Burt Franklin, n.d.); and George W. Van Vleck, *The Panic of 1857: An Analytical Study* (New York: AMS Press, 1967).

2. Van Vleck, *Panic of 1857*, p. 1.

3. Ibid., pp. 5, 14, 24, 36.

4. Evans, *History*, pp. 97–98. Evans precedes this description on p. 94 with: "In act, the crisis was a foregone conclusion, and in proportion as the perils of the future loomed up, the spirit of recklessness which these banks did their best to feed counteracted every influence that made its appeal to timidity and apprehension."

5. The Hutton Papers are in the Quaker Collection of the Haverford College Library. They were the gift of Elizabeth Biddle Yarnall, who employed them in her monograph *Addison Hutton: Quaker Architect, 1834–1916* (Philadelphia: Art Alliance Press, 1974). In 1955 and 1957, Mrs. Yarnall kindly allowed the author to use the Hutton Papers, and all quotations from them are by her permission. The papers of Samuel Sloan were burned before the present author could examine them.

6. Hutton Papers, Quaker Collection, Haverford College Library, Haverford, Pa.

7. Ibid.

8. Ibid. Hutton to his mother, Sept. 25, 1858: "He [Sloan] wrote to us when in Germany desiring us to return to the old office which we did about three weeks ago, and we feel much more at home than in the new building on 3rd St.—that was too far down town *and* the rent was nearly double of this—two very good reasons for returning. This place is not quite so roomy as the other, yet we have ample room for all we have to do *or will have soon*—as this was his office in his palmiest days."

9. Ibid. Hutton to his sister, Mary, Feb. 2, 1858: "Sloan has employed me to write his new work on Street Architecture. . . . Don't say much about it out of the family, if any close questions are asked merely say that I am doing some writing for Sloan. . . . I mean to send him [Hutton's father] the 'Street Architecture' in numbers; we want to get the first out before the first of April. It will be published in four numbers."

10. Ibid. Hutton to his sister, Mary, Dec. 6, 1858; also Yarnall, *Hutton*, p. 28: "We have not now a thing to do in the office, over and above the two books that Sloan is about to publish."

11. Ibid. Hutton to his brother, Finley (date obscured), 1859; also Yarnall, *Hutton*, p. 28: "We have the plates for the first number of the 'City Architecture' all ready for the lithographer and I think it will get issued before long. I mean to send thee a copy if I can raise the dimes, and I will designate all the plates I have drawn for it. I think it will be the best practical work ever published, at least as far as regards street buildings."

12. William L. Whitwell, *The Heritage of Longwood* (Jackson, Miss.: University Press of Mississippi, 1975); Ida May Ogletree McAdams, *The Building of Longwood* (Austin, 1972); Margaret Shields Henderson, *The Legend of Longwood* (Natchez, Miss.: Hudson Printing Co., 1972). There is also a fifteen-minute documentary of Longwood made for educational television by the Natchez Pilgrimage Association. The Haller Nutt papers are in two repositories: Nutt Collections (1,000 pieces, 42 of which deal with the building of Longwood); Henry E. Huntington Library and Art Gallery, San Marino, Calif.; and Nutt Papers (720 pieces and one volume of 206 pages), Manuscript Collection, Duke University Library, Durham, N.C.
13. Sloan, *The Model Architect*, vol. 2, pp. 76–77. The design shows that Sloan had no understanding of Muslim or Byzantine architecture aside from the most obvious clichés of decoration. The essay must have been largely borrowed, but his source has not been determined.
14. Ibid. vol. 1, pp. 76–77, and O. S. Fowler, *A Home for All* (New York: Fowler & Wells, 1854), frontispiece.
15. *Biographical and Historical Memoirs of Mississippi* (Chicago: Goodspeed Publishing Co., 1891), vol. 2, pp. 518–521.
16. Harnett T. Kane, *Natchez on the Mississippi* (New York: William Morrow & Co., 1947), p. 289. See also *Villas on the Hudson* (New York: D. Appleton & Co., 1860), esp. "Fowler Place, Fishkill."
17. The school reports for Mary and Carrie Nutt in the Nutt Papers, Duke University Library, are for the spring of 1860, so they must have entered in the fall of 1859.
18. Yarnall, *Hutton*, p. 33.
19. The Philadelphia newspapers give a much fuller and more detailed report than can be found in the published proceedings of the councils, which leave out—for unexplained reasons—a large part of the discussions and arguments. This is also true for the altercations that followed the awarding of the commission and contract. See *Public Ledger* (Philadelphia), vol. 49, no. 139, Sept. 4, 1860; and ibid., no. 142, Sept. 7, 1860, both p. 2, "Public Buildings."
20. Ibid., vol. 50, no. 4, Sept. 28, 1860, p. 2, "Proceedings in Council."
21. Ibid., no. 6, Oct. 1, 1860; and no. 46, Nov. 16, 1860.
22. Ibid., no. 24, Oct. 22, 1860.
23. George Champlin Manson, "Professional Ancestry of the Philadelphia Chapter," *Journal of the American Institute of Architects*, vol. 1, no. 9, Sept. 1913, pp. 381–583.
24. *Public Ledger*, vol. 50, no. 3, Sept. 27, 1860.
25. Ibid., no. 46, Nov. 16, 1860, p. 2, "Proceedings in Council." Sloan got his full fee, to date, of $1 thousand, but continued employment was tabled. William M. Welch, "The Municipal Hospital for Contagious and Infectious Diseases," in *Founder's Week Memorial Volume*, pp. 517–562. *Annual Report of the Board of Health of the City and County of Philadel-*

phia, 1865 (Philadelphia, 1866) gives the final acceptance date of the building as Apr. 27, 1865.

26. *Statistics of Public Schools in Philadelphia* (Philadelphia, 1864). In the summation Sloan's school buildings of the 1850s are severely criticized, except for the High School and the Normal School.

27. Yarnall, *Hutton*, p. 34. In the Hutton Papers previously cited, there is a reference for Hutton written by Sloan: "Mr. Addison Hutton is an excellent draughtsman, possessed of superior constructive talent and practical experience—and of irreproachable moral character."

CHAPTER VIII: 1859–1869: THE DECADE OF TRANSITION

1. Addison Hutton, letter to his sister, Mary, from "Longwood," dated "8 mo 14, 1860," Hutton Papers.

2. Joseph Jones, "Report to the Committee on Construction for the Johns Hopkins Hospital," *Hospital Construction and Organization* (Baltimore, 1875), Introduction.

3. W. Gill Wylie, *Hospitals: Their History, Organization, and Construction* (New York: D. Appleton & Co., 1877), pp. 211ff.

4. *The Hospital of the Protestant Episcopal Church in Philadelphia*, published by order of the Board of Managers (Philadelphia: J. B. Lippincott & Co., 1869) chap. 2, pp. 16ff.

5. Ibid., and *Public Ledger*, vol. 76, no. 15, Oct. 19, 1871; ibid., no. 92, Jan. 8, 1872.

6. Jones, "Report."

7. *Public Ledger*, vol. 50, no. 46, Nov. 16, 1860. Sloan received his full fee of $1,000, as contracts existing in 1909 show.

8. Welch, "Municipal Hospital," pp. 526–527; *Annual Report of the Board of Health of . . . Philadelphia*, 1866; and *Philadelphia Evening Bulletin*, April 28, 1865.

9. Welch, "Municipal Hospital," p. 527.

10. It was moved from 22nd St. and Lehigh Ave. to a large site in the 33rd Ward bounded by Hunting Park Ave., Luzerne St., Nicetown Lane, and Second St. See Welch, "Municipal Hospital," p. 526.

11. *Public Ledger*, vol. 54, no. 66, Dec. 6, 1862, p. 1; ibid., no. 67, Dec. 8, 1862, p. 1; ibid., no. 69, Dec. 10, 1862, p. 1.

12. *History of Lycoming County, Pa.*, ed. D. J. Stewart (Philadelphia, 1876), pp. 42–43 and frontispiece.

13. Mark Peter Marer and Ruth Rosenberg, *A Picture of Lycoming County* (Naparsteck, 1978), vol. 2, pp. 185–189. Protests over the building's demolition were received from the National Trust, the Victorian Society, the Society of Architectural Historians, and Ada Louise Huxtable, in her column in the *New York Times*.

14. *History of Lycoming County, Pennsylvania*, ed. John F. Meginness (Chicago: Brown, Runk & Co., 1892), p. 272.

15. *History of Northumberland County, Pennsylvania*, ed. Herbert C. Bell (Chicago: Brown, Runk & Co., 1891), p. 160.

16. The "Quarter Sessions Docket/1860–1866," containing the "Presentment" by the Grand Jury and the "Minutes of the Board of Commissioners" documenting the search committee's report and the contract with Rissel (also Risel or Rissell in Lycoming documents) have been found. However, searches by Mr. Leicester Horam, chief clerk of Northumberland County, in 1951, and Mr. Frederick F. Reed, registrar and recorder of Northumberland County, in 1981, did not locate the records covering Sloan's suit or its settlement. Both gentlemen assured me that such records had existed; Mr. Horam said that he had at one time examined them. I am indebted to Mr. H. E. Dickson for making Mr. Horam's research available to me, and to Mr. Samuel J. Dornsife of Williamsport for bringing the suit—mention of which he had discovered in the course of his own researches—to my attention.

17. *The Architectural Review*, vol. 1, Oct. 1868, pp. 278–280.

18. Ibid., pp. 334ff.

19. Sloan, *The Model Architect*, vol. 1:66–67, "A Cottage: Design Fourteenth"; ibid., p. 92, "A Cottage: Design Twenty-Second"; ibid., vol. 2, pp. 63–65, "An Italian Villa: Design Forty-Sixth."

20. Ibid., vol. 1, pp. 55–61.

21. *The Architectural Review*, vol. 1, Oct. 1868, p. 334.

22. Eli Slifer Papers, Dickinson College Library, Carlisle, Pa. Sloan's letters to Slifer are one of only three bodies of Sloan papers as yet known (the other being the Haller Nutt collections). They include an "Estimate in Items" for Slifer's villa, Lewisburg, Pa. (c. 1860); an inquiry into the standing of a planing mill at Lewisburg (July 3, 1861); a request for Slifer's influence in obtaining work at the state capital building (Feb. 14, 1862); a request for Slifer's help in obtaining a promotion for his nephew, "Lewis" (no last name given) to first sergeant in the 29th Reg. Penn. Vol. (Mar. 19, 1863); a request for a recommendation to Peru (Jan. 20, 1864); and a further request for consideration in the improvements to the capital building (Aug. 16, 1869).

23. Yarnall, *Hutton*, pp. 34, 38–39. Addison Hutton, letter to his mother, dated "9 mo. 9, 1863," in Hutton Papers.

24. Finley Hutton, "Memoir," c. 1916, Hutton Papers.

25. Yarnall, *Hutton*, pp. 44ff., and Nos. 130 and 131, Catalogue of Buildings, and Yarnall, *Hutton*, p. 42. Addison Hutton, letter to Finley, dated "2 mo. 1, 1865," Hutton Papers.

26. Caleb I. Cope, *Annual Report of the President of the Philadelphia Saving Fund Society*, published by order of the Board of Managers (Philadelphia, 1868, 1870); Yarnall, *Hutton*, p. 42.

27. Original specifications for the building, in the possession of Mrs. Isabel W. Pons, Librarian, Annie Halenbake Ross Library, Lock Haven, Pa. *Historic Lock Haven: An Architectural Survey*, ed. Dean R. Wagner (Lock Haven, Pa., 1979), p. 80.

28. These are the Fallon House (1854), the L. A. Mackey House (1854), St. Paul's Episcopal Church (1856), the David Carskaddon House (1858), Great Island Presbyterian Church (1863), Mayer's Block on East Water Street (1863), and the C. A. Mayer House (1869).
29. *Historic Lock Haven*, pp. 7, 70.
30. Finley Hutton, "Memoir."
31. Ibid.

CHAPTER IX: *THE ARCHITECTURAL REVIEW* AND THE CENTENNIAL

1. Samuel Sloan's name first appears in the 1868–1869 Roster in the proceedings of the second convention of the AIA, 1868. On page 14 of the proceedings of the third convention (1869), he is listed under "Became Fellow During Term." From 1870 to 1874 he is listed as "Fellow," but not as a member of the Philadelphia Chapter. Between 1876 and 1879 his name appears on AIA membership lists but not in chapter rolls. From 1880 to 1885 he is listed as "Lapsed, Feb. 1876." I am indebted for this information to Susan Cosgrove Holton, Librarian, American Institute of Architects, 1979.
2. The only chapter of the AIA in 1868 was in New York. Therefore, Sloan's membership prior to July 1868 tends to confirm that he did go to New York after Sloan & Hutton was dissolved, as the "Memoir" of Finley Hutton states. Sloan's working editor of the *Review* was Charles J. Lukens (see *American Publisher's Circular and Literary Gazette* [Philadelphia, ed. George W. Childs] vol. 11, Aug. 15, 1868, p. 177; ibid., 12 Nov. 2, 1868).
3. George Champlin Mason, "Professional Ancestry of the Philadelphia Chapter," *Journal of the American Institute of Architects*, vol. 1, no. 9, Sept. 1913, p. 15.
4. It is noticeable that Sloan always uses "Institute of American Architects" rather than American Institute of Architects. He missed no opportunity to emphasize that it was an organization of *American* architects rather than just an American organization of architects.
5. Henry A. Sims, "The American Institute of Architects," *Penn Monthly*, vol. 4, 1873, pp. 499–505.
6. Mason, "Professional Ancestry," p. 16.
7. Ibid.
8. *The Architectural Review*, vol. 11, July 1869, pp. 74–76.
9. *Shippensburg News*, Sept. 17, 1870; *The Shippensburg Story 1730–1970: An Anniversary Publication* (Shippensburg, Pa.: News-Chronicle Co., 1970), pp. 130–131; *Evening Sentinel* (Carlisle, Pa.), "Closing of Dormitories Ends Era at Shippensburg," May 12, 1976; and *Patriot* (Harrisburg, Pa.), "Renovation Slated for Old Main," Oct. 14, 1981. *Note*: All of the above documentation was furnished the author by Mr. Richard L. Arnold of Carlisle, Pa., who has also exhaustively documented the Second Presbyterian Church of Carlisle, a Sloan commission of

1870. See Richard L. Arnold, *A Sesquicentennial Review of the Second Presbyterian Church, Carlisle, Pennsylvania, 1833–1983* (N.p., 1982), pp. 37–39, 188–204.

10. "The New City Hall," *San Francisco Municipal Reports, 1879–1916* (San Francisco, 1917), p. 519.

11. "T. S. Kirkbride and the Kirkbride System," *Institutional Care of the Insane in the United States and Canada*, 2 vols., ed. Henry M. Hurd (Baltimore: Johns Hopkins Press, 1916), vol. 1, pp. 204–213.

12. These are the dwellings for Charles Taylor, Chestnut Hill, Pa. (1861); Eli Slifer, Lewisburg, Pa. (1860–1861); William H. Armstrong, Williamsport, Pa. (1860–1861); and Farmer's Market, Market Street between 11th and 12th Sts., Philadelphia, Pa. (1860–1861).

13. The most flagrant examples are Sloan's obituary in *The American Architect and Building News*, vol. 16, no. 449, Aug. 2, 1884, p. 49. (This periodical openly plagiarized the format and content of Sloan's *Review*); and *Appleton's Cyclopaedia of American Biography*, ed. Wilson and Fiske (New York, 1888), vol. 5, p. 550 (only four years after Sloan's death, this short biography got almost everything wrong).

14. John O. Raum, *History of the City of Trenton, New Jersey . . .* (Trenton, 1871), p. 320; and *The History of New Jersey* (Philadelphia: John E. Potter & Co., n.d.), pp. 214–217.

15. James McClune, *History of the Presbyterian Church in the Forks of the Brandywine from A.D. 1735 to 1885* (Philadelphia, 1885), pp. 48–49. Letters from the Rev. John A. Kauffroth, former pastor of the church, to Richard L. Arnold, Carlisle, Pa., May 25, 1976, and May 18, 1977, giving results of document search (copies in the possession of the present author).

16. *Public Ledger*, vol. 75, no. 118, Aug. 9, 1873, p. 2, under "Local Affairs" carried the full text of the report by the Committee on Plans and Architecture of the U.S. Centennial Commission, giving the names of the ten winning entries in the first competition, their authors, a complete description of their designs, and the additional requirements for entries in the second competition. The committee's decision had been reported the previous day (Aug. 8, 1873) as it was issued later in pamphlet form.

17. *Public Ledger*, vol. 75, no. 118, Aug. 9, 1873. The elevation and plan of "Americanus," together with some marginal notes in script describing it, were found in the "Scrapbook of T. U. Walter," a collection of photographic reductions of some of Sloan's drawings for both the first and second Centennial competitions (together with other unrelated material). The "Scrapbook" is in the collection of the Library of the School of Fine Arts, University of Pennsylvania. Copies of all Sloan material in the "Scrapbook" are in the possession of the present author.

18. Ibid., Aug. 9, 1873; ibid., no. 15, Oct. 10, 1873; ibid., no. 16, Oct. 11, 1873.

19. H. J. Schwarzmann was twenty-three years younger than Sloan (b. 1843 in Munich) and trained as a landscape architect and engineer. When all the entries in the second Centennial competition exceeded the commission's budget (they ran from over 2 million to over 10 million), and after protracted attempts to adapt the designs of the competing architects failed, Schwarzmann was sent by the Fairmount Park Commission to the Vienna International Exhibition of 1873 to study its buildings and plan. He was subsequently hired to design the main exhibition building, fix the site of the subsidiary buildings, and be the Chief Architect of the Exhibition. A full study of the Centennial Exhibition competitions is being done by Mr. David Bahlman. See also *Grounds and Buildings of the Centennial Exhibition, Philadelphia, 1876*, ed. Dorsey Gardner, issued by the U.S. Centennial Commission (Washington, D.C.: Government Printing Office, 1880), pp. 29–30.

20. "Scrapbook of T. U. Walter." This contains the only known reproduction of the interior perspective of Sloan's permanent building proposal. The exterior perspective, elevation, and plan were published in *Description of Design and Drawings for the Proposed Centennial Buildings . . .* , presented by Samuel Sloan (Philadelphia: King & Baird, 1873), pp. 4ff.

21. Sloan, *Description of Design*, cited no. 20. See also Theophilus Ballou White, *Fairmount, Philadelphia's Park* (Philadelphia: Art Alliance Press, 1975), p. 62.

CHAPTER X: 1874–1884: THE FINAL DECADE

1. Samuel Sloan, "Art XV: Heat and Ventilation," in *Church Extension Annual, including the Ninth Annual Report of the Board of Church Extension of the Methodist Episcopal Church for the year 1874* (Philadelphia: Craig, Finley & Co., 1875), pp. 38–44.

2. Mrs. Austin A. Baker, letter to the American Institute of Architects, May 5, 1953, relative to research on Fletcher Sloan, half-brother of Samuel, by his daughter, Carrie Matilda Sloan Foster of Bolivar, Tenn., in the collection of the Library of the AIA, The Octagon, Washington, D.C. This was made available by Mr. George E. Pettengill, Librarian, The Octagon, June 10, 1960. For additional documentation, see the Appendix to the present work.

3. Samuel Sloan, "Art XVI: Our Designs," in *Church Extension Annual*, pp. 44–63.

4. Samuel Sloan, "Our Designs," *Minutes of the General Assembly of the Presbyterian Church in the United States of America, with an Appendix*, n.s., vol. 4 (New York: Presbyterian Board of Publication, pp. 11–16 of the Appendix.

5. *Wooden and Brick Buildings with Details*, 2 vols. (New York: A. J. Bicknell & Co., 1875), vol. 1, Design 17 (plates 23–24), Design 18 (plates 25–27), and Design 19 (plates 28–30). Malinda McGough, "Samuel

Sloan: Three 'Stick Style' Houses in Haddonfield, New Jersey," thesis submitted for the master of arts degree at Tulane University, 1976. Ms. McGough has attributed the houses at 127 Washington Ave., 200 Washington Ave., and 141 Warwick Rd., Haddonfield, N.J., to Sloan, on the basis of comparison with the three designs in Bicknell cited above. See also *The Historical Society of Haddonfield*, vol. 21, no. 2, May 1979, "Spring Meeting Features 'Samuel Sloan, Architect of Haddonfield'"; and Melinda McGough, "Three Houses by Samuel Sloan," mimeographed pamphlet issued by the Historical Society of Haddonfield. The Haddonfield material, together with slides of the attributed houses, was kindly furnished by Ms. McGough.

6. The record of the special meeting is found on page 119 of the Minutes of the Philadelphia Chapter, Book 1; manuscript in the collection of the American Philosophical Society, Philadelphia, Pa. Walter's statement is recorded under "Reports of the Chapters," *Proceedings of the Ninth Annual Convention of the American Institute of Architects*, Baltimore, Nov. 17–19, 1875, ed. George C. Mason Jr. (Newport: Davis & Pitman, 1876).

7. Susan Cosgrove Holton, Librarian, American Institute of Architects, The Octagon, letter to the author, July 26, 1979, giving the results of a document search: "Between 1876 and 1879 he does appear in Institute membership lists, but not in chapter rolls. From 1880 to 1885, he is listed as "Lapsed, Feb. 1876" in Institute lists; he is not in chapter lists."

8. *First Biennial Report of the Commissioners to Build the Western Insane Asylum of North Carolina at Morgantown* (Raleigh: News Job Office and Book Bindery, 1876), pp. 7–8.

9. The Alabama Insane Hospital at Tuscaloosa had recommenced construction on its unfinished building, and Dr. Kirkbride had been solicited for advice as to improvements on their buildings by administrators of the hospitals for the insane in South Carolina and Georgia.

10. Commissioner L. L. Polk, *Handbook of North Carolina embracing Historical and Physiographical Sketches of the State with Statistical and other Information relating to its Industries, Resources and Political Condition* (Raleigh: Raleigh News Steam Book and Job Print, 1879), pp. 176–180. The first building of the Raleigh asylum was built from designs of A. J. Davis. It was authorized in 1848 and opened in 1856. The visit of the delegation to Kirkbride and Sloan, and the commission to Sloan for additions, is documented in *First Biennial Report*.

11. *Report of the Board of Directors and Superintendent of the Insane Asylum of North Carolina* (Raleigh: State Agricultural Journal Book and Job Office, 1874), pp. 39–42.

12. Polk, *Handbook*, p. 180.

13. Ibid., p. 181.

14. The villa was extant and occupied in 1960, and its owner, Mr. Benjamin F. Stahl Jr., was of the opinion that there were other examples in the

vicinity—extant and demolished—which had been built from Sloan's designs in the period immediately following the close of the Centennial Exhibition.

15. Charles Balderston was the son of Mark Balderston, who had gone into business with Finley Hutton, younger brother of Addison Hutton, in 1875 as "Mark Balderston & Co., Builders." In *Gopsill's Philadelphia City Directory*, compiled by Isaac Costa (Philadelphia: James Gopsill, 1869–1895), Charles Balderston is listed in 1874 as "draughtsman," in 1875 as "carp.," in 1876 as "archt.," and in 1877 as "Sloan, Balderston & Young." He retains this listing until 1883, has no listing in 1884, and is listed in 1885 as "archt., 212 S. 3rd, h.3218 Spencer Ter." Young is listed only in 1877 and 1878, under the firm name, with no home address. Mark Balderston is listed as "Mark Balderston & Co. (Mark Balderston and Finley Hutton, Builders)," from 1875 until 1883, when no listing is given. Finley Hutton is listed in 1872 as "draughtsman," in 1873 as "archt.," in 1874 as "builder," and from 1875 to 1883 as associate of Mark Balderston in Mark Balderston & Co., Builders. Addison Hutton's relation with Sloan after their partnership was dissolved is given in Finley Hutton's "Memoir."

16. This is a marble plaque mounted on the wall of the main hallway of the courthouse near the Broad St. entrance (south elevation). I am indebted to Mr. Peter B. Sandbeck of the New Bern Historical Society Foundation, New Bern, N.C., for this documentation. The plaque lists the county commissioners, and the attorney, architects, builder, and painter, and is headed with the inscription: "Aequitas Sequitur Legem."

17. On Sept. 16, 1877, the Philadelphia Chapter of the AIA passed a resolution asking its members not to participate in the asylum competition and to withdraw any entries they had made. However, Sloan's membership in both the chapter and the national organization had already lapsed, Wilson Brothers and Perry & Sedgwick were primarily engineering firms, Stuckert had just opened his office in 1877 and was not a chapter member, and only Hutton was an AIA member in good standing. *American Architect and Building News*, vol. 2, no. 91, Sept. 22, 1877, p. 306, "Correspondence"; ibid., no. 99, Nov. 17, 1877, p. 370, "Correspondence"; ibid., no. 100, Nov. 24, 1877, pp. 373, 378–379.

18. *Institutional Care of the Insane of the United States and Canada*, vol. 1, pp. 38, 41, 208; ibid., vol. 2, p. 224.

19. Polk, *Handbook*, p. 181.

20. Sloan's home address, which had been 508 South 42nd St. since 1866, changed in 1878 to 1910 North 13th St., together with Ellwood P. Sloan. Ellwood moved again in 1881 to 1809 Mervine, where his mother, Mary, is also listed, but not his father, Samuel, who lists no home address. Mary Sloan is listed with Ellwood until after Samuel's death in 1884.

21. Adolphus Gustavus Bauder, "Memoir," manuscript in the possession of

Mrs. Ruth O. Brumbaugh, North Canton, Ohio. Mrs. Brumbaugh is Bauer's granddaughter, and the quotation is used with her kind permission. The "Memoir" was brought to my attention by Professor Carmine Prioli of North Carolina State University. Both he and Mr. William B. Bushong have written studies of Bauer for the *North Carolina Historical Review*, and without their generous help the reconstruction of Sloan's North Carolina period would not have been possible. See Carmine A. Prioli, "The Indian 'Princess' and the Architect: Origin of a North Carolina Legend," *North Carolina Historical Review*, January 1983; and William B. Bushong, "Adolphus G. Bauer, (1858–1898)," unpublished manuscript lent by its author.

22. *News & Observer* (Raleigh, N.C.), vol. 17, no. 170, Sept. 26, 1880, p. 4, "Observations."

23. Ibid., vol. 21, no. 36, Apr. 27, 1883, p. 4.

24. Ibid., no. 24, Apr. 13, 1883, p. 4.

25. Ibid., no. 47, May 9, 1883, p. 3.

26. V. M. Mulholland, "North Carolina's Gingerbread White House," *North Carolina Education*, vol. 24, no. 3, Nov. 1957, pp. 11, 26, 28.

27. Sloan's commuting between Philadelphia, Raleigh, and Columbia caused delays in his North Carolina practice that were sometimes annoying to his clients there. *News & Observer*, vol. 21, no. 104, Nov. 4, 1883, p. 4, under "Observations" commented, "The township school committee await the arrival of Mr. Sloan, the architect, before purchasing the old mansion and grounds." This was in relation to Sloan's commission for a new Graded School in Raleigh, and the "school committee," becoming impatient, bought the old governor's mansion, which changed Sloan's commission from one for a new design to the remodeling of the existing building.

28. Thomas S. Kirkbride, letter "To the Commissioners of the South Carolina Hospital for the Insane," 1854, manuscript in the collection of the College of Physicians, Philadelphia, Pa.

29. *News & Observer* (Raleigh, N.C.), vol. 21, no. 103, Nov. 3, 1883, p. 4, "Business Men."

30. Ibid., no. 104, Nov. 4, 1883, p. 4, "Observations"; and ibid., no. 105, Nov. 6, 1883, p. 6, "Meeting of the Citizens Committee."

31. Ibid., vol. 22, no. 107, Mar. 25, 1884, p. 4, "The Exposition Building"; and ibid., no. 24, June 11, 1884, p. 1, "The State Exposition."

32. *Sketches of the History of the University of North Carolina* (1889), p. 33. Archibald Henderson, *The Campus of the First State University* (Chapel Hill: University of North Carolina Press, 1949), pp. 198–199 and nn. 29 and 32. John McKee, "Spooky Architectural Monstrosity," *Carolina Magazine*, vol. 64, May 1935.

33. *News & Observer* (Raleigh, N.C.), vol. 22, no. 54, July 18, 1884, p. 4, "Personals"; ibid., no. 55, July 19, 1884, p. 4, "Observations"; ibid., no. 56, July 20, 1884, p. 4, "Death of Mr. Samuel Sloan"; ibid., no. 58, July 21, 1884, p. 4, "Funeral."

34. "Burial Records of the Mt. Moriah Cemetery," Permit No. 40625, Feb. 4, 1885, Section 11, Lot No. 20, Grave No. 3rd from East Line, manuscript microfilm, collection of the Historical Society of Pennsylvania, Philadelphia, Pa.

35. *The Press* (Philadelphia), July 23, 1884, p. 4, "His family wish to express their warmest thanks for the sympathy and attention of the people of Raleigh in their time of bereavement, which will ever remain fresh in their remembrances. Every possible need was anticipated and provided for, and no act of kindness which could lessen their sorrow was left unperformed. In the shelter of home, in the bosom of dearest kindred, more thorough and practical thoughtfulness could not have been shown. To Dr. Knox and Mr. Williams, whose exertions have been unremitting, and whose devotion in this hour of trial has been above all price, they wish to express, what is beyond expression, the thankfulness of overflowing hearts." *Note*: It is the opinion of the physicians with whom the notices of Sloan's death have been discussed that he died of heat prostration accompanied by cerebral hemorrhage.

36. *Building*, vol. 2, Sept. 1884, p. 143, "Obituary"; *American Architect and Building News*, vol. 16, no. 449, Aug. 2, 1884, p. 1, "Mr. Samuel Sloan." See also *Cyclopaedia of American Biography*, ed. James Grant Wilson and John Fiske (New York: D. Appleton & Co., 1888), p. 550.

37. *American Architect and Building News*, vol. 16, no. 449, Aug. 2, 1884), p. 1, "Mr. Samuel Sloan."

APPENDIX

Ancestors, Family, and Descendants of Samuel (T.) Sloan

This genealogy is neither complete nor, in the case of several persons, firmly documented. Sloan is so common a name in the counties of southeastern Pennsylvania, and the repetition of given names (John, Charles, James, Samuel, etc.) is so frequent in all the Sloan families investigated, that certain identification of some of the members of the family of Samuel (T.) Sloan could not be made by this author.

Three sources record that Samuel (T.) Sloan was the son of William and Mary (Kirkwood) Sloan and that he was born in Honeybrook Township, Chester County, Pennsylvania, in 1815.[1] However there are among these sources conflicting dates of birth. His birthdate is given on his tombstone in Mount Moriah Cemetery, Philadelphia, Pennsylvania, as March 3. All other sources give his birthday as March 7.[2]

William Sloan, father of Samuel, is first documented as living in Honeybrook Township by the census of 1810, wherein he is listed as the tenant of a house owned by (*defaced*) Gibbons, formerly also occupied by Thomas Sloan. Succeeding census and tax records give the following information:

In 1810 the tax records of Honeybrook list Samuel and Robert Sloan as freemen.

In 1813 William and James Sloan were taxed as "inmates" of the house of Samuel Kirkwood. Samuel and John Sloan are listed as freemen.

In 1815 William Sloan was listed as "inmate" of the house of John Sloan, who was taxed for six acres of land. Samuel and Robert Sloan were listed as freemen. Samuel Kirkwood was no longer listed.

In 1817, William Sloan is no longer listed in Honeybrook. Samuel, Robert, and James are listed as freemen.[3]

The relationships among these men have not been documented, but in view of the names given by William Sloan to his own sons, it seems likely that they were closely connected (brothers, uncles, first cousins, etc.). All of them were probably descendants of a Samuel Sloan who came to Chester

County, Pennsylvania, from Worcester, Massachusetts, in time for his son, William, to be born there in 1760.[4] This William may have been the grandfather of Samuel (T.) Sloan.

Samuel Kirkwood, father of Mary (Kirkwood) Sloan, is documented by the 1810 census as residing in Sadsbury Township, Lancaster County, Pennsylvania.[5] As the 1813 Honeybrook records show, he was by then a resident of that township and housing both William Sloan (and presumably William's family) and James Sloan. By 1815 he had either died or moved from Honeybrook. Samuel Kirkwood was a descendant, possibly a son, of Robert Kirkwood, who came from Londonderry, Ireland, to New Castle, Delaware, in 1731, later settling in Hartford County, Maryland. His large family of children lived in or near the valley of the Susquehanna River on both sides of the Pennsylvania-Maryland line. One branch settled in Lancaster County, Pennsylvania, and a grandson, Daniel Kirkwood (1814–1895), almost an exact contemporary of Samuel (T.) Sloan, became principal of the high school in the county seat of Lancaster.[6]

Three sources credit William Sloan with having sired ten sons and one daughter.[7] Of these, it seems that the four eldest (William, born July 9, 1806; Charles, born November 9, 1811; *Samuel*, born March 7, 1815; and John, born July 16, 1816) were the children of Mary (Kirkwood) Sloan. There are, however, two sons and one daughter for whom no birthdate has been found; these are Robert, Thomas (died June 2, 1869), and Elizabeth.[8] Two other children—Wesley (born 1821) and Fletcher (born April 8, 1826)—are known to have been the issue of his second wife, Keziah Diffidiffy (or Diffenderffer), member of a Pennsylvania-German family long settled in Lancaster County, Pennsylvania.[9] One son of the ten credited to William Sloan has not been identified.

Both substantiation and confusion of these relationships is found in two wills, that of Margaret Sloan, "Singlewoman," who died May 10, 1888, and that of Thomas Sloan (died May 1869), which was probated June 2, 1869.[10] Margaret made bequests to the following persons:

Ellwood Sloan, identified as "nephew, son of my brother Samuel"
Wesley Sloan, identified as "brother"
John Sloan, identified as "brother"
Louisa Sloan, identified as "daughter of John"
William Sloan, identified as "nephew, of West Philadelphia," and to his wife, Adeline, and daughter, Clara
Samuel Bodkin, identified as "nephew, of West Philadelphia," and to his son, Frank
Rebecca Lane, identified as "widow of Joel Lane, of West Philadelphia"

These identifications substantiate the relationship of Samuel (T.) Sloan, Wesley, John, and Margaret and indicate that the maiden name of a wife of one of the Sloan brothers was Bodkin. In the documents collected during the settlement of the estate of Mrs. Carrie Matilda Sloan Foster of Bolivar, Tennessee, granddaughter of Fletcher Sloan, youngest half-brother of Samuel (T.) Sloan, there is a letter from Mrs. Wesley Sloan of Media, Pennsylvania, containing the phrase "My late husband's Grandfather, Wesley Sloan, was a brother to Elizabeth and Fletcher Sloan." Another letter in the same collection, from Fred Hanson (or Hansen), records, "Fletcher and Mrs. Amy Snyder's Grandmother were brother and sister" and identifies the grandmother as Elizabeth Sloan.[11] If the repeated attribution of only one daughter to William and Mary (Kirkwood) Sloan is correct, then only Margaret could have been that daughter, and Elizabeth was another sister-in-law, whose maiden name could have been Bodkin. In the records of the Wesley Sloan family under the heading "Family Deaths" is the entry "Jane Bodkin—Born April 26, 1810—Died, Feb. 22, 1818." This would suggest that intermarriage had occurred between the Sloan and Bodkin families at an early date. As of this writing, no satisfactory solution to the Bodkin "problem" has been found, and as a result the exact status of Elizabeth Sloan is still in doubt.

William Sloan, who is called in Margaret's will "nephew," was the son of Thomas Sloan, the probate of whose will lists

Robert Sloan, identified as "brother"
William Sloan, identified as "son"
Wesley Sloan, identified as "brother" and "witness"

This substantiates the relationship between Samuel (T.) Sloan and Robert and Thomas Sloan, for whom, however, no other documentation has been found. Thomas' death in May 1869 might seem to indicate that he was an older son, child of Mary (Kirkwood) Sloan; however, in a period when the average life expectancy of males in the United States was under fifty years, this need not have been the case.

Margaret Sloan's bequest to "Rebecca Lane, widow of Joel" is explained by the tombstones in the Pennell lot in Mount Moriah Cemetery. There, adjacent to the stones of James Pennell (1786–1875) and his wife Mary (1792–1871) (the father and mother of Mary [Pennell] Sloan, wife of Samuel [T.] Sloan) are the stones of Rebecca Pennell Lane (1829–1913) and her husband Joel Lane (1810–1884).[12] Rebecca Lane was thus a sister of Mary (Pennell) Sloan, wife of Samuel (T.) Sloan, and the sister-in-law of Margaret Sloan.

Further documentation of William Sloan, the supposed oldest brother of Samuel, is almost entirely lacking. There is a marginal note in the family records of the Wesley Sloans: "Several of the brothers settled in the South. [Then, in pencil]: One settled in St. Louis, Mo." As the only half-brother known to have settled in the South was Fletcher, the youngest child in the family (who settled in Bolivar, Tennessee), it is possible that William was another southwestern migrant.

For Charles Sloan, the second son of Mary (Kirkwood) Sloan, there are only two references. He is listed in the records of the Wesley Sloan family as "brother" and was said by Mrs. Carrie Matilda Sloan Foster, granddaughter of Fletcher Sloan, to have been a resident of West Decatur, Pennsylvania, and "an authority on ventilation."[13]

The letter of Fred Hanson, previously cited, which identifies Elizabeth Sloan, gives her daughter's married name as Alice Dimeling (or Dimling) Morrow. A letter of Alice D. Morrow (dated December 27, 1927), which is among the Foster documents, gives the name of her daughter as Amy and states that Amy had three children at that time, two boys (unnamed) and a girl, of two years nine months, named Alice. The Fred Hanson letter and the letter of Mrs. Wesley Sloan, previously cited, give Amy's married name as Amy Morrow Snyder. A letter of Amy Morrow Snyder (dated August 6, 1955) among the Foster documents records the name of one son, Thomas, who is living in Norristown, Pennsylvania, at that date, the father of one son of six years (unnamed) and a recently born daughter (unnamed) and also states that her daughter, Alice, is married (name not given), is living in Phillipsburg, Pennsylvania, and has one son of three years (unnamed). The letters of both Mrs. Morrow and Mrs. Snyder give West Decatur, Pennsylvania, as the writers' address, which gives rise to the possibility that Elizabeth Sloan was the wife of Charles Sloan.

The only direct reference to John Sloan, Samuel's next younger brother, are his dates in the Wesley Sloan records (July 11, 1816–October 31, 1879). There is a listing for him in *McElroy's Philadelphia Directory* of 1859 as "Carpenter," his address being the same as that of Wesley Sloan, "Chestnut ab Rose, W.P." The name John Sloan is so common in the Philadelphia directories of the period that only when John is associated with Wesley can one be certain that the reference is to the brother of Samuel. One entry in the *Registry of Deeds and Mortgages* for the City and County of Philadelphia may refer to John; in Book 197, page 524, the record of a transaction on May 22, 1875, lists Samuel Sloan as "Grantor" and J. H. Sloan as "Grantee." This could be Samuel's brother, John, since he did not die until 1879. No will or notice of administration has been found for John or J. H. Sloan in the Philadelphia records.

The death notice and burial record of Margaret Sloan both give her age at death as seventy years. She would therefore have been born in 1818. If she was the full sister of Samuel, then Samuel, John, and Margaret were all born within three years (March 7, 1815; July 16, 1816; ? 1818). This short span between births is not in accord with the spans between Mary (Kirkwood) Sloan's first three children (William–Charles, five years three months; Charles–Samuel, three years four months), nor that of William Sloan's children by Keziah Diffenderffer (Wesley–Fletcher, five years). A reasonable hypothesis would be that John was an unplanned child, whose birth, only one year and three months after that of Samuel, caused the death of his mother. This speculation is partially borne out by the census and tax records of Honeybrook Township. In 1815 they show that William Sloan was a resident of Honeybrook, living with John Sloan. Samuel is recorded, without exception, as having been born in Honeybrook (either March 3 or March 7, 1815); however, he is said by one source to have been taken to Lancaster at an early age and to have received his schooling and carpenter's apprenticeship there.[14] Wesley and Fletcher Sloan, children of Keziah (Diffenderffer) Sloan, William's second wife, are known to have been born in Lancaster. The census and tax records of Honeybrook for 1817 do not list William Sloan; he had moved at some time between 1815 and 1817. If Mary (Kirkwood) Sloan died at or soon after the birth of John (July 16, 1816), William Sloan would have been left with a family of small children, one a newborn infant. It is reasonable to assume that he would have remarried as quickly as possible, that is, before the end of 1816. Keziah Diffenderffer came from an old Lancaster family whose members have been influential in local affairs from the eighteenth century to the present day. William's chances of finding work to support his family would have been greater in Lancaster—with the help of his wife's family—than in Honeybrook; hence, it seems likely that William married Keziah and moved to her home city of Lancaster before the year 1817. Margaret, then, would be the first child of William and Keziah, and the half-sister of Samuel. As the birthdates and places of Robert and Thomas Sloan are not known, their exact relationship to Samuel cannot be determined.

There is one further unsolved puzzle relative to Margaret Sloan. The interment records of Mount Moriah Cemetery in Philadelphia show that she was buried on May 12, 1888, in Section 138, Lot No. 187, Center Grave.[15] However, a careful survey of this site and all adjoining sites (as well as, Lot Nos. 18 and 87, and the same lot numbers in Sections 13 and 38) has not located her grave. Margaret has vanished: there is no record of her body having been disinterred and moved to another cemetery (the records of West Laurel Hill, the family cemetery of the Wesley Sloan family, do not list her, nor do those of any other Philadelphia cemetery for which the 1888 records are extant). The administration of Mount Moriah can give no explanation for this.

Wesley Sloan (1821–1904), half-brother of Samuel, is soundly documented. He was born in Lancaster and came to Philadelphia as a young man, probably after having served his carpenter's apprenticeship in Lancaster under John Walter Sloan, his father's cousin, a carpenter and cabinetmaker of Lancaster who also trained Samuel.[16] Wesley is first listed in *McElroy's Philadelphia Directory* for 1846, as a carpenter. In 1859 he is again listed as "carpenter" in *McElroy's*, with the same home address as John Sloan, presumably his older half-brother. From 1887 to 1890 he is listed in *Gopsill's Philadelphia City Directory* as a partner of "Sloan and Son (carp. and builders)" together with Thomas C. Sloan, the address of the firm being the same as Wesley's home address. The *Registry of Deeds and Mortgages* of the city and county of Philadelphia lists sixteen registries with Wesley as "Grantee" (the earliest being December 29, 1854, the latest November 5, 1884) and sixteen with him as "Grantor" (the earliest being December 29, 1854, the latest June 1, 1883). In 1900, Wesley moved from Philadelphia to Media, Pennsylvania.

Wesley married Margaret Curran (1822–1890), who had been born and raised in England. Of their three children, Eliza Sloan (December 9, 1847– June 8, 1849), Charles Fletcher Sloan (May 7, 1850–July 11, 1850), and Thomas Curran Sloan (April 19, 1853–? 1918), only Thomas C. survived past early childhood.[17] He is first listed in *Gopsill's* in 1887 as a partner with his father, Wesley, in the firm of "Sloan and Son (carp. and builders)" and continues to be so listed until 1890. Thomas C. Sloan married Gulielma T. Garrett (1852–1933), by whom he had seven children; three died in infancy: Anna G. Sloan (1880–1888), T. Clarence Sloan (1884–1888), and J. Rodger Sloan (1886–1888).[18] The surviving children were Louella (1891–), Wesley (1878–1957), Elmer (1888–1945), and Raymond (dates unknown). Louella Sloan married Dennis Marshall Woodson (1886–1955) and had two children, Wesley Sloan (1916–1975) and Sue (1918–). Wesley Sloan Woodson married Noel Johnson (dates unknown), by whom he had two children, Dennis Marshall (1947–) and Nancy Sloan (1949–). Sue Woodson married Glenn Diehl Rohrbaugh (1911–1949), by whom she had three sons, Glenn Dennis (1943–), David Woodson (1945–) and Richard Sloan (1948–). Raymond Sloan married Mary Swartz Fiscel (1886–1960), by whom he had one son, Garrett (1919–) who in 1982 was director of the Miami-Dade Water and Sewer Authority. Elmer Sloan married Marion Fronfield (1889–1945), by whom he had three children, Frances Fronfield (1920–1924), Harvy Fronfield (1917–) and Mildred Garrett (Milliken) (1925–).

The second Wesley Sloan (1878–1957) married Alice Mary Whann (1879–1977), by whom he had three children, Edith Louella (1904–1973), Elanor Garrett (1907–) and Ralph Thomas (b. 1905). Edith Louella Sloan married Charles Edwin Fellows (1904–1973), Ralph Thomas Sloan married Pauline Anderson Kane (1919–) and Elanor Garrett Sloan married Mark Brooke Williamson (1904–). It has been through the kind help of Mr. and Mrs. Ralph T. Sloan and Mrs. Sue Rohrbaugh that the majority of this latter genealogical material has been gathered.

Fletcher Sloan (April 8, 1862–March 26, 1883), the last child of William Sloan and Keziah Diffenderffer, was born in Lancaster, Pennsylvania, but was taken as a child in arms to Hamilton Village, just west across the Schuylkill River from Philadelphia. William Sloan had moved to Hamiltonville (as it was also called) at some time either before or immediately after Fletcher's birth. Other evidence seems to indicate that the move took place before that event; hence, Keziah Sloan returned home to Lancaster to have her child.[19] Mrs. Carrie Matilda Sloan Foster, granddaughter of Fletcher Sloan, gave his birthplace as Philadelphia. This is in conflict with all other sources, but if he was taken to Hamilton Village as a child of a few weeks or months, Fletcher would have remembered it as his "home," and it was a suburb of Philadelphia by his tenth year. The next certain reference to Fletcher is a note in the column "Local Affairs" of the *Philadelphia Public Ledger* of September 7, 1853 (vol. 35, no. 143), which reported that Fletcher Sloan was to accompany John Stewart, of the firm of Sloan & Stewart, to Tuscaloosa, Alabama, for the purpose of supervising the new Alabama Insane Hospital, the commission for which had recently been awarded to the firm. A second notice, in the same column, appeared on April 28, 1857 (vol. 43, no. 31) and reported that Stewart was now the field architect on the job and Fletcher Sloan was chief superintendent in charge of construction.

Exactly when Samuel Sloan began to employ his half-brother, Fletcher, is not known. For the firm to entrust even the assistant supervision of such an important commission as Sloan's first insane hospital to Fletcher without Fletcher having had some years of experience with Sloan & Stewart, both in the office and in the field, is improbable. Moreover, Fletcher set himself up as an "Architect" in Tuscaloosa as soon as the initial funding for the hospital ran out, which argues for office as well as field experience. He obviously had determined to remain in the South by 1856, when he married Mary Elizabeth (W.) Crane of Tuscaloosa (February 3, 1827–February 5, 1888) and opened an independent practice. Two sources credit Fletcher with having "built" an Episcopal church (no name given) and several residences in Tuscaloosa.[20] One source credits him with the design of "some" of the buildings on the campus of the University of Alabama at Tuscaloosa and with having been, for a short time, the assistant state architect of Mississippi.[21] This later attribution is supported by the general agreement that Fletcher was the architect for the courthouses in Holly Springs and Oxford, Mississippi, and possibly an Episcopal church (unnamed) in Oxford.[22]

At some time in the late 1860s, Fletcher moved to Memphis, Tennessee, but he remained there only a short time before removing to Bolivar, Tennessee, where he resided for the remainder of his life. There seem to have been two reasons for the move; first, his firm, "Willis, Sloan and Trigg, builders and architects," was awarded the commission for the Hardeman County Courthouse, Bolivar, in 1867; the building was completed in 1868 and is still standing (with additions and alterations).[23] Second, he may have lost two of his five children in the yellow fever epidemic that swept Memphis in the late 1860s. Whatever the reasons, Fletcher was a resident of Bolivar in 1868 (or 1869) when he received the commission for St. James Episcopal Church.[24] For the remainder of his active career he was a successful architect.

Fletcher and Mary Sloan had five children, of which three—Carrie Matilda (1860–1960), Sophie W. (1862–1903), and George I. (1864–1903)—survived childhood. George I. Sloan is said to have moved to Chicago, but the records of Union Cemetery, Bolivar, list his interment there.[25] Sophie W. Sloan married James Andrew Foster (1901), by whom she had one son, George Fletcher Sloan Foster (?–1902). Carrie M. Sloan also married James Andrew Foster (1907), but there were no children of the marriage. There are no direct descendants of Fletcher Sloan living.

Samuel (T., probably Thomas) Sloan married (c. 1843) Mary Pennell, the daughter of James and Mary Pennell of West Hamiltonville, Pennsylvania. Mary (Pennell) Sloan is known to have had three brothers (Nathan, Henry H., and Jonathan [who had died by October 30, 1874]) and three sisters (Sarah [Mrs. John V. Wright], Sidney [Mrs. William J. Loflin], and Rebecca [Mrs. Joel M. Lane]).[26] Mary's gravestone in Mount Moriah Cemetery, Philadelphia, bears the dates "Oct. 3, 1820–Nov. 10, 1891." This birthdate is not in accord with the records of the 1870 and 1880 federal census, in which Mary's age is given as forty-five and fifty-six years respectively; this would make her birth year 1825 or 1824. There is also a contradiction on Samuel's gravestone, where his birthday is given as "March 3, 1815"; all other sources give the day as March 7. Samuel and Mary Sloan had two sons—Ellwood Pennell Sloan (1846–1912) and Howard L. (probably Loflin) Sloan (April 25, 1849–June 28, 1875)—and one daughter, Ada Sloan, whose age is given in the 1870 and 1880 federal census as twelve and twenty years respectively, making her birth year either 1858 and 1860; however, on her baptismal record her birthdate is recorded as April 7, 1858.

Ellwood P. Sloan married Laura M. McCaskey (1850–1917); he is recorded as unmarried in the 1870 federal census, but as married with three children—the oldest, Maurice, being seven years old—in the 1880 census.[27] The earliest possible date for his marriage is therefore some time in 1872, when he would have been twenty-six years old. The children of Ellwood and Laura Sloan were Maurice (June 20, 1873–?), Helen Sloan (whose gravestone in Mount Moriah Cemetery bears the dates 1875–1928 and her maiden name, so she apparently did not marry) and Samuel A. (May 19, 1878–?). The lot in Mount Moriah containing the graves of Samuel, Mary, Ellwood P., Laura M., Helen and Howard L. Sloan is identified on the threshold of its granite surround as "SLOAN–LOFLIN"; however, there is possibly one Loflin grave, and the lot, which is a large one, is relatively empty, the six Sloan graves occupying only its right-hand edge.

Ellwood P. Sloan is first listed by *McElroy's* in 1867 as "bookkeeper," with a home address the same as his father, Samuel. In 1869, he is listed by *Gopsill's* as a member of the firm of Powell, Drayton & Co., but with the same home address, which he retains until 1879. In that year he changed his home address and is listed as "supt" (superintendent), no firm being given. Beginning in 1880 he is listed as a member of the firm of G. S. Sloan, Color and Paint Works; in 1883 he is "Manager" of that firm; and in 1885 the firm is listed under his name alone. He continues to be so listed by *Gopsill's*, with the home address "h. 1833 N. 11," until his death in 1912.

Despite diligent and protracted search, almost nothing has been found about the life of Ada Sloan, only daughter of Samuel. She is listed, and her age given, in the federal census of 1870 and 1880 (twelve and twenty years respectively). Her baptismal record exists in the papers of the Calvary Presbyterian Church, Philadelphia, with the date December 7, 1858, and her birthdate given as April 7, 1858. She is mentioned in all of Samuel Sloan's obituaries, beginning with the first from the *Raleigh (N.C.) News & Ob-*

server, July 20, 1884, but in none of them is her name given, so it is not known whether she married or remained single. No will or order of administration for Ada Sloan has been found, and she is not buried in the SLOAN–LOFLIN lot at Mount Moriah Cemetery, which leads to the assumption that she did marry.

Aside from their listing in the federal census report of 1880, very little is known about the youth of Maurice M. Sloan and Samuel A. Sloan, sons of Ellwood and Laura Sloan, grandsons of Samuel. Maurice Macaskey Sloan (b. June 20, 1873) married Jessica Carlotta Cramer on May 2, 1898. From 1895 to 1897 he is listed in the Philadelphia directories as "draftsman" with a home address of "Leverington near Selig," Roxborough, Pennsylvania. He seems to have moved to Scranton, Pennsylvania, in 1897 or 1898 (just before or upon his marriage) and remained there until 1911. However, he was listed as an associate of the Philadelphia firm of Stuckert & Sloan (that is, F. Russel Stuckert, son of J. Franklin Stuckert) in 1910, although still living in Scranton. In 1911 he returned to Philadelphia as a full partner in Stuckert & Sloan (1911–1915), residing in Ardmore, Pennsylvania. In 1914 or 1915 he moved to Atlantic City, New Jersey, and dissolved his partnership with Stuckert, and further record of him has not been found.

Samuel A. (Alan?) Sloan (b. 1878) married Ann (or Anna) Thorn on October 12, 1904. He was a civil engineer by profession and until 1915 resided at 33 Roxborough Avenue, Roxborough, Pennsylvania. A son, Samuel Alan Sloan (Jr.?) was born in 1906. No records after 1915 have been found.

Howard L. Sloan, son of Samuel, who died in his twenty-sixth year, does not seem to have married.[28]

Several random pieces of data which may bear upon the names and relationships of the descendants of William Sloan, father of Samuel, have been found, but they are without substantiation and are given here only as possibilities. In the will of Thomas Sloan, brother of Samuel, previously cited, there is a bequest to Ellen Sloan, "widow of Capt. John B. Sloan." As this will was probated on June 2, 1869, and John B. Sloan is given the rank of "Capt.," it can be assumed that he died in the Civil War. This could be John, the next older brother of Samuel, for whom only the birth date (July 16, 1816) is known. John B. Sloan's dates would then be (1816–c. 1865).

In a letter from Samuel Sloan to Eli Slifer, dated March 19, 1863, Samuel refers to his "Nephew" in the "29th Reg. Penna. Volts.," commanded by "Col. Murphy," calling him only by his first name, "Lewis."[29] A survey of the roster of the 29th Regiment shows this to have been Lewis S. Gibson, son of a Mrs. Gibson of Philadelphia, who is referred to in the will of William B. Sloan as "widdow, of Philadelphia." As Margaret is the only documented sister of Samuel, how Lewis S. Gibson could have been his "Nephew" is a puzzle. One possibility could be that "Mrs." Gibson was the widow of one of Samuel's brothers who remarried a Gibson and whose son took the name of his stepfather.

The present author makes his apologies for the incompleteness of this genealogy but wishes to point out that it is the product of almost thirty years of research in which sound leads to the collateral descendants of Samuel (T.) Sloan were not discovered until all of the first generation, and many of the second, had died. Moreover, official records of marriages, deaths, births, and so on, of a majority of its early members had suffered various disasters from fire and flood to just "cleaning out the basement." The greatest problem was the destruction of Samuel's personal papers before this author could see them.

NOTES

1. Harry Rush Kervey, "Notes on Chester County Authors," manuscript and clippings in the collection of the Chester County Historical Society, West Chester, Pa. Obituaries: *Public Ledger* (Philadelphia), July 23, 1884; *Building*, vol. 2, Sept. 1884, p. 143; *Cyclopaedia of American Biography* (New York: D. Appleton & Co., 1888), p. 550.

2. See sources cited in no. 1. Also, the family records of the Wesley Sloan family, which were kindly made available to me by Wesley Sloan's great-grandson, Mr. Ralph Thomas Sloan, of Media, Pa.

3. The census and tax records of Honeybrook Township, Chester County, Pa., and Sadsbury Township, Lancaster County, Pa., were researched for the author by Ms. Barbara L. Weir of West Chester, Pa. I am also indebted to Ms. Naomi C. Hite, Assistant Archivist, Lancaster County Court of Common Pleas, Lancaster, Pa., for her research into wills and death records in Lancaster County.

4. *Abridged Compendium of American Genealogy*, ed. F. A. Virkus (Chicago, 1925–1942), vol. 1, p. 828.

5. Census and tax records, Honeybrook Township.

6. *National Cyclopaedia of American Biography* (New York: James T. White & Co., 1877), vol. 4, pp. 282, 349.

7. Wesley Sloan family records (n. 2). Mrs. Austin A. Baker, Bolivar, Tenn., letter dated May 5, 1953 to the American Institute of Architects, requesting information on Fletcher Sloan, brother of Samuel Sloan; copy made available to the present author on June 10, 1960, by Mr. George E. Pettengill, Librarian, The Octagon, Washington, D.C. Letters in the documents relative to the settlement of the estate of Mrs. Carrie Matilda Sloan Foster, Bolivar, Tenn.; copies made available to the present author by Mr. Ewing J. Harris, Attorney at Law, Bolivar, Tenn., Apr. 21, 1982.

8. The Wesley Sloan family records (n. 2), document William, Charles, Samuel, and John. Thomas and Robert are documented in the will of Thomas Sloan, probated on June 2, 1869 (*Registry of Wills*, City and County of Philadelphia, vol. 65, p. 214). Elizabeth is documented in the Foster Papers (n. 7).

9. Mrs. Austin A. Baker letter.

10. Will of Margaret Sloan, died May 10, 1888 (*Registry of Wills*, City and County of Philadelphia, vol. 139, no. 685 [1888], p. 101).

11. Foster Papers (n. 7).

12. Rebecca Pennell is also documented as the sister of Mary Pennell Sloan, together with her other living sisters and brothers, in the *Registry of Deeds and Mortgages*, City and County of Philadelphia, book 158, p. 500 (Grantor, Samuel Sloan; Grantee, A. M. Beitler; date, Oct. 30, 1874).

13. Mrs. Austin A. Baker letter.

14. "Notes on Chester County Authors."

15. *Register of Interment*, Mount Moriah Cemetery, Philadelphia, Pa., p. 487 (microfilm in the collection of the Historical Society of Pennsylvania, call no. XR 777:2).

16. *National Cyclopaedia of American Biography*, vol. 28, p. 443; *Abridged Compendium of American Genealogy*, vol. 6, p. 331.

17. Wesley Sloan family records (n. 2).

18. Ibid.

19. The birthplace of Fletcher Sloan is variously given as Philadelphia and Lancaster, Pa. However, all of his obituaries give Lancaster (see unidentified newspaper clippings, Foster papers [n. 7]). William Sloan's move to Hamilton Village is documented in "Old West Philadelphia," *West Philadelphia Telephone* (newspaper), Nov. 24, 1894, and "Miss Clara E. Pennell," *Proceedings of the Delaware County Historical Society*, ed. Frank Grant Lewis, vol. 3 (1922–1929), pp. 138–139.

20. Mrs. Sam W. L. Thompson, Bolivar, Tenn., letter to the author, Sept. 18, 1982; Mrs. Martha C. Adams, Archival Technician, Tennessee State Library and Archives, letter to the author (together with copies of documents in the collection of the archives), Sept. 25, 1981.

21. Mrs. Martha C. Adams.

22. Mrs. Sam W. L. Thompson and Mrs. Martha C. Adams.

23. "Hardeman County," *History of Tennessee* (Nashville: Goodspeed Publishing Co., 1887), p. 839; "Hardeman County, Tennessee," *General History* (n.p., n.d.), p. 14, collection of the Tennessee State Library and Archives.

24. See sources cited in no. 23.

25. Owens, Boyd, and Davidson, *The Cemetery Records of Hardeman County, Tennessee*, vol. 2: *City of Bolivar* (Fort Worth: Miran Publishers, 1971), pp. 46–47.

26. See n. 12.

27. Federal census data for 1850, 1860, 1870, and 1880, microfilm and original documents in the collection of the Historical Society of Pennsylvania.

28. Samuel Sloan, in an August 1861 letter to Haller Nutt (Nutt Papers, Huntington Library, San Marino, Calif.), refers to Howard as "sickly."

No wife of Howard's has been found in the records of the City and County of Philadelphia or those of Calvary Presbyterian Church, Philadelphia, of which he was a communicant.

29. Samuel Sloan, letter to Eli Slifer, Mar. 19, 1863, collection of the Dickinson College Library, Carlisle, Pa.

Catalogue of Buildings and Publications by Samuel Sloan

INTRODUCTION

This Catalogue is tabulated chronologically, the order determined by the date of the earliest known reference to each building. Following the tabular number (*No. 12*), the date of that earliest reference is given (Jan. 22, 1853), followed by abbreviations for the Architect (S & S), the Building Type (*RS*), and the Condition of the building, as known to the author or as reported to him by qualified researchers (Ea). If the condition of the building at present is unknown, but was known at some date within the time during which the author carried out his research, that date will be noted. Below the tabular line are listed the building's *Commission* (giving its identification and location as found in the earliest reference, and its commissioner), *Documentation* (in order of primary, secondary, etc., sources and chronologically within those categories), *Illustration* (in the same manner), *Description* when available and significant (abstracted from the source best able to describe the building in its original form), and *History* (insofar as it is known to the author), except where data is lacking. To condense this material, a number of abbreviations and symbols are used; they are listed below. An example of an entry is given here first.

EXAMPLE

No. 12: Jan. 22, 1853, S & S, *RS* (Ea)

(The building is the twelfth known work; its earliest date of reference is January 22, 1853; the architects are the firm of Samuel Sloan and John Stewart; it is a residence that is extant but altered.)

COMMISSION

Private residence, 120 Spruce St., Phila., Pa., for John Doe.

DOCUMENTATION

PPL, vol. 24, no. 16, Jan. 22, 1853.

(First referenced in the *Public Ledger*, Philadelphia, Pa., of January 22, 1853, in the daily column "Local Affairs" [unless otherwise noted], which column appeared on page 2, column 2 from the opening of Sloan's practice, 1851, until 1862.)

ILLUSTRATION

Photograph, PP-FLP.

(Photograph of the building's exterior [unless otherwise noted] in black-and-white [unless otherwise noted] in the Print and Photograph collection of The Free Library of Philadelphia, Logan Circle, Philadelphia, Pa.)

DESCRIPTION

PPL, op. cit., "40' × 60' with semi-circular veranda."

(The earliest description is that of the *Public Ledger*, previously cited, giving the dimensions of the building and its most salient feature.)

HISTORY

Sold to Richard Roe 1854; converted to a roominghouse 1912; purchased by the University of Pennsylvania date unk.; converted to a woman's dormitory before 1955, at which time it was extant but altered.

ABBREVIATIONS

ARCHITECT(S)

S	Samuel Sloan, in individual practice
S & B	Firm of Samuel Sloan and Charles Balderston
S, B & Y	Firm of Samuel Sloan, Charles Balderston, and Isaiah B. Young
S & H	Firm of Samuel Sloan and Addison Hutton
S & S	Firm of Samuel Sloan and John Stewart

BUILDING TYPES

C	Commercial building (retail and wholesale stores, markets, office buildings, warehouses, and factories)
E	Educational (elementary and secondary schools, colleges, academies, nonreligious seminaries, and special schools)
M	Medical (hospitals, asylums, orphanages, and training schools)

P	Public buildings (local, state, and national government buildings, libraries, charitable and fraternal buildings, exhibitions and monuments)
RE	Religious (churches, church schools, and seminaries)
RS	Residential (private and speculative housing)

BUILDING CONDITION

(D)	Building demolished
(E)	Building extant
(Ea)	Building extant but altered
(U)	Condition unknown
(Ud)	Unknown, believed demolished

SOURCES OF DOCUMENTATION

AABN	*American Architect and Building News*, ed. James R. Osgood (Boston: James R. Osgood & Co.)
AJE	*American Journal of Education*, ed. Henry Barnard (Hartford, Philadelphia, New York, and London: Putnam & Co.)
ARABJ	*The Architectural Review and American Builder's Journal*, ed. Samuel Sloan and Charles J. Lukens (Philadelphia: Claxton, Remson & Haffelfinger, July 1868–November 1870)
BP	DeWitt C. Baxter, *Baxter's Panoramic Business Directory of Philadelphia for 1856–1859*, Phila., occasionally published from 1857 to 1882.
CC-FLP	Castner Collection (Scrapbooks) in The Free Library of Philadelphia
CC-HSP	Campbell Collection, Historical Society of Pennsylvania
Controllers	Controllers of the Public Schools for the City and County of Philadelphia
CSP	*Common Schools of Pennsylvania*, ed. Thomas H. Burrowes (Harrisburg, Pa.: A. Boyd Hamilton, 1855)
FLP	The Free Library of Philadelphia, Logan Circle, Philadelphia, Pa.
FWMV	*Founder's Week Memorial Volume*, ed. Fredric P. Henry (Philadelphia, 1909)
Gleason's	*Gleason's Pictorial Drawing Room Companion*, ed. and pub. F. Gleason (Boston, Mass.)
Gopsill's	*Gopsill's Philadelphia City Directory*, ed. Isaac Costa (Philadelphia: James Gopsill, 1869–1895)

HABS	Historic American Building Survey, Library of Congress, Washington, D.C.
HABS-PA	HABS Pennsylvania Survey
H-*AM*	S. F. Hotchkin, *Ancient and Modern Germantown, Mount Airy, and Chestnut Hill* (Philadelphia: P. W. Ziegler & Co., 1889)
H-*BP*	S. F. Hotchkin, *The Bristol Pike* (Philadelphia: George W. Jacobs & Co., 1893)
HP	Hutton Papers, Quaker Collection, Haverford College Library, Haverford, Pa.
H-*RP*	S. F. Hotchkin, *Rural Pennsylvania in the Vicinity of Philadelphia* (Philadelphia: George W. Jacobs & Co., 1897)
HSP	The Historical Society of Pennsylvania, Philadelphia, Pa.
ICIUSC	*The Institutional Care of the Insane in the United States and Canada*, 2 vols., ed. Henry M. Hurd (Baltimore: Johns Hopkins Press, 1916)
Jackson	Joseph Jackson, *Encyclopaedia of Philadelphia*, 4 vols. (Harrisburg, Pa.: National Historical Association, 1931–1933)
K-*H*	Thomas S. Kirkbride, *Hospitals for the Insane* (Philadelphia: J. B. Lippincott & Co., 1854, 1st ed.; 1880, 2nd ed.)
McElroy's	*McElroy's Philadelphia Directory*, ed. and pub. A. McElroy (Philadelphia, 1837–1867)
PC-HSP	Penrose Collection (Scrapbooks), collection of the Historical Society of Pennsylvania
PCP	*The Presbyterian Church in Philadelphia* (Philadelphia: Allen, Lane & Scott, 1895)
PE	*Philadelphia and Its Environs* (Philadelphia: J. B. Lippincott & Co., 1874)
PHC	Philadelphia Historical Commission
Poulson	Collection of panoramic views of Philadelphia Streets (including sections from *Baxter's Panoramic Business Directory of Philadelphia*) in the collection of the Library Company, Philadelphia, Pa.
PP-FLP	Print and Photograph Collection, The Free Library of Philadelphia
PP-HSP	Print and Photograph Collection, Historical Society of Pennsylvania
PPL	*Public Ledger* (later *and Examiner*), newspaper, Philadelphia, Pa., all references, unless otherwise noted, are to daily column "Local Affairs," p. 2, col. 2

PSP   Franklin Davenport Edmunds, *The Public School Buildings of the City of Philadelphia*, 3 vols. (Philadelphia: Privately printed, 1913–1917)

RCPS   (Annual) *Report*(s) *of the Controllers of the Public Schools for the City and County of Philadelphia* (Philadelphia: Crissy & Markley, 1851–1867)

RN&O   *News & Observer*, Raleigh, N.C.

S-CA   Samuel Sloan, *Sloan's Constructive Architecture* (Philadelphia: J. B. Lippincott & Co., 1859, 1st ed.; 1866, 2nd ed.; 1873, 3rd ed.)

S-CSA   Samuel Sloan, *City and Suburban Architecture* (Philadelphia: J. B. Lippincott & Co., 1859, 1st ed.; 1867, 2nd ed.)

S-HA   Samuel Sloan, *Sloan's Homestead Architecture* (Philadelphia: J. B. Lippincott & Co., 1861, 1st ed.; 1867, 2nd ed.; 1870, 3rd ed.)

S-MA   Samuel Sloan, *The Model Architect*, 2 vols. (Philadelphia: E. S. Jones & Co., 1851–1852, 1853, 1st ed.; E. H. Butler & Co., 1860, 2nd ed.; J. B. Lippincott & Co., 1862, 3rd ed.; and 1873, 4th ed.)

S-RB   Samuel Sloan, *American Houses: A Variety of Designs for Rural Buildings* (Philadelphia: B. Ashmead, 1861, 1st ed.; Henry Carey Baird, 1868, 2nd ed.)

SRL   Scrapbooks of the Ridgway Branch of The Library Company of Philadelphia

S&W   Thomas J. Scharf and Thompson Westcott, *History of Philadelphia, 1609–1884*, 3 vols. (Philadelphia: L. H. Everts & Co., 1884)

Tatum   George B. Tatum, *Penn's Great Town* (Philadelphia: University of Pennsylvania Press, 1961)

TLC   The Library Company of Philadelphia, Pa.

Westcott   *Official Guidebook to Philadelphia, 1875*, ed. Thomas Westcott (Philadelphia: Porter & Coates, 1875)

W-PP   Richard J. Webster, *Philadelphia Preserved* (Philadelphia: Temple University Press, 1976)

Yarnall   Elizabeth Biddle Yarnall, *Addison Hutton: Quaker Architect, 1834–1916* (Philadelphia: Art Alliance Press, 1974)

DIVISION I: CONFIRMED COMMISSIONS

No. 1: June 8, 1849, S, P(Ea)

COMMISSION

Court House and jail for Delaware County, Pa., on the Square bounded by Front, Second, Orange and Olive Sts., Media, Pa., for the Commissioners of Delaware County.

DOCUMENTATION

Thomas U. Walter, drafts of letters to the Commissioners, May 28, June 16, July 5 and 30, 1849; Diary, vol. 3, p. 66, entries May 26, June 12, 1849, Walter Papers, collection of The Athenaeum, Philadelphia, Pa. (2) Mark Bartleston, letters to Thomas U. Walter, July 3, 9, 14, 1849, Walter Papers, op. cit. (3) John P. Crozer, letters to Thomas U. Walter, May 17, June 18, 1849, Walter Papers, op. cit. (4) Circular, announcement of competition for public buildings in Media, May 14, 1849, Walter Papers, op. cit. (5) George C. Smith, *History of Delaware County, Pennsylvania* (Philadelphia: Henry B. Ashmead, 1862), pp. 368–377. (6) William H. Engle, *History of the Commonwealth of Pennsylvania*, 3rd ed. (Philadelphia: E. M. Gardner, 1883), p. 678. (7) *History of Delaware County, Pennsylvania*, ed. Henry Graham Ashmead (Philadelphia: L. H. Everts & Co., 1884), pp. 591–594. (8) *A History of Delaware County Pennsylvania and Its People*, ed. John W. Jordan (New York: Lewis Historical Publishing Co., 1914), pp. 301–302. (9) *Chester Times*, Chester, Pa., "Courthouse Completed in August, 1851," June 2, 1950, and "Court in Media," Aug. 24, 1951.

ILLUSTRATION

Lithograph, "Public Buildings at Media," C. P. Tholey, artist, Bowen & Co. litho., George C. Smith, op. cit., p. 369. (2) Photograph, c. 1913, "Court House, Media, Pa.," collection Delaware County Historical Society, Chester, Pa. (3) Photographs, "Court House, Media, Pa." and "The County Jail," A. Lewis Smith, "Media's Past," *Semi-Centennial of the Borough of Media, Penna., May 19, 1910*, pamphlet, n.p., collection of Delaware County Historical Society. (4) Photograph, "County Courthouse, After 1913 Enlargements," *Chester Times*, op. cit.

DESCRIPTION

George C. Smith, op. cit., p. 396, original building. (2) William H. Egle, op. cit., pp. 678–679, after alterations of 1868, 1877–78. (3) *Chester Times*, op. cit., after alterations of 1913, 1928–32.

HISTORY

Competition announced May 14, 1849; entries received May 29, 1849; commission June 8, 1849; contract Aug. 28, 1849; cornerstone Sept. 24, 1849; Courthouse accepted May 1, 1851; jail enlarged 1877; new jail, 1878; two wings added to courthouse and clock-tower removed 1913; courthouse renovated and enlarged, 1929–32; dedication of new building Jan. 9, 1932; building extant, altered.

No. 2: Jan. 24, 1851, S, *RS*(D)

COMMISSION

"Bartram Hall," villa on the site of "Bartram's Gardens," 170 acres west of Schuylkill River, 24th (now 40th) Ward, Kingsessing, Philadelphia, Pa., for Andrew M. Eastwick.

DOCUMENTATION

PPL, vol. 30, no. 85, Jan. 25, 1851. (2) *S-MA*, vol. 2, pp. 49–52. (3) *Gleason's*, vol. 6, Jan. 7, 1854, p. 328. (4) *Survey No. 9118*, July 18, 1854, Philadelphia Contributorship. (5) Thomas Westcott, *The Historical Mansions and Buildings of Philadelphia* (Philadelphia: Porter & Coates, 1877), p. 188. (6) "Eastwick Castle for Public Use," newspaper clipping (n.p., n.d.), "Philadelphia Sketches," scrapbook, 1886–96, collection HSP. (7) CC-HSP, vol. 2, "W Philadelphia, South of Market St.," newspaper clipping (n.p., n.d.), "A Noted House Burned: The Eastwick Mansion." (8) *Bartram Hall*, paper delivered by Mrs. Andrew M. Eastwick to City Historical Society, Dec. 14, 1910, pub. by the Society, 1930. (9) Tatum, pp. 93, 185.

ILLUSTRATION

Lithographs, plans, elevations, and sections, *S-MA*, vol. 1, plates 29–45, Sloan delin., P. S. Duval & Co., litho. (2) Photograph, "Eastwick Villa, Kingsessing, Adjoining Bartram's Gardens to the South," PP-FLP. (3) Photograph, front view, PP-HSP. (4) Photograph, *Bartram Hall*, op. cit., frontispiece.

DESCRIPTION

S-MA, op. cit. (2) *Gleason's*, op. cit. (3) *Bartram Hall*, op. cit.

HISTORY

Commission c. Aug. 1850; ground broken Feb. 1851; occupied Dec. 1851; sold to City of Philadelphia 1890; burned May 29, 1896.

No. 3: Feb. 22, 1851, S, *RS*(D)

COMMISSION

Row of nine dwellings, west side Logan Square, Philadelphia, Pa., client unknown.

DOCUMENTATION

PPL, vol. 30, no. 145, Feb. 22, 1851.

NOTE: No other documentation has been found. The buildings would have been demolished when the Parkway was constructed in 1918, or before.

No. 4: Feb. 22, 1851, S, *C*(D)

COMMISSION

"Harrison's Buildings," four stores, 9th and Spring Garden Sts., Philadelphia, Pa., for S. A. Harrison.

PPL, vol. 30, no. 145, Feb. 22, 1851. (2) CC-HSP, vol. 25, "8th–12th Sts.," advertisement, "Harrison's Buildings," n.p., dated in ink "1856."
ILLUSTRATION
Wood engraving, "Harrison's Buildings," CC-FLP, vol. 14.
HISTORY
Demolished and new building erected on site 1895.

No. 5: Mar. 20, 1851, S, *E*(D)

COMMISSION
North-East (or North-Eastern) Grammar School (after 1868, New Street Primary School), south side of New St. west of Front St. between 1st and 2nd Sts., Philadelphia, Pa., for the Controllers.
DOCUMENTATION
PPL, vol. 30, no. 171, Mar. 20; vol. 31, no. 6, Apr. 2, 1851. (2) *RCPS*, June 30, 1851, p. 12. (3) *RCPS*, June 30, 1852, p. 10. (4) *CSP*, pp. 103–35. (5) *AJE*, vol. 33, Mar.–Dec. 1863, pp. 826–835. (6) *PSP*, vol. 2, pp. 161–63.
ILLUSTRATION
Engraving, front elevation and ground-floor plan, *RCPS*, June 30, 1852, p. 10. (2) Photograph and drawing, front view and plans, *PSP*, pp. 161, 163.
DESCRIPTION
PPL, op. cit. (2) *PSP*, op. cit., as of 1913.
HISTORY
Cornerstone July 1851; new building erected c. 1914.

No. 6: Apr. 2, 1851, S, *E*(D)

COMMISSION
Warner Primary School, Robertson St. between 7th and 8th Sts. (also given as east side 8th St. north of Parrish St.), Philadelphia, Pa., for the Controllers.
DOCUMENTATION
PPL, vol. 31, no. 6, Apr. 2, 1851. (2) *RCPS*, June 30, 1851, p. 12. (3) *RCPS*, June 30, 1852, p. 10. (4) *AJE*, vol. 33, (n.s., vol. 3), Mar.–Dec. 1863, p. 828. (5) *PSP*, vol. 2, pp. 141–143.
ILLUSTRATION
Engraving, elevation and floor plan, *RCPS*, June 30, 1852, p. 10. (2) Photograph and drawing, front view and floor plan, *PSP*, op. cit., pp. 141, 143.
DESCRIPTION
AJE, op. cit., identical with North-Eastern School. (2) *PSP*, op. cit., lists twelve classrooms for 240 pupils.

Commission Mar. 1851; cornerstone July 4, 1851; occupied Dec. 9, 1851; damaged by fire 1870; remodeled May 19, 1903; largely rebuilt July 10, 1914; demolished date unk.

No. 7: Apr. 2, 1851, S, E(D)

COMMISSION

South-West Primary School, 19th and Addison Sts., Philadelphia, Pa., for the Controllers.

DOCUMENTATION

PPL, vol. 31, no. 6, Apr. 2, 1851. (2) *RCPS*, June 30, 1852, p. 10. (3) *PSP*, vol. 2, pp. 145–147.

ILLUSTRATION

Photograph, front view, *PSP*, op. cit., p. 145.

HISTORY

Demolished date unk.

No. 8: Apr. 2, 1851, S, E(D)

COMMISSION

Lyons Secondary School, Catherine St. north of 10th St., Moyamansing, Philadelphia, Pa., for the Controllers.

DOCUMENTATION

PPL, vol. 31, no. 6, Apr. 2, 1851. (2) *RCPS*, June 30, 1852, p. 10. (3) *PSP*, vol. 2, pp. 153–155.

ILLUSTRATION

Photograph, front view, *PSP*, op. cit., p. 145.

DESCRIPTION

PPL, op. cit., as of 1851. (2) *PSP*, op. cit., as of 1913.

HISTORY

Demolished date unk.

No. 9: Apr. 9, 5, 1851, RS(Ea)

COMMISSION

Town plan, wharf, stationhouse, and ten villas, Riverton, N.J., for the Riverton Improvement Co. (Daniel L. Miller Jr., Rodman Wharton, Dillwyn Parrish, William D. Parrish, Caleb Clothier, Charles D. Cleveland, William C. Biddle, Robert Biddle, and Chalkley Gillingham).

DOCUMENTATION

PPL, vol. 31, no. 12, Apr. 9; no. 18, Apr. 16; no. 137, Sept. 4, 1851. (2) "Riverton," *New Jersey Mirror*, Mount Holly, N.J., vol. 32, no. 1702, May 1, 1852. (3) "Deed Q-5," Aug. 23, 1852, recorded June 3, 1854, Office of the

County Clerk, Mount Holly, N.J., pp. 263ff. (4) *Act of Incorporation and By-laws of the Riverton Improvement Company*, pamphlet (n.p.), Apr. 13, 1852, collection of Mrs. Therese Stockman Barclay, Riverton, N.J. (original ms. documents in the State Archives, Trenton, N.J.). (5) Documentation and re-cording of all extant buildings by Mrs. Joseph W. Hahle, Riverton, N.J., to whom the writer is greatly indebted for the use of her research.

ILLUSTRATION

Lithograph, *Plan of the New Town of Riverton, N.J., Beautifully Situated on the Cinnaminson Shore on the River Delaware, Eight Miles Above Philada* (Phila-delphia: Killner, Camp & Co., 1851), collection of Porch Club, Riverton, N.J. (2) Lithograph, "Riverton, N.J., 1890," isometric map, Riverton, N.J., Otto Koehler litho., collection Riverton Library, Riverton, N.J. (3) Photo-graphs, of all extant buildings (a) collection Mrs. Joseph W. Hahle, op. cit., and (b) collection College of Architecture, Clemson University, Clem-son, S.C.

HISTORY

Improvement Company formed c. Feb. 1851; commission c. Mar. 1851; vil-las for Caleb Clothier (503 Bank Ave.), Dillwyn Parrish (501 Bank Ave.), Rodman Wharton (407 Bank Ave.), William D. Parrish (311 Bank Ave.), Robert Biddle (307 Bank Ave.), Caleb Clothier (101 Main St., purchased from Rodman Wharton, 1853), Charles P. Miller (100 Main St.) all extant but altered; villa for Daniel L. Miller (Lot 4) demolished; villa for Prof. Charles Dexter Cleveland (originally Lot 9, moved to Lot 13, 1940) extant, altered; original wooden wharf replaced with iron pier by Riverton Iron Pier Co. 1868; stationhouse replaced 1909 and replacement demolished 1955.

No. 10: May 1, 1851, S, *RS*(Ea, 1955)

COMMISSION

Speculative dwelling, Locust St. between Mary (38) and William (39) Sts. (later 3812 Locust St.), West Philadelphia, Pa., for N. B. Browne.

DOCUMENTATION

PPL, vol. 31, no. 31, May 1, 1851.

ILLUSTRATION

Photograph, 1955, front view, collection of the author.

HISTORY

Commission c. Apr. 1851; sold to Marcus M. Taswell 1854; converted to rooming house 1912; purchased by the University of Pennsylvania, date unk., for use as a women's residence hall; extant 1955, altered.

No. 11: May 1, 1851, S, *RS*(D)

COMMISSION

Speculative dwelling, corner of Spruce and Hamilton (41) Sts., West Phila-delphia, Pa., for N. B. Browne.

DOCUMENTATION
PPL, vol. 31, no. 31, May 1, 1851.
HISTORY
Demolished date unk.

No. 12: May 1, 1851, S, *RS*(Ud)

COMMISSION
Two adjacent speculative dwellings, Westminster Ave., West Philadelphia, Pa., for Andrew D. Cash.

DOCUMENTATION
PPL, vol. 31, no. 31, May 1, 1851.

DESCRIPTION
PPL, op. cit., "Summer residences, on lots $100' \times 120'$, in the Gothic style, of stone masticked to look like brown-stone."

HISTORY
Demolished date unk.

No. 13: May 1, 1851, S, *RS*(Ud)

COMMISSION
Four speculative dwellings, Oneida (46) St., West Philadelphia, Pa., for Andrew D. Cash.

DOCUMENTATION
PPL, vol. 31, no. 31, May 1, 1851.

DESCRIPTION
PPL, op. cit., "Summer residences, in blocks of two, each block on a lot $160' \times 160'$, in the Gothic style, of stone masticked to look like brown-stone."

HISTORY
Demolished date unk.

No. 14: May 1, 1851, S, *RS*(U)

COMMISSION
Six speculative dwellings, Locust St. between William (39) and Till (40) Sts., West Philadelphia, Pa., for Samuel A. Harrison.

DOCUMENTATION
PPL, vol. 31, no. 31, May 1, 1851.

ILLUSTRATION
Photographs (1955) in the collection of the writer.

DESCRIPTION
PPL, op. cit., "In blocks of two, each $20' \times 70'$, with side yards $30'$ wide, in the Italian style of masticked stone."

HISTORY
One block of these was extant, and occupied, in 1955.

No. 15: May 1, 1851, S, *RS*(E, 1955)

COMMISSION

Two speculative dwellings, 3803 and 3805 Locust St. between Mary (38) and William (39) Sts., West Philadelphia, Pa., for Samuel A. Harrison.

DOCUMENTATION

PPL, vol. 31, no. 31, May 1, 1851.

ILLUSTRATION

Photographs (1955) in the collection of the author.

DESCRIPTION

PPL, op. cit., "Suburban mansions, 44' fronts, bay-windows on two stories, in Pointed Gothic style."

HISTORY

In 1955 these were (1) the residence of the University of Pennsylvania Chaplain and (2) the Kappa Alpha Fraternity.

No. 16: May 30, 1851, S, *RE*(D)

COMMISSION

Ebenezer Methodist Episcopal Church, Christian St. above 3rd St., Philadelphia, Pa., for the Building Committee of the church (the Rev. John Ruth, Samuel Tudor, W. E. Pidgeon, R. L. Flanigen, and James S. Bell).

DOCUMENTATION

PPL, vol. 31, no. 56, May 30, 1851. (2) *History of EBENEZER Methodist Episcopal Church of Southwark, Philadelphia*, pub. by the Centennial Publishing Committee (Philadelphia: J. B. Lippincott & Co., 1890), pp. 119–121 and Appendix. (3) CC-HSP, vol. 17, "Churches," two newspaper clippings, annotated in ink "Telegraph, Jan. 15, 1916" and "Record, Jan. 17, 1916," both reporting the 125th anniversary of the church.

ILLUSTRATION

Engraving (small), "Ebenezer, M. E. Church, Erected 1852," signed "F. M. Welsh, So.," annotated, in ink, "S. 2nd St., Southwark," CC-FLP, vol. 23, "Churches," p. 0.

DESCRIPTION

History, op. cit., p. 119, "The new church, 55 × 70 feet, exceeded the dimensions of the old building. Samuel Sloan was the architect, and adhered in his design to what seems to have been considered the orthodox style of Methodist architecture."

HISTORY

Commissioned May 2, 1851; erected by Samuel Tudor for $10,700; dedicated June 24, 1852; congregation moved to 52nd and Parrish Sts. in 1903 and old church demolished.

No. 17: May 30, 1851, S, E(D)

COMMISSION

Wood and West Streets Secondary School, corner of Wood and West Sts., Kensington, Philadelphia, Pa., for the Controllers.

DOCUMENTATION

PPL, vol. 31, no. 56, May 30, 1851. (2) Edward Robert Robson, *School Architecture* (London: John Murray, 1877), p. 35. (3) *PSP*, vol. 2, pp. 189–191.

ILLUSTRATION

Engravings, front elevation and floor plan, Robson, op. cit., plates 23 and 24.

DESCRIPTION

PPL, op. cit., "It is on Mr. Sloan's improved plan, adopted by the Board of Controllers for the Public Schools, for the new schoolhouses now commenced, or under contract, to be built in the city and various districts." "Each story will be divided into 4 rooms by moveable glass partitions, so as to be thrown into one at pleasure." (2) Robson, op. cit., p. 35.

HISTORY

Demolished date unk.

No. 18: May 30, 1851, S, E(D)

COMMISSION

West Jersey Academy, in the square bounded by Commerce, Lawrence, Broad, and West Sts., Bridgeton, N.J., for the Presbytery of West Jersey.

DOCUMENTATION

PPL, vol. 31, no. 56, May 30, 1851. (2) Thomas Cushing and Charles E. Sheppard, *Histories of the Counties of Gloucester, Salem, and Cumberland, New Jersey* (Philadelphia: Everts & Peck, 1883), p. 592. (3) Isaac T. Nichols, *The City of Bridgeton, New Jersey* (Philadelphia: Burk & McFetridge, 1889), pp. 16, 52–56. (4) *Art Issue of the Bridgeton Evening News*, ed. William B. Kirby, 1895, p. 4.

ILLUSTRATION

Photograph, "West Jersey Academy at Bridgeton, N.J.," Nichols, op. cit., p. 56. (2) Engraving and three photographs, collection of the Cumberland County Historical Society, Greenwich, N.J. (3) Engraving, frontispiece, Dr. S. P. Jones, *Responsibilities and Duties of Teachers*, pamphlet (n.p., n.d.), collection of the Cumberland County Historical Society, Greenwich, N.J.

DESCRIPTION

PPL, op. cit., "Of brick, three stories in height, 48½' × 56' with a tower." (2) Cushing and Sheppard, op. cit., p. 592, "Of native stone, 53½' × 60', three stories with basement."

HISTORY

Cornerstone Aug. 9, 1852 (Nichols, op. cit.), Aug. 8, 1852 (Cushing and Sheppard, op. cit.); opened 1854; closed for a number of years but "re-opened within the last few years" (Cushing and Sheppard, op. cit.); "was demolished in the late twenties or early thirties to make room for a new high school" (Carl L. West, Cumberland County Historical Society).

No. 19: May 30, 1851, S, RS(D)

COMMISSION

City residence, 103 Walnut St., below 4th St., Philadelphia, Pa., for William J. Johnson.

DOCUMENTATION

PPL, vol. 31, no. 56, May 30, 1851. (2) PC-HSP, box 26, "Walnut Street."

ILLUSTRATION

Lithograph, BP, 1856, "Walnut Street," collection of TLC.

DESCRIPTION

PPL, op. cit., "Four stories, street floor offices for Johnson, first story in brown-stone, upper stories in brick, veranda at second story supported by stone brackets, elaborate cornice, terminal balustrade."

NOTE: This may be the same as "Johnson's Court," Brenner Scrapbook, 14, 106/3.163, collection of HSP.

HISTORY

Demolished date unk.

No. 20: June 10, 1851, S, E(Ud)

COMMISSION

Haddington School, corner of Washington (Market) St. and Merion Rd., Haddington (later West Philadelphia), Pa., for the Controllers.

DOCUMENTATION

PPL, vol. 31, no. 65, June 10, 1851. (2) RCPS, June 30, 1851, p. 12. (3) PSP, vol. 2, p. 157.

HISTORY

Demolished date unk.

No. 21: June 10, 1851, S, E(Ud)

COMMISSION

Watson Primary School, League St. east of 2nd St., Southwark, Philadelphia, Pa., for the Controllers.

DOCUMENTATION

PPL, vol. 31, no. 65, June 10, 1851. (2) RCPS, June 30, 1851, p. 12. (3) PSP, vol. 2, p. 159.

HISTORY

Demolished date unk.

No. 22: June 30, 1851, S, *E*(D)

COMMISSION

Glenwood School, corner of Ridge Ave. and York St., Philadelphia, Pa., for the Controllers.

DOCUMENTATION

RCPS, June 30, 1851, p. 12 (2) *RCPS*, June 30, 1852, p. 10. (3) Henry Barnard, *School Architecture* (New York: Charles B. Norton, 1854), pp. 11ff. (4) *AJE*, vol. 13 (n.s., vol. 3), Mar.–Dec. 1863, p. 829. (5) *PSP*, vol. 2, pp. 125–127.

ILLUSTRATION

Engraving, *RCPS*, June 30, 1851, p. 12. (2) Engraving, principal elevation and ground-floor plan, *RCPS*, June 30, 1852, p. 10. (3) Engraving, *AJE*, op. cit., p. 829. (4) Photograph, exterior, and ground-floor plan, *PSP*, vol. 2, p. 125.

DESCRIPTION

RCPS, June 30, 1852, p. 10. (2) *PSP*, vol. 2, pp. 125–127, "two stories, two class-rooms in each story, class-rooms separated by glazed partitions."

NOTE: All descriptions refer to the building as "erected and arranged upon the new plan."

HISTORY

Demolished 1899.

No. 23: Aug. 9, 1851, S, *P*(D)

COMMISSION

Odd Fellows Hall (later Commissioners' Hall and Town Hall), corner Park (37) St. and Washington (Market) St., West Philadelphia, Pa., for Livingston Lodge No. 135 of the Independent Order of Odd Fellows.

DOCUMENTATION

PPL, vol. 31, no. 116, Aug. 9, 1851; vol. 36, no. 86, Jan. 2, 1854. (2) CC-HSP, vol. 1, "West Philadelphia, North of Market Street," newspaper clippings; annotated in ink (a) *"Times*; Philadelphia, Pa., Oct., 1900" story "West Philadelphia Commissioners' Hall," (b) *"Record*, Philadelphia, Pa., Aug. 28, 1910" story of building's demolition. (3) Scrapbook of J. B. Merritt, 1907–16, p. 145, unidentified newspaper clipping, "Last of Commissioners' Hall," collection of HSP (Wg*998v.2). (4) Joseph Jackson, *America's Most Historic Highway*, new ed. (Philadelphia: John Wanamaker, 1926), p. 340.

ILLUSTRATION

Photograph, "Old Commissioner's Hall, West Philadelphia," Merritt Scrapbook, op. cit.

DESCRIPTION

PPL, op. cit., description of original building, "building 60' × 86', stores on ground floor, saloon on second floor, meeting rooms and offices on third floor, both street facades ornamented with rich brackets and elaborate cornice."

HISTORY

Commissioned c. Aug. 1951; building purchased from the Odd Fellows by the Commissioners of West Philadelphia Jan. 1854; converted to office building prior to 1900; demolished Aug. 1910.

No. 24: Aug. 19, 1851, S, RS(D)

COMMISSION

Double dwelling, northeast corner of 11th and Filbert Sts., Philadelphia, Pa., for Dr. Walter Williamson.

DOCUMENTATION

PPL, vol. 31, no. 124, Aug. 19, 1851. (2) Brenner Scrapbooks, 9/117, unidentified newspaper clipping, n.d., reporting demolition of building, collection of HSP.

ILLUSTRATION

Sketch of building (c. 1865), Brenner Scrapbook, op. cit.

DESCRIPTION

PPL, op. cit., "building 37' × 50', each dwelling having a fine marble door frame on 11th St. entrance."

HISTORY

Demolished c. 1936 and replaced by Bell Telephone Building.

No. 25: Aug. 25, 1851, S, project unexecuted.

COMMISSION

Suburban mansion, corner of Germantown Ave. and School House Lane, Germantown, Pa., for Mr. E. K. Tryon.

DOCUMENTATION

PPL, vol. 31, no. 130, Aug. 26, 1851, "Local Affairs."

NOTE: S. F. Hotchkin, H-AM, does not describe this building; he identifies buildings at the southwest corner of the intersection (Bank of Germantown) and northeast corner (No. 4801, the De la Plane House) and lists all the houses on School House Lane from Germantown Ave. to Town Line. Hotchkin does not mention Tryon in the entire book.

NOTE ALSO: Mark Frazier Lloyd, director of the Germantown Historical Society, says, "There can be no doubt that Sloan never erected a . . . residence for E. K. Tryon at the corner of School House Lane and Germantown Avenue in Germantown."

No. 26: Sept. 12, 1851, S, C(D)

COMMISSION

"Simes Block," northwest corner of 12th and Chestnut Sts., Philadelphia, Pa., for Samuel Simes.

DOCUMENTATION
PPL, vol. 31, no. 145, Sept. 12, 1851. (2) Brenner Scrapbooks, 17/43, newspaper clipping, identified in ink "Phila. *Record*, Oct. 17, 1909," "Chestnut Street of Former Days," collection of HSP. (3) Poulson, vol. 1, 1859, p. 12, and SRL, vol. 8, p. 19, items 74–78, collection of TLC.

ILLUSTRATION
Engraving, "Samuel Simes," *McElroy's*, 1855. (2) Lithograph, "Chestnut Street," *BP*, 1856, collection of TLC. (3) Woodcut, "Samuel Simes' Block," n.d., CC-HSP, vol. 13, "Chestnut Street." (4) Engraving, "N.W. corner of 12th and Chestnut," Brenner Scrapbooks, op. cit. (5) Photograph, collection of Dr. Winston Weisman.

DESCRIPTION
PPL, op. cit., "Store 60' on Chestnut, 75' on 12th St., of Pictou [Nova Scotia] stone, four large 'bulk' windows, exquisite mineral water stand designed by Sloan, Simes' house attached to the store which has an observatory 84' high." (2) Brenner Scrapbooks, op. cit., "In the early 40's Simes drug store was well known in the city, then about 1853 a more imposing four-story edifice was erected, made of stone from the Pictou quarry."

HISTORY
Commissioned c. Sept. 1851; Simes retired 1865; building continued as drugstore and offices until 1901; 1901 John Wanamaker, who then owned the building, sold it to the Commonwealth Title Insurance and Trust Co., who demolished the building and erected their offices on the site.

No. 27: Sept. 21, 1851, S, C(D)

COMMISSION
Jones, White & Co. (1853, Jones, White & M'Curdy), corner of Arch and 6th Sts. (later 116 Arch St. and 528 Arch St.), Philadelphia, Pa., for Dr. John D. White.

DOCUMENTATION
PPL, vol. 31, no. 163, Sept. 21, 1851; vol. 32, no. 68, Nov. 6, 1851. (2) Harold L. Faggart, "Beginning of Dental Education in Philadelphia," *Journal of the American College of Dentists*, vol. 17, no. 4, Dec. 1950, pp. 390–393. (3) Poulson, vol. 1, p. 51, collection of the Library Company, Philadelphia, Pa. (4) PC-HSP, box 17, "N. Arch, West from 6th."

ILLUSTRATION
Engraving, "The Philadelphia College of Dental Surgery," Faggart, op. cit., p. 393. (2) Engraving (small), source unk., PC-HSP, op. cit.

DESCRIPTION
PPL, op. cit., "five stories, iron front, street floor with large windows fitted with revolving slats like those of Bailey & Co., offices and workrooms above."

HISTORY
Second floor of building was location of the first school of dental surgery in Pennsylvania, the Philadelphia College of Dental Surgery, whose first session

was held in Nov. 1852; continued as dental laboratory and supply house until 1895; subsequent history unk.; demolished date unk.

No. 28: Oct. 8, 1851, S, C(U)

COMMISSION

Commercial store, 103 Walnut St., Philadelphia, Pa., for unknown client.

DOCUMENTATION

PPL, vol. 32, no. 38, Oct. 8, 1851. (2) PC-HSP, box 23, clipping (n.p.,
n.d.), "Improvements on Walnut Street."

ILLUSTRATION

BP, 1856, "Walnut Street," collection of TLC.

HISTORY

Demolished date unk.

No. 29: Nov. 22, 1851, S, C(E)

COMMISSION

Iron-fronted store (later Keen Building), 75 Chestnut St. (later 217 Chestnut St.), Phila., Pa., for unknown client.

DOCUMENTATION

PPL, vol. 32, no. 84, Nov. 22, 1851. (2) SRL, vol. 8, p. 19, items 74–78,
and p. 23, items 90–92. (3) PC-HSP, box 18, "Chestnut St." W-*PP*, p. 66,
"Chestnut Street Area Study."

ILLUSTRATION

Engravings and photographs, PC-HSP, op. cit. (2) Woodcut (small), SRL,
op. cit. (3) Lithograph, "Chestnut Street," *BP*, 1856, collection of TLC.

DESCRIPTION

PPL, op. cit., "store of four stories, facade of iron with doors and win-
dows of revolving slats similar to those of Bailey & Co." (2) W-*PP*, p. 66,
"One of the few surviving examples of a formerly stylish mid-19th-century
wholesale-retail block. Includes: Keen Building (No. 217), built 1851,
Samuel Sloan, architect, cast-iron storefront by Architectural Iron Works
(Daniel D. Badger), New York."

HISTORY

Extant 1976.

No. 30: Dec. 11, 1851, S, RS(D)

COMMISSION

Private dwelling, corner of Broad St. and Girard Ave., Philadelphia, Pa., for
Joseph S. Silver.

DOCUMENTATION

PPL, vol. 32, no. 102, Dec. 11, 1851.

DESCRIPTION

PPL, op. cit., "in the richest Itallian style."

HISTORY

Joseph Silver moved to Broad and Parrish Sts. in 1860; the mansion of
P. A. B. Widener was built on the site of the Silver house in 1887; demolished date unk.

No. 31: Late 1851 or early 1852, S, *RS*(D)

COMMISSION

Private dwelling, northwest corner of Perry St. and Madison Ave., Montgomery, Ala., for J. S. Winter.

DOCUMENTATION

S-MA, vol. 2, pp. 81–82, "A Southern House: Design Fifty-Third." (2)
Willis Brewer, *Alabama: Her History, Resources, War Record, and Public Men
from 1540 to 1872* (Spartanburg, S.C.: Reprint Co., 1975), p. 293. (3) Robert D. Thorington, Montgomery, Ala., letters to the author, Aug. 20, Sept.
5, 1980.

ILLUSTRATION

Lithographs, plates 74–78, *S-MA*, op. cit. Photographs in the collection of
Robert D. Thorington, copies in the possession of the present author.

DESCRIPTION

S-MA, op. cit., "It is in the Itallian style, and the campanile or tower is a
marked feature of the elevation."

HISTORY

Thorington, op. cit., "It was located on the northwest corner of the intersection of Perry Street and Madison Avenue in Montgomery. Winter's house
was built before 1852"; demolished.

No. 32: Feb. 4, 1852, S(? & S), *E*(D)

COMMISSION

Shunk School (later Beth Eden House), east side of New Market St. north
of Brown St. (also listed as above Coates St., later as 807 New Market St.),
Philadelphia, Pa., for the Controllers.

DOCUMENTATION

PPL, vol. 32, no. 114, Feb. 4, 1852, vol. 34, no. 61, Dec. 3, 1852. (2)
RCPS, June 30, 1852, p. 9. (3) *PSP*, vol. 2, pp. 169–171. (4) W-*PP*,
p. 338.

ILLUSTRATION

Photograph, *PSP*, op. cit., p. 169. (2) Plot plan, floor plans, elevations (3
sheets), HABS, PA-18000. (3) Photographs (2), 1967, Pennsylvania Historical Salvage Council.

DESCRIPTION

PSP, op. cit., "two floors, four class-rooms to each floor separated by sliding glazed partitions, building 40' × 64', three-bay front elevation, gable roof."

HISTORY

Commissioned Feb. 1852; cornerstone June 23, 1852; interior altered 1916; converted to Settlement House of Second Presbyterian Church in Philadelphia 1916–68; demolished 1969.

No. 33: Feb. 4, 1852, S (? & S), *E*(D)

COMMISSION

Filbert Street School, north side of Filbert St. west of 20th St., Philadelphia, Pa., for the Controllers.

DOCUMENTATION

PPL, vol. 32, no. 114, Feb. 4, 1852. (2) *RCPS*, June 30, 1852, p. 9. (3) *PSP*, vol. 2, pp. 188–191.

DESCRIPTION

PPL, "eight class-rooms, four on each of two floors, separated by sliding glazed partitions."

HISTORY

Building accepted Sept. 14, 1852; altered Nov. 12, 1870; building sold to Pennsylvania Railroad June 30, 1904, and demolished.

No. 34: Feb. 6, 1852, S & S, *M*(Ea)

COMMISSION

Alabama Insane Hospital (later Bryce Hospital), on a tract of 326 acres two miles east of Tuscaloosa, Ala., for the State of Alabama.

DOCUMENTATION

Acts of the Third Biennial Session of the General Assembly of Alabama, 1851–52, (Montgomery: State Printer, 1853), pp. 10–19. (2) "An Act to establish a State Hospital for Insane persons in Alabama," *Report(s) of the Controller of Public Accounts of the State of Alabama to the General Assembly, 1851–1863* (Montgomery: State Printer): no. 14 (1851–53), p. 7; (1854–55), p. 7; (1855–56), p. 39; (1858–59), p. 35; (1859–60), p. 15; (1862–63), p. 23. (3) *Annual Report(s) of the Officers of the Alabama Insane Hospital at Tuscaloosa for the Year(s) 1862, 1867, 1869, 1870–1888* (Tuscaloosa: John F. Warren). (4) *Report of the Trustees of the Alabama Insane Hospital, November 29, 1855* (n.p., n.d.). (5) *PPL*, vol. 34, no. 58, Nov. 30, 1852; no. 122, Feb. 12, 1853; vol. 42, no. 31, Apr. 28, 1857. (6) *K-H*, 1st ed., pp. 34ff.; 2nd ed., (1880), pp. 110, 121–143, 147–152. (7) "History of Education in Alabama, 1702–1889," *Circular of Information No. 3, 1889*, ed. Herbert B. Adams (Washington, D.C.: Government Printing Office, 1889), pp. 156–157. (8) *Hand-Book of Alabama*, comp. Saffold Berney (Birmingham: Roberts & Sons, 1892), pp. 245–249. (9) R. A. Powell, "A Sketch of Psychiatry in the Southern States," *Transactions of the American Medico-Psychological Association*, vol. 4. (10) *ICIUSC*, vol. 1, pp. 5ff. (11) Kathrine Vickery, *A History of Mental Health in Alabama*, Department of Mental Health publication, 1972, pp. 30–35.

ILLUSTRATION

Engraving, perspective, *Circular of Information No. 3, 1889*, op. cit., p. 165. (2) Photograph, exterior, *Hand-Book of Alabama*, op. cit., p. 247. (3) Engravings, plans and elevations, K-*H*, pp. 35, 37. (4) Photograph, exterior, *ICIUSC*, op. cit., p. 30.

DESCRIPTION

Report of the Trustees of the Alabama Insane Hospital, op. cit., and K-*H*, are the best descriptions of the original building.

HISTORY

Act of establishment Feb. 6, 1852; commissioned Nov. 30, 1852; cornerstone July 14, 1853; John Stewart and Fletcher Sloan superintendents of construction Autumn 1853–Mar. 1858; patients received in unfinished building July 6, 1861; used as military hospital 1862–65; construction resumed 1869; completed 1876; many additions and alterations 1876 to present; portions of original building extant, but majority greatly altered.

No. 35: Feb. 10, 1852, S & S, P(D)

COMMISSION

Court House for Camden County, N.J., on the plot bounded by Broad, Sixth, Market, and Frontal Sts., Camden, N.J. for the Board of Chosen Freeholders of the County of Camden.

DOCUMENTATION

"First Minute Book of Chosen Freeholders of the County of Camden," manuscript, entries for Feb. 10 and May 3, 1852, and Mar. 21, 1853. (2) "Articles of Agreement" between the Board and Daniel A. Hall for the erection of the courthouse, with all specifications, manuscript, May 26, 1852. (*Note*: Both documents (1) and (2), in the records of the City of Camden, N.J., were located and recorded by Mrs. R. I. Greenberg of Moorestown, N.J.) (3) *The West Jerseyman*, Camden, N.J., May 5, 1852, p. 2; Aug. 4, 1852, p. 2; Mar. 23, 1853, p. 2. (4) *PPL*, vol. 33, no. 53, May 12, 1852; no. 55, May 14, 1852. (5) George R. Prowell, *The History of Camden County, New Jersey* (Philadelphia: L. J. Richards & Co., 1886), pp. 183–185.

ILLUSTRATION

Photographs, engravings, and newspaper cuts in the collection of the Camden County Historical Society, Camden, N.J.

DESCRIPTION

Prowell, op. cit., "The building is of brick, rough-cast, fifty by one hundred and five feet in length and width. The first design included a dome, but this was omitted in the building. The jail, containing twelve cells, is in the basement, below the level of the streets. The county officers were on the first floor, the only ones remaining being the sheriff and the county collector. The court-rooms are on the second floor, while the third floor comprised apartments for the sheriff and family who formerly resided in the court-house."

HISTORY

Competition drawings received by the Board Feb. 10, 1852; submissions made by Button, Le Brun, Frazier, Sloan, and Lefevre; commission awarded May 3, 1852; contract for erection to Daniel A. Hall for $26,800 May 26, 1852; completed Mar. 19, 1855; alterations by S. D. Button 1885; demolished 1906 and replaced by extant building.

No. 36: Feb. 20, 1852, S & S, RS(Ud)

COMMISSION

Private dwelling, southeast Schuylkill 5th (18th) and Chestnut Sts., Philadelphia, Pa., for Charles Stokes.

DOCUMENTATION

PPL, vol. 32, no. 128, Feb. 20, 1852.

DESCRIPTION

PPL, op. cit., "of brown stone in the Grecian style, richly ornamented."

HISTORY

Unknown; demolished date unk.

No. 37: Apr. 7, 1852, S & S, C(D)

COMMISSION

Retail store (later incorporated into the block of buildings known as the Smythe Building c. 1855–67), 101 Arch St. above 3rd St., Philadelphia, Pa., for Samuel Townsend.

DOCUMENTATION

PPL, vol. 33, no. 11, Apr. 7, 1852. (2) W-PP, p. 98.

ILLUSTRATION

Photograph (1966), PHC.

DESCRIPTION

HABS, PA-1479, 6 data pages, including 1873–95 insurance surveys, "five stories, arched window on each story, brick with cast-iron facade."

HISTORY

Demolished 1975; front dismantled and stored by Fairmount Park Commission; certified by PHC 1976.

No. 38: Apr. 7, 1852, S & S, C(U)

COMMISSION

Retail store, 99 Arch St. above 3rd St., Philadelphia, Pa., for McDowell & Day.

DOCUMENTATION

PPL, vol. 33, no. 11, Apr. 7, 1852.

NOTE: No additional documentation for this building has been found. It may have been an announced project that was never constructed.

No. 39: May 1, 1852, S & S, *P*(Ea)

COMMISSION

Court House of Lancaster County, Pa., corner of E. King and Duke Sts., Lancaster, Pa., for the Commissioners of Lancaster County.

DOCUMENTATION

PPL, vol. 33, no. 35, May 1, 1852. (2) J. I. Mombert, *An Authentic History of Lancaster County in the State of Pennsylvania* (Lancaster, Pa.: J. E. Barr & Co., 1869), pp. 427–429. (3) Ellis and Evans, *History of Lancaster County* (Philadelphia, 1883), p. 206. (4) *Journal of the Lancaster County Historical Society*, vol. 22, 1918, pp. 142ff.

ILLUSTRATION

Lithograph, "The Court House at Lancaster," L. Haugg, litho., Mombert, op. cit., p. 427. (2) Engravings and photographs in the collection of the Lancaster County Historical Society, Lancaster, Pa.

DESCRIPTION

Mombert, op. cit., description of building in original form.

HISTORY

Commission May 1852; cornerstone Aug. 23, 1852; accepted Sept. 7, 1854; two wings added c. 1920; enlargements and additions 1976–80; building extant, altered.

No. 40: May 2, 1852, S & S, *P*(E)

COMMISSION

Fulton Hall (Fulton Opera House after Oct. 1873), Prince St. between Orange and W. King Sts., Lancaster, Pa., for Christopher Hager.

DOCUMENTATION

Examiner and Herald, Lancaster, Pa., May 5, Aug. 4, Sept. 1, Oct. 20, 1852. (2) "Fulton Hall and Its Graven Image," *Papers Read Before the Lancaster County Historical Society, Friday, December 6, 1918*, vol. 22, no. 9, pp. 141–146. (3) Ellis and Evans, *History of Lancaster County*, Phila., 1883, p. 206. (4) Felix Reichmann, "Amusements in Lancaster, 1750–1940," *Papers Read etc.*, op. cit., vol. 45, no. 2, 1941, pp. 47–53. (5) Joseph L. Kingston, "History of Fulton Opera House," *Historical Papers and Addresses of the Lancaster County Historical Society*, vol. 54, no. 6, 1952, pp. 142–153.

ILLUSTRATION

Architects drawings, in the collection (1932) of Mrs. Charles I. Landis, Lancaster, Pa., reproduced as "Architect's Drawings of Fulton Hall," William Frederic Worner, "Ole Bull and Adelina Patti in Lancaster," *Historical Papers*, op. cit., vol. 36, no. 6, 1962. (2) Photographs (a) "Fulton Opera House—Prince Street in 1862," p. 145, (b) "Interior Fulton Opera House—Remodeled 1873," p. 148. (3) Photograph, "Fulton Opera House—Prince Street in 1862," collection of Lancaster County Historical Society.

DESCRIPTION

Examiner and Herald, op. cit., and Kingston, op. cit., for the building in its original form. (2) Doris Burns, "Reminiscences of the Fulton Opera House," *Journal of the Lancaster County Historical Society*, vol. 76, no. 3, 1972, pp. 117–135, for description of interior after 1873.

HISTORY

Commissioned Apr. 1852; opened Oct. 14, 1852; conveyed to the Fulton Hall Association Oct. 8, 1855; sold to Hilaire Zaeppel and Blasius Yecker Sept. 7, 1865; remodeled by Edwain Forrest Durang, Architect, into Fulton Opera House 1873; Fulton Opera House opened Oct. 1873; began showing motion pictures Apr. 22, 1903; converted to motion picture theater 1930; Centennial restoration of building 1952; Centenary celebration Oct. 14, 1952; extant, restored.

No. 41: June 9, 1852, S & S, *RE*(Ea)

COMMISSION

First Baptist Church of Germantown, 36–42 E. Price St., Germantown, Pa., for the Building Committee of the First Baptist Church of Germantown, Pa.

DOCUMENTATION

PPL, vol. 33, no. 66, June 9, 1852. (2) H-*AM*, p. 136. (3) CC-HSP, vol. 17, "Churches," newspaper clipping (n.p., dated in ink Apr. 26, 1912, "Church Sixty Years Old." (4) W-*PP*, p. 265.

ILLUSTRATION

Newspaper cut (n.p.), dated in ink 1902; and postcard, n.d., CC-HSP, vol. 17, "Churches." (2) Two exterior photographs, HABS, PA-1688 (1973). (3) Photographs and clippings, collection of the Germantown Historical Society.

DESCRIPTION

W-*PP*, op. cit.; despite being the latest, this is the best description of the original form of the building.

HISTORY

Commissioned June 1852; completed June 1853, except for steeple; steeple added 1862, removed 1887; building remodeled 1892, 1897; sold to the Polite Temple Baptist Church 1955; certified by PHC 1965.

No. 42: June 30, 1852, S & S, *E*(U)

COMMISSION

George Wolfe School, Charlotte St. above Poplar St. (also given as Charlotte St. north from Brown to Masters Sts.), Philadelphia, Pa., for the Controllers.

DOCUMENTATION

RCPS, June 30, 1852, p. 9. (2)*PPL*, vol. 34, no. 61, Dec. 3, 1852. (3) *CSP*, class 4, no. 4, pp. 103–110. (4) *PSP*, vol. 2, pp. 181–183.

ILLUSTRATION

CSP, op. cit.

DESCRIPTION

PSP, op. cit., the only description yet found, unless the general specifications in *CSP*, op. cit., apply specifically to this building.

HISTORY

Unknown.

No. 43: June 30, 1852, S & S, *E*(U)

COMMISSION

Penn Grammar School, southwest corner of 8th and Thompson Sts., Philadelphia, Pa., for the Controllers.

DOCUMENTATION

RCPS, June 30, 1852, p. 9. (2)*PPL*, vol. 33, no. 140, Sept. 4, 1852.

NOTE: Except for the brief announcements in the *RCPS* and *PPL*, no other documentation for the building has been found. Edmunds does not list it in *PSP*, and it is never mentioned in the *AJE*.

No. 44: Aug. 11, 1852, S & S, *RS*(D)

COMMISSION

Suburban villa, Indian Queen Lane near Town Line, Germantown, Pa., for Robert K. Wright.

DOCUMENTATION

Deed Books, City of Philadelphia, Deeds GWC.81.347, TH.143.101, TH.143–103, and RDW.106.189, Philadelphia City Archives. (2) G. M. Hopkins, "*Atlas of Twenty-Eighth Ward of the City of Philadelphia*," 1875, vol. 2, plate 50, pp. 50–51. (3) *PPL*, vol. 33, no. 119, Aug. 1, 1852. (4) H-*AM*, p. 106.

NOTE: The writer is indebted to Anna Coxe Toogood and Mark Frazier Lloyd of the Germantown Historical Society for the documentation of this building.

DESCRIPTION

PPL, op. cit., gives the only description of the building's original form, "English Gothic Style, of stone rough-cast, 30′ × 90′ with ornamental dormers, the roof slates applied in decorative patterns."

HISTORY

Commission Aug. 1852; sold to Wistar Morris Apr. 1, 1854; repurchased by Wright from Morris Apr. 1854; sold to Sarah T. Allen and Emma L. Taylor Nov. 12, 1856; remained in Taylor family (called "Cedron") until 1915; demolished c. 1945; site now occupied by Muhlenberg Building (Board of

Publication of the Lutheran Church in America), 2900 West Queen Lane, Philadelphia, Pa.

No. 45: Aug. 11, 1852, S & S, RS(D)

COMMISSION

"Bella Vista" (later "Summit Place"), suburban villa, Abbotsford Lane, Germantown (later S. Indian Queen Lane, Falls of the Schuylkill), Pa., for the Rev. John M. Richards, minister of the First Baptist Church, Germantown.

DOCUMENTATION

PPL, vol. 33, no. 119, Aug. 11, 1852. (2) G. M. Hopkins, *Atlas of the Twenty-Eighth Ward (etc.) 1875*, op. cit., and *Atlas of the Twenty-Second Ward (etc.) 1885*. (3) "Germantown Who's Who," scrapbook, collection of the Germantown Historical Society, newspaper clipping, identified as "*Ind. Gaz.* 1/4/26." (4) H-*AM*, p. 136.

NOTE: The writer is indebted to Anna Coxe Toogood and Mark Frazier Lloyd of the Germantown Historical Society for the documentation of this building.

DESCRIPTION

PPL, "Norman Villa, 70' × 50', with circular bay windows and an octagonal entrance tower 100' high."

HISTORY

Commissioned Aug. 1852 (or earlier); continued in the Richards family until after 1906; burned c. 1924; ruins demolished before 1945.

No. 46: Aug. 11, 1852, S & S, RS(Ud)

COMMISSION

Speculative dwelling, Spruce and William (39) Sts., West Philadelphia, Pa., for J. J. Woodward.

DOCUMENTATION

PPL, vol. 33, no. 119, Aug. 11, 1852.

DESCRIPTION

PPL, "42' × 65', of rough stone masticked, brackets under eaves."

HISTORY

Unknown; demolished date unk.

No. 47: Aug. 11, 1852, S & S, RS(Ud)

COMMISSION

Speculative dwelling, Spruce St. adjoining J. J. Woodward lot, West Philadelphia, Pa., for J. L. Goddard.

DOCUMENTATION

PPL, vol. 33, no. 119, Aug. 11, 1852.

DESCRIPTION

PPL, op. cit., "25' × 54', of stone rough-cast."

HISTORY

Unknown; demolished date unk.

No. 48: Aug. 11, 1852, S & S, RS(Ud)

COMMISSION

Private dwelling, corner of Spruce and Till (40) Sts., West Philadelphia, Pa., for Nathaniel B. Browne.

DOCUMENTATION

PPL, vol. 33, no. 119, Aug. 11, 1852.

ILLUSTRATION

Photograph, "40th St. looking toward Spruce," n.d., PC-HSP, box 22.

DESCRIPTION

PPL, op. cit., "Itallian style with a tower 60' high."

HISTORY

Unknown; demolished date unk.

No. 49: Aug. 11, 1852, S & S, RS(Ud)

COMMISSION

Private dwelling, Spruce St. adjoining the lot of N. B. Browne, West Philadelphia, Pa., for Samuel A. Harrison.

DOCUMENTATION

PPL, vol. 33, no. 119, Aug. 11, 1852; vol. 35, no. 72, June 15, 1853.

ILLUSTRATION

Photograph, "40th St. looking toward Spruce," PC-HSP, box 22.

DESCRIPTION

PPL, op. cit., "Roman Corinthian style, six column portico, column capitals and window pediments, in terra-cotta."

HISTORY

Unknown; demolished date unk.

No. 50: Aug. 11, 1852, S & S, RS(Ud)

COMMISSION

Private dwelling, corner of Till (40) and Pine Sts., West Philadelphia, Pa., for Mr. Sexton of Deal, Sexton & Co.

DOCUMENTATION

PPL, vol. 33, no. 119, Aug. 11, 1852.

DESCRIPTION

PPL, op. cit., "Florentine style, verandas on both street fronts."

HISTORY

Unknown; demolished date unk.

NOTE: The entire block of dwellings on Till (40) St. between Spruce and Pine Sts. is given to Sloan (*PPL*, vol. 35, no. 72, June 15, 1853), but the intermediate buildings between those of Harrison and Sexton are not announced until June 1853. It seems that both sides of 40th St. were developed by Browne and Harrison from Spruce to Pine Sts.

No. 51: Nov. 5, 1852, S & S, *E*(Ud)

COMMISSION

Webster School, Hancock St. above Franklin Ave. (also given as Girard Ave. east from 6th St.), Kensington, Philadelphia, Pa., for the Controllers.

DOCUMENTATION

PPL, vol. 34, no. 37, Nov. 5; no. 56, Nov. 27, 1852. (2) *PSP*, vol. 2, pp. 145–147.

ILLUSTRATION

Photograph, exterior, *PSP*, op. cit., p. 146.

DESCRIPTION

PSP, op. cit., pp. 145–146.

HISTORY

Cornerstone Nov. 6, 1852; demolished date unk.

No. 52: Nov. 5, 1852, S & S, *E*(Ud)

COMMISSION

John Quincy Adams School, Garden St. below Buttonwood St., Philadelphia, Pa., for the Controllers.

DOCUMENTATION

PPL, vol. 34, no. 37, Nov. 5, 1852; vol. 35, no. 5, Sept. 28, 1853. (2) *RCPS*, June 30, 1853, p. 11. (3) *PSP*, vol. 2, pp. 177–179.

ILLUSTRATION

Photograph, exterior, *PSP*, op. cit., p. 178.

DESCRIPTION

PSP, op. cit., p. 178.

HISTORY

Commissioned c. Spring 1853; dedication Sept. 27, 1853; demolished date unk.

No. 53: Nov. 5, 1852, S & S, *E*(D)

COMMISSION

The Normal School (after 1859 Girls' High School, from 1860 to 1869 Girls' High and Normal School, from 1869 to 1876 Girls' Normal School), south side Sergeant (Spring) St. between 9th and 10th Sts., Philadelphia, Pa., for the Controllers.

DOCUMENTATION

PPL, vol. 34, no. 37, Nov. 5, 1852; vol. 35, no. 60, June 1, 1853; vol. 37, no. 16, Mar. 30, 1854; no. 21, Apr. 5, 1854. (2) *S-MA*, vol. 2, pp. 48–49. (3) *RCPS*, June 30, 1853, pp. 1–9. (4) John Trevor Custis, *The Public*

Schools of Philadelphia: Historical, Biographical, Statistical (Philadelphia: Burk & McFetridge Co., 1897), pp. 157–158. (5) *PSP*, vol. 3, pp. 1–4; (6) *AJE*, vol. 14, 1864, pp. 737–738.

ILLUSTRATION

Lithographs, perspective, section, plans, *S-MA*, op. cit., plates 44–46. (2) Engravings, elevations, plans, *AJE*, vol. 14, 1864, figs. 1–5, pp. 737–738. (3) Photograph, exterior, Custis, op. cit., p. 1. (4) Photographs, woodcuts, and engravings, collections of FLP.

DESCRIPTION

PPL, vol. 37, no. 16, Mar. 30, 1854, gives a full description of the building in its original form.

HISTORY

Commission c. Autumn 1852; cornerstone May 31, 1853; dedication Apr. 4, 1854; removal of school to new building, 17th and Spring Garden Sts., Nov. 1876; demolished date unk.

No. 54: Dec. 14, 1852, S & S, C(D)

COMMISSION

Retail store, 213 Market Sts. (513 Market St. after 1858), Philadelphia, Pa., for Hoskins, Hieskell & Co.

DOCUMENTATION

PPL, vol. 34, no. 70, Dec. 14, 1852. (2) PC-HSP, box 20, newspaper clipping (n.p., n.d.), announcement of new building.

ILLUSTRATION

Lithograph, "Hoskins, Hieskell & Co., Importers & Jobbers of Fancy & Staple Dry Goods, No. 213 Market & 34 Commerce St. Philad.," Inger & Haugg, litho., P. D. Duval, printer, c. 1854, in color, 35″ × 22¾″, collection of The Library Company, Philadelphia, Pa. (2) Woodcut, newspaper advertisement, John McAllister Scrapbook, vol. 15, p. 75, collection of HSP.

DESCRIPTION

PPL, op. cit., "The most ornamental iron front yet projected in our city, occupying the sites of two stores, 32 feet by 200 feet, extending to Commerce Street. It is to be of Norman Itallian style with no interior brick lining to the iron front, no interior columns, the floors supported by trussed girders."

HISTORY

Commissioned c. Autumn 1852; occupied c. Autumn 1953; demolished date unk.

No. 55: Dec. 14, 1852, S & S, E(D)

COMMISSION

The Philadelphia High School, east side of Broad St. from Green to Brandywine St., Philadelphia, Pa., for the Controllers.

DOCUMENTATION

PPL, vol. 34, no. 70, Dec. 14, 1852; no. 96, Jan. 13, 1853; vol. 36, no. 84, June 29, 1854. (2) *RCPS*, June 30, 1853, pp. 1–9. (3) *RCPS*, Dec. 31, 1854, pp. 1–9. (4) *S-CSA*, pp. 79–81. (5) *AJE*, vol. 13, Mar.–Dec. 1863, pp. 830–833. (6) *PSP*, vol. 3, pp. 5–8. (7) Numerous guidebooks and encyclopedias published between 1854 and 1902.

ILLUSTRATION

Lithographs, elevation and plan, *S-CSA*, plates 104 and 105. (2) Lithograph and drawing, elevation and plan, *CSP*, example 10, p. 135. (3) Woodcut, elevation and plan, *AJE*, vol. 1, Mar.–Dec. 1855, pp. 92, 95. (4) Numerous photographs, engravings, and lithographs, collections of FLP, TLC, and HSP.

DESCRIPTION

PPL, op. cit., Jan. 13, 1853, "The building is of brick, 100′ × 74′, four stories in height, with window and door surrounds of white marble, the brick-work will be broken after the style adopted in the Assembly Building, and the tower, 96′ high, will be used as an observatory."

HISTORY

Commissioned Jan. 12, 1853; cornerstone May 31, 1853; dedication June 28, 1854; supplemental building dedicated June 25, 1874; new building on southwest corner of Broad and Green Sts. commissioned 1897; school relocated Feb. 1939 and Sloan building demolished.

No. 56: June 3, 1853, S & S, C(Ud)

COMMISSION

Three stores, 2nd and Little Dock Sts., Philadelphia, Pa., for Joseph M. Bennett.

DOCUMENTATION

PPL, vol. 35, no. 62, June 3, 1853.

DESCRIPTION

PPL, op. cit., "Improvements to replace the Loxley House and adjoining properties. Each store 18′ × 76′, fronting on 2nd St., the corner store having 26′ frontage on Little Dock St., with show-rooms for cabinet makers and workshop in the rear; the lower stories of iron, and the four upper stories of pressed brick."

HISTORY

Unknown; demolished date unk.

No. 57: June 3, 1853, S & S, RE(D)

COMMISSION

Tabernacle Methodist-Episcopal Church, 11th and Green Sts. (also given as 11th above Jefferson St.), Philadelphia, Pa., for the building committee of the church.

NOTE: The commission was withdrawn during preliminary construction and awarded to S. D. Button.

DOCUMENTATION

PPL, vol. 35, no. 62, June 3, 1853; vol. 41, no. 122, Aug. 13, 1856. (2) Brenner Scrapbooks, p. 176, newspaper clipping (n.p., n.d.), "Methodists Plan A Golden Jubilee," HSP(4.122). (3) Tatum, p. 177.

ILLUSTRATION

Lithograph, perspective, signed "Sloan & Stewart archts.," "Tabernacle M. E. Church, 11th St. above Jefferson, Philadelphia," J. F. Watson litho., Wagnar & McGuigan, printer, c. 1854, in color, 23″ × 19″, collection of TLC. (2) Photograph, front, CC-HSP, vol. 15, "Churches," date and source unknown.

DESCRIPTION

PPL, op. cit., "Ornamental Portico of four columns, semi-circular wings to each side containing stairs to hall."

HISTORY

Church chartered 1853; commission to Sloan & Stewart c. Spring 1853; commission withdrawn 1854; temporary frame structure until July 1856; new building, architect S. D. Button, dedicated Oct. 26, 1856; church burned to ground Jan. 1857; rebuilding completed Nov. 1858; building demolished date unknown.

No. 58: June 3, 1853, S & S, RE(U)

COMMISSION

Zion Episcopal Church, 8th St. and Columbia Ave., Philadelphia, Pa., for the building committee of the church.

DOCUMENTATION

PPL, vol. 35, no. 62, June 3, 1853.

DESCRIPTION

PPL, op. cit., "building 50′ × 78′, tower 22′ square and 135′ tall."

HISTORY

NOTE: The lack of any further documentation on this building seems to indicate that it was a project never erected or for which the commission was withdrawn.

No. 59: June 3, 1853, S & S, RE(Ud)

COMMISSION

Completion of the Second Baptist Church, 5th St. below Carpenter St., Philadelphia, Pa., for the building committee of the church.

DOCUMENTATION

PPL, vol. 35, no. 62, June 3, 1853. (2) CC-HSP, vol. 15, "Churches," newspaper clipping (n.p.), dated in ink May 11, 1911, "Passing of Calvary Church."

HISTORY

Occupied until 1889, when the congregation removed to 7th and Snyder Sts.; the name was changed to Calvary Baptist Church at some time before the remove; the Sloan building was demolished date unk.

No. 60: June 3, 1853, S & S, P(D)

COMMISSION

City Literary Institute for Young Men (also known as City Institute and Philadelphia Institute), northeast corner Schuylkill 5th (18th St.) and Chestnut Sts. (also given as 218 S. 18th St.), Philadelphia, Pa., for the Board of Managers of the Institute.

DOCUMENTATION

PPL, vol. 35, no. 62, June 3, 1853; no. 79, June 23, 1853; vol. 39, no. 2, Mar. 25, 1855. (2) Westcott, p. 205. (3) *PE*, p. 85. (4) Jackson, p. 468. (5) CC-HSP, vol. 14, "Chestnut Street," *Sixty-Third Annual Report of the Philadelphia Institute: Philadelphia's Oldest Free Library, Erected 1854*, front page only (n.p., n.d.).

ILLUSTRATION

Woodcut, front elevation, CC-HSP, op. cit. (2) Photographs, collection of FLP.

DESCRIPTION

PPL, op. cit., June 3, 1853, "building 44′ × 96′, first floor with two stores, second floor reading room, and apartments for the school of design and manager, third floor lecture rooms."

NOTE: Westcott gives the dimensions as 44′ × 120′.

HISTORY

Institute founded 1852; commission for building 1853; opened Mar. 23, 1855; building enlarged before 1875; sold and Institute moved to 218 S. 19th St. in 1926; building demolished thereafter, date unk.

No. 61: June 3, 1853, S & S, RS(D)

COMMISSION

Adjoining town residences, southeast corner of Logan Square at 18th St., Philadelphia, Pa., for Mr. Kimbal and Mr. Gordon.

DOCUMENTATION

PPL, vol. 35, no. 62, June 3, 1853.

ILLUSTRATION

Photograph, "18th Street at Logan Square," Robert F. Looney, *Old Philadelphia in Early Photographs, 1839–1914* (New York: Dover Publications, 1976), plate 110, p. 113.

DESCRIPTION

PPL, op. cit., "each dwelling 32′ × 88′, ground floor of Pictou Stone, upper floors mastick over brick."

HISTORY

Buildings demolished 1918 for the construction of the Benjamin Franklin Parkway.

No. 62: June 15, 1853, S & S, *RS*(Ud)

COMMISSION

Private dwelling, Till (40) St. between Spruce and Pine Sts., West Philadelphia, Pa., for Mr. Malony.

DOCUMENTATION

PPL, vol. 35, no. 74, June 15, 1853. (2) CC-HSP, vol. 2, "West Philadelphia," newspaper clipping (n.p.), dated in ink Mar. 4, 1907, "Swiss Villa at the corner of 40th and Spruce Streets."

ILLUSTRATION

Newspaper cut, CC-HSP, op. cit.

HISTORY

Unknown; demolished date unk.

No. 63: June 15, 1853, S & S, *RS*(Ud)

COMMISSION

Speculative dwelling, Till (40) St. between Spruce and Pine Sts., West Philadelphia, Pa., for N. B. Browne.

DOCUMENTATION

PPL, vol. 35, no. 74, June 15, 1853.

DESCRIPTION

PPL, op. cit., "building in the Elizabethan Style."

HISTORY

Demolished date unk.

No. 64: June 17, 1853, S & S, *P*(D)

COMMISSION

Second Masonic Temple (also called New Masonic Temple and Masonic Hall), corner of Chestnut and 7th Sts., Philadelphia, Pa., for the Right Worshipful Grand Lodge.

DOCUMENTATION

Minutes of the Right Worshipful Grand Lodge (Philadelphia: Grand Lodge, 1905), vol. 8, 1849–54, p. 351; vol. 9, 1855–58, pp. 123–127, 329–348. (2) *PPL*, vol. 36, no. 72, June 17; no. 50, Nov. 19; no. 83, Dec. 29, 1853; vol. 38, no. 112, 1855; vol. 39, no. 56, May 28; no. 130, Aug. 23; no. 154, Sept. 20; no. 155, Sept. 21, 1855. (3) S & W, vol. 1, p. 74. (4) *Freemasonry in Pennsylvania*, ed. Julius F. Suchse (Philadelphia, 1919), vol. 3, pp. 414, 419, 446. (5) Tatum, pp. 78, 178–179. (6) SRL, vol. 1, p. 1 (tickets to laying of cornerstone and formal opening); vol. 6, pp. 9, 10, 11, 22, 23; vol. 7, pp. 3, 7, 37, 68, 77; vol. 8, pp. 25, 27, 37; vol. 9, pp. 39, 41. (7) *AABN*, vol. 16, no. 449, p. 49. (8) John McAllister's Scrapbooks, HSP, W22 5346, vol. 5, pp. 66–67.

ILLUSTRATION

Lithograph, "New Masonic Hall," Tholey litho., Friend & Aub. printer, J. G. Simpson publisher, 23″ × 19″, in color, c. 1855, collection of Library of Congress, Washington, D.C. (2) Woodcut, "Masonic Hall Chestnut Street between Seventh and Eighth," n.d., Perkins Collection, HSP, vol. 8B, item 813. (3) *BP*, 1856, 1859, 1860, "Chestnut Street," Collection of TLC. (4) Photographs, engravings, and woodcuts in the collections of FLP, TLC, and HSP.

DESCRIPTION

The contemporary descriptions of the building in its original form are in John McAllister's Scrapbooks, op. cit., and *PPL*, op. cit., Aug. 23 and Sept. 20, 1855.

NOTE: The interior of the Grand Lodge Room was executed by Collins & Authenrieth, Architects. For an illustration, see (1) Lithograph, "Grand Lodge Room of the New Masonic Temple," Max Rosenthal delin. (Philadelphia, 1855), 21″ × 16⅞″, in color, collection of Library of Congress. (2) Photograph, black-and-white, Kenneth Finkle, *Nineteenth-Century Photography in Philadelphia* (New York: Dover Publications, 1980), plate 101, p. 97.

HISTORY

Commissioned June 16, 1853; cornerstone Sept. 29, 1853; spire approved Jan. 1855; dedication Sept. 1855; sold to William M. Singerly 1882; converted to "Temple Theatre and Egyptian Musee" 1883–85; theater opened Sept. 14, 1885; burned Dec. 26, 1886 and ruins demolished.

No. 65: June 17, 1853, S & S, *P*(D)

COMMISSION

Enlargement, Odd Fellows' Broadway Hall, Broad and Spring Garden Sts., Philadelphia, Pa., for the Independent Order of Odd Fellows.

DOCUMENTATION

First Annual Report of the Board of Managers of the Spring Garden Institute (Philadelphia, 1852), pp. 4ff. (2) *PPL*, vol. 35, no. 74, June 17, 1853. (3) CC-HSP, vol. 23, "Diagonal Avenues," p. 1, newspaper clipping (n.p., n.d.), "Odd Fellows Temple at Broad and Spring Garden." (4) *Philadelphia as It Is in 1852*, ed. R. A. Smith (Philadelphia: Lindsay & Blakiston, 1852), p. 45. (5) *Laying the Cornerstone of the Odd Fellows' Temple*, pamphlet, ed. Geo. F. Borie (Philadelphia: Crosscup & West, 1893), p. 50, HSP. (6) W-*PP* p. 287, n. 20.

ILLUSTRATION

Lithograph, "Odd Fellows' Broadway Hall, Broad & Spring Garden Streets, Philadelphia," drawn and printed by Rease & Schell, c. 1855, in color, 13″ × 20½″, HSP. (2) Woodcut, "N. Broad" (n.p.), dated in ink 1855, CC-HSP, vol. 60. (3) Engraving, John McAllister's Scrapbooks, HSP, W22 5346, vol. 17, p. 79. (4) Photograph in *Laying the Cornerstone etc.*, op. cit., p. 50.

DESCRIPTION

PPL, op. cit., and John McAllister's Scrapbooks, op. cit., are the only contemporary descriptions of the building in its original form.

HISTORY

First building commissioned from Hoxie & Button, 1851; enlargement commissioned from Sloan & Stewart May 13, 1853; building sold 1893 and subsequently demolished.

No. 66: July 4, 1853, S & S, P(D)

COMMISSION

West Philadelphia Institute, northwest corner 40th and Ludlow Sts., West Philadelphia, Pa., for the Managers of the West Philadelphia Institute.

DOCUMENTATION

An Appeal in Behalf of the West Philadelphia Institute, pamphlet (Philadelphia: Isaac Ashmead, 1853), HSP, Wn*79, vol. 1, p. 6. (2) *Annual Report of the Managers of the West Philadelphia Institute, 1854*, pamphlet, n.d., HSP, Wn*79, vol. 1, p. 4. (3) *PPL*, vol. 35, no. 88, July 4, 1853; vol. 36, no. 12, Oct. 12, 1853; no. 86, Jan. 2, 1854. (4) Joseph Jackson, *America's Most Historic Highway* (Philadelphia: John Wanamaker, 1926), p. 340.

ILLUSTRATION

Lithograph, perspective of proposed building, *An Appeal etc.*, op. cit., frontispiece. (2) Woodcut, "West Philad. Institute" (n.p., n.d.), CC-FLP, vol. 17, "Education," p. 16.

DESCRIPTION

An Appeal etc., op. cit., the architect's own description of proposed building. (2) *PPL*, op. cit., Oct. 12, 1853, description of building as realized.

HISTORY

Institute organized Jan. 2, 1853; commission Spring 1853; cornerstone July 4, 1853; occupied Jan. 1854; building sold c. 1910 and subsequently demolished.

No. 67: July 4, 1853, S & S, RS(Ud)

COMMISSION

Two adjoining town residences, Broad St. between Girard and Columbia Aves., Philadelphia, Pa., for former sheriff William Deal.

DOCUMENTATION

PPL, vol. 35, no. 88, July 4, 1853.

DESCRIPTION

PPL, op. cit., "with 25' fronts, of brown stone, the first floor elevated with a balustrade before windows, roof with cornice and terminal balustrade."

HISTORY

One of these may have been extant in 1974; see Edward Teitelman and Richard W. Longstreth, *Architecture in Philadelphia: A Guide* (Cambridge, Mass.: MIT Press, 1974), p. 132.

No. 68: July 4, 1853, S & S, RS(Ud)

COMMISSION

Block of ten town residences in New York style, Broad St. and Columbia Ave., Philadelphia, Pa., for an unknown client.

DOCUMENTATION

PPL, vol. 35, no. 8, July 4, 1853.

ILLUSTRATION

S-CSA may illustrate this project, Design XVII, "A Block of Dwellings."

DESCRIPTION

PPL, op. cit., "with 25' fronts, bay windows at first and second floors crowned with balustrade, basement of granite, upper floors of brick, rough cast in imitation of granite, balustrade at roof line of entire block with observatories at each corner in the center."

HISTORY

This could be Nos. 1620–1636 North Broad St., which was extant in 1974. See Edward Teitelman and Richard W. Longstreth, *Architecture in Philadelphia: A Guide* (Cambridge, Mass.: MIT Press, 1974), p. 143.

No. 69: Aug. 25, 1853, S & S, RS(U)

COMMISSION

Entire block of town residences, 8th St. between Green and Spring Garden Sts., Philadelphia, Pa., for Joseph Harrison Jr.

NOTE: There is a contradiction in the location of this development, which is also given as Green St. between 16th and 18th Sts. (Poulson, 7:137, TLC, and W-*PP*, p. 288).

DOCUMENTATION

PPL, vol. 35, no. 132, Aug. 25, 1853; vol. 36, no. 130, Feb. 22, 1854.

NOTE: The Aug. 25 notice calls this "Mr. Harrison's improvements on Green Street" and states that he has already begun a similar project on the north side of Spring Garden above 8th St. It seems that the *Public Ledger* got the two projects confused.

DESCRIPTION

W-*PP*, p. 287, "The main feature of these semidetached houses was the small grass plot in front of each dwelling."

HISTORY

Harrison brought fifteen two-story houses on this site and demolished them in the autumn of 1853. The commission to Sloan & Stewart was given in August 1853, and the project was ready for occupancy by late Summer

1854. This was one of the low-cost housing projects which Harrison and Sloan collaborated on. How much of it is extant is uncertain. In 1955 at least three, much modified, examples were still standing.

No. 70: Aug. 1853, S & S, P(D)

COMMISSION
Court House of Westmoreland County, Pa., northwest corner of Main and W. Pittsburgh Sts., Greensburg, Pa., for the Commissioners of Westmoreland County.

DOCUMENTATION
Addison Hutton, letter to his sister, Mary, dated "6/12/57," Hutton Papers, Quaker Collection, Haverford College Library, Haverford, Pa. (2) *History of the County of Westmoreland, Pennsylvania*, ed. George Dallas Albert (Philadelphia: L. H. Everts & Co., 1882), pp. 425–428. (3) John N. Boucher, *History of Westmoreland County, Pennsylvania* (Chicago: Lewis Publishing Co., 1906), pp. 437–439.

ILLUSTRATION
Lithographs, elevations, plans, S-CSA, Design VII, "A Court-House," pp. 50–51. (2) Lithograph, "Court-House, Greensburg, Westmoreland County," *History of the County of Westmoreland etc.*, op. cit., p. 426. (3) Photograph, "The Court House, Built 1854," Boucher, op. cit., p. 438.

DESCRIPTION
Boucher, op. cit., although the latest, is the best description of the building in its original state. Boucher had access to documents no longer in existence.

HISTORY
First commissioned from J. Edgar, whose plans were rejected by the Commissioners; commission to Sloan & Stewart, Aug. 1853; contract 1854; cornerstone Oct. 24, 1854; building accepted Aug. 1855; building demolished 1901.

No. 71: Sept. 7, 1853, S & S, M(D)

COMMISSION
Kalamazoo State Hospital (later Building 15, Female Center, Annex, kitchen, dining room and passage, Kalamazoo Regional Psychiatric Hospital), on the site bounded by Stadium Dr., Howard St., Oakland Dr., and Oliver St., Kalamazoo, Mich., for the State of Michigan.

DOCUMENTATION
First Report on Michigan Asylums for the Insane and for the Deaf, Dumb, and Blind for the years 1855–1856 (Lansing: State Printer, 1856). (2) *PPL*, vol. 35, no. 143, Sept. 7, 1853. (3) *ICIUSC*, vol. 2, p. 766. (4) K-H, 2nd ed., pp. 86–87. (5) Harley J. McKee, "Glimpses of Architecture in Michigan," *Michigan History*, vol. 50, no. 1, Mar. 1966, pp. 9, 40.

ILLUSTRATION

Painting, dated 1874, Michigan Historical Collection, University of Michigan, Ann Arbor, Mich. (2) Photographs and plans, Survey of facility, 1943, Michigan State Administrative Board (Department of Management and Budget), Buildings and Construction Division, Lansing, Mich.

DESCRIPTION

Survey, 1943, op. cit., Randall Wagner, Registered Architect, full description.

HISTORY

Commission c. Autumn 1853 (*PPL*, op. cit., Sept. 7, 1853, "On the recommendation of Dr. Kirkbride, and the evidence of the Alabama Hospital, and the Committee from Michigan offered the commission to Mr. Sloan"); center building and south wing completed 1856; north wing completed 1859; annex and kitchen completed 1860; dining room and passage completed 1860; alterations 1883–1945; demolished July 5, 1966–Nov. 10, 1967.

No. 72: Oct. 12, 1853, S & S, *RS*(U)

COMMISSION

Private dwelling, Mantua St. north from 40th St. near Lancaster Ave. (Mantua Ave.), West Philadelphia, Pa., for James C. Vodges.

DOCUMENTATION

PPL, vol. 36, no. 17, Oct. 12, 1853.

NOTE: No other documentation, illustration, or record of this building has been found. The announcement of its commission in the *PPL*, op. cit., may have been that of a project which was never constructed.

No. 73: Nov. 15, 1853, S & S, *C*(Ud)

COMMISSION

Printing establishment, George (Sansom) St. above 11th St. (later 1859 Sansom St.), Philadelphia, Pa., for Isaac Ashmead.

DOCUMENTATION

PPL, vol. 36, no. 46, Nov. 15, 1853.

ILLUSTRATION

Lithograph (n.p., n.d.), collection of prints and photographs, FLP.

DESCRIPTION

PPL, op. cit., "building now in progress, of five stories with three exposures."

HISTORY

Demolished date unk.

No. 74: Jan. 2, 1854, S & S, *RS*(U)

COMMISSION

Speculative dwelling, Spruce St. "near" William (39) St., West Philadelphia, Pa., for N. B. Browne.

DOCUMENTATION

PPL, vol. 36, no. 86, Jan. 2, 1854, no description.

NOTE: No other documentation for this building has been found; it may have been a project that was never constructed. It is one of nine residences reported, as a group, in *PPL*, op. cit., Jan. 2, 1854, under "Improvements in West Philadelphia." The remaining eight follow.

No. 75: Jan. 2, 1854, S & S, *RS*(U)

COMMISSION

Speculative dwelling, Till (40) St. above Pine St., West Philadelphia, Pa., for James T. Allen.

DOCUMENTATION

PPL, vol. 36, no. 86, Jan. 2, 1854, called "Itallian Cottage."

No. 76: Jan. 2, 1854, S & S, *RS*(D)

COMMISSION

Speculative dwelling, Pine St. above Till (40) St., West Philadelphia, Pa., for James T. Allen.

DOCUMENTATION

PPL, vol. 36, no. 86, Jan. 2, 1854, called "Gothic Cottage."

NOTE: In 1955 a stable, assumed to be contemporary with the house, was still standing.

No. 77: Jan. 2, 1854, S & S, *RS*(U)

COMMISSION

"Mansion," Pine St. above William (40) St., West Philadelphia, Pa., for Thomas White.

DOCUMENTATION

PPL, vol. 36, no. 86, Jan. 2, 1854, no description.

No. 78: Jan. 2, 1854, S & S, *RS*(U)

COMMISSION

Speculative dwelling, Hamilton (41) St., West Philadelphia, Pa., for William Lofland.

DOCUMENTATION

PPL, vol. 36, no. 86, Jan. 2, 1854, called "Itallian Cottage."

HISTORY

Edward Teitelman and Richard W. Longstreth, *Architecture in Philadelphia: A Guide* (Cambridge, Mass.: MIT Press, 1974), list this house extant in 1974, as 4100 Pine St.

No. 79: Jan. 2, 1854, S & S, *RS*(U)

COMMISSION

Speculative dwelling, Hamilton (41) St., West Philadelphia, Pa., for S. A. Harrison.

DOCUMENTATION

PPL, vol. 36, no. 86, Jan. 2, 1854, called "Gothic Cottage."

No. 80: Jan. 2, 1854, S & S, *RS*(U)

COMMISSION

Speculative dwelling, northeast corner of Walnut and 41st Sts., West Philadelphia, Pa., for the Rev. Albert Barnes.

DOCUMENTATION

PPL, vol. 36, no. 86, Jan. 2, 1854, no description.

No. 81: Jan. 2, 1854, S & S, *RS*(U)

COMMISSION

Private dwelling, north side of Walnut St. "adjoining" the Rev. Albert Barnes (given in *McElroy's*, 1859, as Walnut, north side, west of Chestnut Ave.), West Philadelphia, Pa., for Judge Joseph Allison.

DOCUMENTATION

PPL, vol. 36, no. 86, Jan. 2, 1854, no description.

No. 82: Jan. 2, 1854, S & S, *RS*(U)

COMMISSION

Private dwelling, Walnut St. above Chestnut Ave., West Philadelphia, Pa., for William D. Baker.

DOCUMENTATION

PPL, vol. 36, no. 86, Jan. 2, 1854, no description.

HISTORY

Edward Teitelman and Richard W. Longstreth, *Architecture in Philadelphia: A Guide* (Cambridge, Mass.: MIT Press, 1974), p. 196, list this house extant in 1974, as 4207 Walnut St.

No. 83: Feb. 2, 1854, S & S, *C*(Ud)

COMMISSION

Commercial building, 5th and Market Sts., Philadelphia, Pa., for Thurlor, Hughes & Co.

DOCUMENTATION

PPL, vol. 36, no. 113, Feb. 2, 1854.

ILLUSTRATION
BP, 1856, "5th Street," TLC.

DESCRIPTION
PPL, op. cit., "in the Byzantine style, with the front in Quincy granite."

HISTORY
Demolished date unk.

No. 84: Feb. 14, 1854, S & S, *E*(D)

COMMISSION
Northern Home for Friendless Children, north side of Brown St. extending from Nixon to Reservoir Sts. (also given as Corner of Brown and 23rd Sts.), Philadelphia, Pa., for the Managers of the Northern Home for Friendless Children.

DOCUMENTATION
Second Annual Report, Northern Home for Friendless Children (Philadelphia: S. Clarkson, 1855), p. 11. (NOTE: This report lists Sloan as a life member, together with Joseph Harrison Jr. and Messrs. H. and A. Cope.) (2) *PPL*, vol. 36, no. 123, Feb. 14, 1854; vol. 39, no. 56, May 28, 1855. (3) *Third Annual Report etc.* (Philadelphia: H. B. Ashmead, 1856), pp. 11–12.

ILLUSTRATION
Engraving, perspective of building without lantern, *Second Annual Report etc.*, op. cit., back cover. (2) Engraving, perspective of building with lantern, *Third Annual Report etc.*, op. cit., back cover. (3) Photograph, exterior, *Sixty-Sixth Annual Report etc.* (Philadelphia, 1919), p. 14.

DESCRIPTION
Second Annual Report etc., op. cit., p. 11, "The design and specifications were furnished by Messrs. Sloan and Stewart, Architects, and the contract given to Messrs. Brown and Embly, Builders."
NOTE: This was a reissue of the design for the West Jersey Academy, Bridgetown, N.J., of 1851, donated to the managers by Sloan and Stewart.

HISTORY
Cornerstone June 17, 1854; dedication May 1, 1855; the *Sixty-Sixth Annual Report*, 1919, gives the original location for the building; the *Eighty-Second Annual Report*, 1935, gives its address as 5301 Ridge Ave., Wissahickon, Philadelphia; old building demolished 1936 and the Orthopedic Hospital erected on the site.

No. 85: Feb. 22, 1854, S & S, *RS*(D)

COMMISSION
"Riverdale," country villa, on the Bristol Pike, in the 26th Ward, "near" Holmsburg, Bucks County, Pa., for Joseph Harrison Jr.

DOCUMENTATION

PPL, vol. 36, no. 130, Feb. 22, 1854. (2) H-*BP*, p. 213. (3) The Rev. Dr. F. M. Beasley, *Papers from Overlook House* (n.p., n.d.), chapter entitled "Riverdale."

DESCRIPTION

Hotchkin, *Bristol Pike*, "Riverdale—A long white fence on the State Road marks the estate of Joseph Harrison, now rented to the city for the use of the House of Correction, and tilled by the inmates." "Here is the Russian mansion with its dome built by Mr. Harrison, who was engaged in railway work. . . ." (2) *PPL*, op. cit., states that Harrison "was building" a "new Delaware villa, 'Riverdale.'"

HISTORY

Demolished for the new House of Correction, date unk.

No. 86: Feb. 23, 1854, S & S, C(Ud)

COMMISSION

Commercial building, 3rd St. above Spruce St., Philadelphia, Pa., for Wendell & Espy.

DOCUMENTATION

PPL, vol. 36, no. 134, Feb. 23, 1854.

DESCRIPTION

PPL, op. cit., "in the Norman style, with three doors on the street having circular heads and keystones carved into lions' heads, the roof with elaborate cornice and brackets."

HISTORY

Demolished date unk.

No. 87: Apr. 15, 1854, S & S, RE(E)

COMMISSION

First Baptist Church (now Downtown Baptist Church), 101 W. McBee Ave., Greenville, S.C., for the building committee of the First Baptist Church.

DOCUMENTATION

Addison Hutton, letter dated "6/21/57," HP. (2) Robert Norman Daniel, *A Century of Progress, Being the History of the First Baptist Church, Greenville, South Carolina* (Privately printed, 1957), pp. 8, 22, 30, 32.

ILLUSTRATION

Photocopy, original drawing of elevation (original formerly in the possession of the First Baptist Church), signed "Sloan & Stewart, Architects, 154 Walnut St., Philad., April 15/54," copy in the collection of the author. (2) Photograph (1858), exterior, p. 8, and photograph (1890), interior, p. 22, in Daniel, op. cit.

HISTORY

Dedication Feb. 21, 1858; part of congregation removed to new site and church renamed Sept. 1947; placed on National Register Aug. 16, 1977; extant.

No. 88: May 31, 1854, S & S, *E*(Ud)

COMMISSION

Fayette School (after 1916 the William C. Jacobs School), Somerton Turnpike Rd., Bustleton, Philadelphia, Pa., for the Controllers.

DOCUMENTATION

RCPS, Dec. 31, 1854, p. 9. (2) *PPL*, vol. 37, no. 59, May 31, 1854. (3) *PSP*, vol. 3, pp. 21–24.

DESCRIPTION

PPL, op. cit., "the building being 44' × 44', of 2 stories each floor divided into 2 rooms separated from each other by moveable glazed partitions."

HISTORY

Demolished date unk.

No. 89: May 31, 1854, S & S, *E*(Ud)

COMMISSION

Manayunk School, Manayunk, Pa., for the Controllers.

DOCUMENTATION

RCPS, Dec. 31, 1854, p. 9. *RCPS*, Dec. 31, 1855, p. 12. (2) *PPL*, vol. 37, no. 59, May 31, 1854.

DESCRIPTION

PPL, op. cit., "the building being 44' × 70', of 2 stories with 4 rooms on each floor separated by moveable glazed partitions."

HISTORY

Demolished date unk.

No. 90: July 4, 1854, S & S, *RE*(Ea)

COMMISSION

Baptist Church of West Chester (also known as First Baptist Church), 221 S. High St., West Chester, Pa., for the building committee of the congregation.

DOCUMENTATION

Addison Hutton, letter to his brother, dated "6/21/57," HP. (2) J. Smith Futley and Gilbert Cofe, *History of Chester County, Pennsylvania* (Philadelphia: Louis H. Everts & Co., 1881). (3) *West Chester Past and Present, Centennial Souvenir with Celebration Proceedings*, published by the *Daily Local News*, West Chester, Pa., 1899, pp. 117–118. (4) Classified printed manuscript files, heading "West Chester Churches—Baptist," Chester County Historical Society, West Chester, Pa.

NOTE: Documentation for this building was researched by Mr. Bart Anderson in the process of an HABS survey, 1959.

ILLUSTRATION

Lithograph, "Baptist Church," perspective of building in original form, Charlie C. Taylor delineator and publisher, W. H. Rease, litho. and printer, c. 1860. (2) Photograph, "West front and South side Baptist Church of West Chester," showing additions of 1886 (since removed), both (1) and (2) in the collection of the Chester County Historical Society, West Chester, Pa. (3) Photograph, west front in original form, *Centennial Souvenir*, op. cit., p. 117.

HISTORY

Cornerstone July 4, 1854; basement (c. 12' clear of ground level), containing a lecture room, completed and in use by Sept. 1857; addition to south side for baptistry, pulpit replaced and pews replaced with chairs (the Rev. Clarence Larken of Kennett Square, "architect"), 1886; pulpit removed to east end of sanctuary 1899; portico of four Doric columns added to west front, Sunday school wing (40' × 50') attached to east side and extensive interior remodeling (Ralph Minich and George E. Merrill, architects) 1930; portico and additions to south side removed before 1959; building extant almost in original form.

No. 91: Aug. 3, 1854, S & S, RS(Ea)

COMMISSION

"Hamilton Terrace," five suburban villas, Hamilton (41) St. between Baltimore Pike and Becket St. (Chester Ave.), West Philadelphia, Pa., for S. A. Harrison.

DOCUMENTATION

PPL, vol. 38, no. 113, Aug. 3, 1854; vol. 41, no. 110, July 30, 1856. (2) W-*PP*, p. 199.

ILLUSTRATION

Photostat, original, a large watercolor drawing, "Hamilton Terrace, W. P., built for S. A. Harrison," unsigned, PP-HSP.

DESCRIPTION

See Chapt. 6 (final paragraph) of this work.

HISTORY

In 1955 three of the buildings were still in use, much altered.

No. 92: Aug. 31, 1854, S & S, RE(D)

COMMISSION

Scotch Associate Presbyterian Church (later First United Presbyterian Church), southwest corner of Broad and Lombard Sts., Philadelphia, Pa., for the building committee of the congregation.

DOCUMENTATION

PPL, vol. 38, no. 137, Aug. 31, 1854; vol. 40, no. 118, Feb. 8, 1856. (2) *PCP*, pp. 242–243. (3) W. B. J. Edger, *Historical Sketch of the First United Presbyterian Church of Philadelphia* (Philadelphia, 1902), in the collection of the Presbyterian Historical Society, Philadelphia, Pa.

ILLUSTRATION

Photograph, undated, building in original condition, *PCP*, p. 242. (2) Photograph, undated, building in original condition, SRL, vol. 4, p. 41. (3) Photograph, building in ruinous condition, PC-HSP, box 17.

DESCRIPTION

PPL, op. cit., "dimensions 55′ × 78′, of brick covered with mastic, with white marble dressing."

HISTORY

Building accepted 1855; dedicated Feb. 10, 1856; demolished date unk.

No. 93: Dec. 31, 1854, S & S, E(D)

COMMISSION

James Pollock School, Fitzwater St. above 15th St. (also given as south side Fitzwater west of 15th), Philadelphia, Pa., for the Controllers.

DOCUMENTATION

RCPS, Dec. 31, 1854, p. 10. (2) *PPL*, vol. 39, no. 142, Sept. 6, 1855. (3) *RCPS*, Dec. 31, 1855, p. 9. (4) *CSP*, class 4, no. 4, pp. 103–110. (5) *PSP*, vol. 3, pp. 33–36.

ILLUSTRATION

Photograph, exterior, p. 33, and drawings, plans of first and second floors, p. 36, *PSP*, op. cit.

HISTORY

Contract let 1854; dedication Sept. 5, 1855; altered Sept. 29, 1868; building vacated c. 1916 and demolished thereafter date unk.

No. 94: Dec. 31, 1854, S & S, E(D)

COMMISSION

Henry Clay School, Lancaster St. between Wharton and Reed Sts. (also given as west side of Howard St. north of Reed St.), Philadelphia, Pa., for the Controllers.

DOCUMENTATION

RCPS, Dec. 31, 1854, p. 10. (2) *CSP*, class 4, no. 4, pp. 103–110. (3) *PSP*, vol. 3, pp. 13–15, building identical with James Pollock School.

ILLUSTRATION

Photograph, exterior, *PSP*, op. cit., p. 13.

HISTORY

Contract let 1854; accepted 1855; demolished date unk.

No. 95: 1854/1856, S & S, *RE*(E)

COMMISSION

Leigh Street Baptist Church, Leigh St. and 25th St. (also given as 517 N. 25th St.), Richmond, Va., commissioners unknown.

DOCUMENTATION

Mary Wingfield Scott, *Old Richmond Neighborhoods* (Richmond, Va., 1950), p. 44. (2) *Leigh Street Baptist Church* (Richmond, Va., 1954), p. 26. (3) William J. Murtagh, letter to the author, Mar. 9, 1960, referencing the building in the Historic American Building Inventory of the National Trust for Historic Preservation.

ILLUSTRATION

Photograph, exterior, *Leigh Street Baptist Church*, op. cit., fig. 33. (2) Photographs (1964, 1969) in the collection of the author.

HISTORY

Building extant, altered 1969.

No. 96: May 16, 1855, S & S, *C*(D)

COMMISSION

"Tower Hall," Clothing Store of Bennett & Co., 518 Market St. above 5th St., Philadelphia, Pa., for Joseph M. Bennett.

DOCUMENTATION

PPL, vol. 39, no. 46, May 16, 1855; vol. 41, no. 148, Sept. 27, 1856. (2) *S-CSA*, p. 58. (3) Poulson, vol. 3, p. 23. (4) *PE*, p. 6. (5) *Bennett's Illustrated Toilet of Fashion, Published At Tower Hall, 518 Market Street, Bet'wn 5 & 6, Philadelphia*, advertising pamphlet (n.d.), collection of HSP (wf81 B471). (6) Robert F. Looney, *Old Philadelphia in Early Photographs, 1839–1914* (New York: Dover Publications, 1976), pp. 78–79.

ILLUSTRATION

Lithograph, elevation, rendered in color, *S-CSA*, plate 56. (2) *BP*, panoramic drawing, elevations along Market St., 1856, collection of TLC. (3) Engraving, "View on Market Street," *PE*, p. 6. (4) Photograph, dated in ink 1890, PC-HSP, box 20. (5) Woodcut, cover illustration, *Bennett's Illustrated*, op. cit. (6) Photograph, facade, Looney, op. cit., p. 78.

DESCRIPTION

Bennett's Illustrated, op. cit., "The edifice is five stories in height, surmounted with a castelated tower, the most elevated point of which is 135 feet above the ground. It is 180 feet deep, with two fronts of 23 feet each on Market and Minor streets. The Market street front is entirely of granite, in the Norman style of architecture, with circular headed windows deeply recessed."

NOTE: This source describes the entire building in detail.

HISTORY

Commissioned May 1856; opened Sept. 1857; sold to Garitee & Son 1879; demolished after 1902.

No. 97: July 14, 1855, S & S, *RE*(U)

COMMISSION

Episcopal Church of Our Savior, 8th and Reed St., Philadelphia, Pa.

DOCUMENTATION

PPL, vol. 39, no. 96, July 14, 1855.

NOTE: No other documentation for this building has been found, although the *PPL* report gives it to the firm of Sloan & Stewart.

No. 98: Oct. 30, 1855 (also Oct. 16, 1855), S & S, *RE*(D)

COMMISSION

Protestant Episcopal Church of The Savior, Mary (38) St. between Oak (Ludlow) and Chestnut Sts., West Philadelphia, Pa., for the building committee.

DOCUMENTATION

Addison Hutton, letter to his brother, dated "6/21/57," HP. (2) *PPL*, vol. 11, no. 32, Oct. 30, 1855. (3) M. Lafitte Vieira, *West Philadelphia's Historic Churches and Burial Grounds* (Philadelphia: Avil Printing Co., 1903), pp. 54–58, CC-FLP, vol. 28, p. 72. (4) Cornerstone of existing building bearing three dates, 1855, 1861, and 1906.

ILLUSTRATION

Photograph, *Telegraph*, Philadelphia, Apr. 17, 1902, clipping, CC-HSP, vol. 17, "Churches," showing alterations made in 1861. (2) Photograph, "Old Church of The Savior," CC-FLP, vol. 28, p. 72. (3) Photograph, front and one flank, Vieira, op. cit., p. 54.

DESCRIPTION

PPL, op. cit., "in the Norman style."

HISTORY

Contract Oct. 16, 1855; cornerstone Nov. 24, 1855; dedicated Apr. 26, 1857; alterations 1861; enlarged Apr. 2–Nov. 17, 1889; burned Apr. 16, 1902; new building on same site extant.

NOTE: The commission was given in 1854 but construction was delayed until 1855. The "alterations" of 1860–61 were so extensive that little, if anything, remained of Sloan's building after they were completed.

No. 99: Nov. 7, 1855, S & S, *M*(E, 1976)

COMMISSION

Department for Males, Pennsylvania Hospital for the Insane, former estate of Paul Busti between West Chester and Haverford Rds. (later 111 N. 49th St.), West Philadelphia, Pa., for the board of managers of the Pennsylvania Hospital.

DOCUMENTATION

"Minutes of a Meeting of the Board of Managers of the Hospital for the Insane, March 3, 1856," ms., collection of the Pennsylvania Hospital. (2)

Proceedings at the Laying of the Cornerstone of the New Pennsylvania Hospital for the Insane, etc. (Philadelphia: T. K. and P. G. Collins, 1856), p. 5. (3) Addison Hutton, letter to his brother Finley, dated "Jul. 6, 1857," HP. (4) *PPL*, vol. 40, no. 39, Nov. 7, 1855; vol. 42, no. 10, Oct. 2, 1856; no. 116, Feb. 4, 1857; vol. 46, no: 132, Feb. 21, 1859; vol. 48, no. 29, Oct. 28, 1859. (5) K-*H*, 2nd ed., pp. 108–129. (6) Thomas G. Morton and Frank Woodbury, *The History of the Pennsylvania Hospital, 1751–1895* (Philadelphia: Times Printing House, 1895), pp. 173–175. (6) *ARABJ*, vol. 1, Apr. 1869, pp. 626–642. (7) W-*PP*, pp. 212, 309.

ILLUSTRATION

Photographs, exterior and interior, by F. Langenheim, *Annual Report (etc) 1858*, pp. 104, 120, 121. (2) Engraving, perspective, *Report (etc) 1859*, frontispiece, plan, p. 9. (3) Engravings, perspective and plans (identical with those of no. 2, above), *ARABJ*, op. cit., p. 626. (4) Photographs, exterior and interior, Morton and Woodbury, op. cit., pp. 176, 177. (5) Lithograph, perspective exterior, Francis R. Packard, *Some Account of the Pennsylvania Hospital* (Philadelphia: Engle Press, 1938), p. 120. (6) Photographs, two exterior, HABS, PA-1635.

DESCRIPTION

Original appearance, *The Stranger's Guide in Philadelphia* (Philadelphia: Lindsay & Blakiston, 1864), p. 139. (2) Morton and Woodbury, op. cit., describe the additions of 1870 and the rebuilding of 1885–86. (3) W-*PP* gives the enlargements of 1929 and 1931.

HISTORY

Department proposed 1853; erection approved 1854; commission Mar. 3, 1856; cornerstone July 7, 1856; patients received Oct. 27, 1859; alterations 1870, 1886; enlarged 1929, 1931; certified by PHC 1957; designated National Historical Landmark 1965; extant as Institute of the Pennsylvania Hospital, 1985.

No. 100: Apr. 21, 1856, S & S, *M*(D)

COMMISSION

Municipal Hospital for Contagious and Infectious Diseases, Lehigh Ave., between 20th and 21st Sts. (also given as 22nd St. and Lehigh Ave.), Philadelphia, Pa., for the Commissioners of the Board of Health of the City and County of Philadelphia.

DOCUMENTATION

Annual Report of the Board of Health of the City and County of Philadelphia, 1865 (Philadelphia, 1866). (2) *PPL*, vol. 41, no. 25, Apr. 21, 1856; vol. 50, no. 46, Nov. 16, 1860, "Proceedings in Council." (3) William W. Welch, "The Municipal Hospital for Contagious and Infectious Diseases," *FWMV*, pp. 526–528.

ILLUSTRATION

Photographs, two exterior, Welch, op. cit., pp. 526, 527.

DESCRIPTION

The only known description of Sloan's building is in Welch, op. cit.

HISTORY

The Board of Health adopted Sloan's plans for the replacement of the old hospital at Bush Hill in Apr. 1856; however, they were not "approved" until Nov. 24, 1862; building given over to the Board of Health Apr. 27, 1865; dedicated Apr. 28, 1865; facility moved to site in the 33rd Ward bounded by Hunting Park Ave., Luzerne St., Nicetown Lane, and Second St. shortly after 1909.

No. 101: July 31, 1856, S & S, RS(D)

COMMISSION

Town mansion, northeast corner 18th and Locust Sts. (later 221 S. 18th St.), Rittenhouse Square, Philadelphia, Pa., for Joseph Harrison Jr.

DOCUMENTATION

PPL, vol. 41, no. 111, July 31, 1865; vol. 44, no. 70, Dec. 10, 1857. (2) *S-CSA*, design XXIV, "A Suburban Mansion," pp. 84–89. (3) *Estate of Joseph Harrison, Jr., Case N. 271, January Term, 1883* (Philadelphia: Collins, 1883), collection of TLC. (4) *PE*, p. 87. (5) Charles J. Cohen, *Rittenhouse Square Past and Present* (Philadelphia, 1922), pp. 258–262. (7) Tatum, p. 36. (8) Robert F. Looney, *Old Philadelphia in Early Photographs, 1839–1914* (New York: Dover Publications, 1976), p. 152.

ILLUSTRATION

Lithographs and line drawings, elevations, sections, and plans, *S-CSA*, plates 107–118, pp. 84–89. (2) Lithograph, "Residence of Joseph Harrison, Esq. Rittenhouse Square, Phila.," perspective, in color, John Frampton delin., L(ouis) N(apoleon) Rosenthal, 10″ × 12″ (smaller ed. 8″ × 12″), 1859, collection of FLP. (3) Photograph, front elevation, n.d., PC-HSP, box 18. (4) Photograph, "Joseph Harrison Residence," Looney, op. cit., plate 148, p. 152.

DESCRIPTION

S-CSA, op. cit., architect's description. (2) *PPL*, July 31, 1856, the fullest reportorial description. (3) Cohen, op. cit., description of building in later years.

HISTORY

Harrison seems to have discussed the project with Sloan as early as 1852 or 1853; however, construction did not begin until 1855, and the family did not occupy the house until 1857 or 1858. Harrison died on Mar. 27, 1874, but the property remained intact until 1925, when the building was demolished and replaced by the Penn Athletic Club (now the Signal Corps Building).

No. 102: July 31, 1856, S & S, *RE*(D)

COMMISSION

"Harrison's Row," ten row houses, Locust St., entire block from 17th to 18th Sts., Philadelphia, Pa., for Joseph Harrison Jr.

DOCUMENTATION

PPL, vol. 41, no. 111, July 31, 1856; vol. 44, no. 70, Dec. 10, 1857. (2) Cohen, *Rittenhouse Square* (Phila., 1922), pp. 258–262. (3) Tatum, p. 36.

ILLUSTRATION

Photograph, showing common garden and rear elevation, SRL, vol. 8, p. 17. (2) Photograph, front elevation, Tatum, op. cit., p. 95.

DESCRIPTION

PPL, July 31, 1856, "each dwelling 25' × 60', in New York style of plan and Itallian style elevations." (2) Tatum, op. cit., describes the common facilities.

HISTORY

Demolished date unk.

No. 103: Dec. 9, 1856, S & S, *C*(U)

COMMISSION

Commercial building, Walnut St., below 3rd St., Philadelphia, Pa., for John Grigg.

DOCUMENTATION

PPL, vol. 41, no. 68, Dec. 9, 1856.

NOTE: No other documentation for this building has been found, and this notice contained no description; therefore, it may be the announcement of a project that was never erected.

No. 104: Dec. 11, 1856, S & S, *C*(D)

COMMISSION

"Washington Building," Office Building, 3rd St. above Spruce St., on the site of "Washington Hall" (also called "Old Masonic Hall"), Philadelphia, Pa., for Joseph Harrison Jr.

DOCUMENTATION

PPL, vol. 42, no. 70, Dec. 11, 1856; vol. 44, no. 39, Nov. 4, 1857. (2) *ARABJ*, vol. 1, Mar. 1869, p. 573. (3) John McAllister Scrapbooks, HSP, vol. 5, p. 79, newspaper clipping, *Ledger & Transcript*, Philadelphia, Nov. 4, 1857, "The Washington Building."

DESCRIPTION

PPL, Nov. 4, 1857, "building is 50' × 118', of four stories, with a hall 50' × 34' on the second floor and restaurant in the basement, offices above, at the rear an arcade with glass roof, street front of brick 'sanded to look like stone' with cornices and door surrounds in Pictou stone, the style is Itallian."

There may be a representation of the front elevation in *BP*, 1857, but the identification is not certain.

HISTORY
Harrison purchased "Washington Hall" in May 1856; the old building had been demolished and Sloan & Stewart's building erected by Nov. 4, 1857; the "Washington Building" was demolished date unk.

No. 105: May 12, 1857, S & S, *P*(Ea)

COMMISSION
Jail (later County Prison), Market St., New Castle, Del., for the committee appointed by the Levy Court of New Castle County.

DOCUMENTATION
Delaware Gazette, Wilmington, May 12, 1857, p. 1, "New Castle County Jail"; May 29, 1857, p. 4, "The New Jail." (2) Dedication tablet, east wall, County Prison, New Castle, Del., "BUILT, A.D. 1857, Architect, Samuel Sloan" (this tablet was still in place in June 1960). (3) J. Thomas Sharf, *History of Delaware* (Wilmington, n.d.), vol. 2, p. 1038.

ILLUSTRATION
Photograph, elevation, in the collection of the writer. (2) Photographs, collection of the Historical Society of Delaware.

DESCRIPTION
Delaware Gazette, op. cit., "They [the committee] propose to adopt a plan somewhat similar to the jail of Montgomery County at Norristown, Pa., and have engaged S. D. Sloan, Esq., an architect well known to our people, to furnish a design."

NOTE: Sloan's middle initial is given as *D*.

HISTORY
The site was that of the "old jail"; Sloan went to New Castle to see the site on May 11, 1857, and he delivered the plans and specifications on June 2, 1857; the building served as the county prison until the early 1880s; the State of Delaware now leases the building to the city for use as a police station; extant.

No. 106: June 21, 1857, S & S, *RE*(D)

COMMISSION
First Presbyterian Church, 418 E. Girard Ave., Philadelphia, Pa., for the building committee of the church.

DOCUMENTATION
Addison Hutton, letter dated "6/21/57," HP. (2) Ernest M. Fiend, *A History of the First Presbyterian Church of Kensington in Philadelphia*, pamphlet (n.p., n.d.), pp. 10–11, collection of HSP. (3) "A Sermon Preached at the Dedica-

tion of the New House of Worship . . . of the Congregation in Kensington," May 22, 1859, pamphlet (Philadelphia: Henry B. Ashmead, 1859), collection of HSP. (4) John Matlack, son of the builder of the church, a series of articles in the *Philadelphia Herald*, 1908 (no other identification), clippings in the collection of HSP.

ILLUSTRATION

Photograph, interior, Ernest M. Fiend, op. cit., p. 5. (2) Possible photograph, elevation, *PCP*, p. 43.

HISTORY

Cornerstone Aug. 31, 1857; dedication May 22, 1859; cost $24,000; entirely rebuilt 1893.

NOTE: W-*PP*, p. 315, "in Kensington Samuel Sloan supplied the plans for the First Presbyterian Church (1857–59), which initially had a high steeple where the incongruous ogee dome now rests" (1976). If this is the case, then only the steeple was removed in 1893, and the photograph on p. 43 of *PCP* is of the Sloan building.

No. 107: Apr. 3, 1857, S & S, *RE*(D)

COMMISSION

First Presbyterian Church, German St., below 3rd St., Southwark, Philadelphia, Pa., for the building committee of the church.

DOCUMENTATION

PPL, vol. 42, no. 10, Apr. 3, 1857; vol. 46, no. 37, Nov. 2, 1857; vol. 48, no. 15, Oct. 12, 1859. (2) *PCP*, p. 14. (3) *Minutes of the General Assembly of the Presbyterian Church*, n.s., vol. 14 (Philadelphia, 1891), p. 572.

ILLUSTRATION

Lithograph, in color, "First Presbyterian Church, Southwark, Phila.," J. F. Watson, printer, c. 1858, 11⅞″ × 8½″, collection of HSP.

DESCRIPTION

PPL, op. cit., Apr. 3, 1857, "building 60′ × 97½′, cupola 65′, towers at corners of front elevation 25′ above roof line." (2) Nicholas B. Wainright, *Philadelphia in the Romantic Age of Lithography* (Philadelphia: Historical Society of Pennsylvania, 1958), p. 135, item 131.

HISTORY

Cornerstone Apr. 2, 1857; measures taken to complete the church Oct. 12, 1859; congregation removed to 755 S. 2nd St. (date unk.) and then to 735 Passyunk Rd. (date unk.); building demolished date unk.

No. 108: June 21, 1857, S & S, *RE*(Ea)

COMMISSION

Emmanuel Episcopal Church, Frankford Ave. and Hickory St. (later 8118 Frankford Ave.), Holmsburg, Pa., for the building committee of the vestry.

Addison Hutton, letter dated "6/21/57," HP. (2) *50th Anniversary of Emmanuel Church, Holmsburg, Pennsylvania,* pamphlet (1894), in the possession (1963) of the Rev. Tage Teisen, Bethesda-by-the-Sea, Palm Beach, Fla. (3) CC-HSP, vol. 16, "Churches," newspaper clipping, n.p., dated "9/25/1857," reports cornerstone laying. (4) H-*BP*, pp. 145–146.

ILLUSTRATION
Print, in color, perspective of building, in the vestry of the present building. (2) Photograph; front, H-*BP*, opp. p. 145. (3) Photograph, dated "1911," front elevation, CC-HSP, vol. 16, "Churches." (4) Photographs, present building, collection of the author.

HISTORY
Cornerstone Sept. 21, 1857; first service held July 4, 1858; original chancel demolished and larger rebuilt 1899; church extant (1959), altered.

NOTE: Joseph Harrison was a member of the building committee.

No. 109: June 21, 1857, S & S, *RE*(E, 1959)

COMMISSION
Protestant Episcopal Church of St. James the Greater, Cedar and Walnut Sts., Bristol, Pa., for the building committee of the vestry.

DOCUMENTATION
Addison Hutton, letter dated "6/21/57," HP. (2) *50th Anniversary of Emmanuel Church, Holmsburg, Pennsylvania,* pamphlet (1894), "The Vestry asked Samuel Sloan, an architect, to prepare designs for the Church similar to the design of the Church in Bristol (Pa.) with agreed upon alterations." (2) The Rev. Tage Teisen, Rector, Bethesda-by-the-Sea, Palm Beach, Fla., letters to the author, 1957–59.

NOTE: This church, Emmanuel Church, Holmsburg, and "a church" in Frankford, Pa. (probably St. Mark's Protestant Episcopal Church, demolished c. 1910–11) are all referred to in the Hutton letter of June 21, 1857, as "in progress." Documentation for St. James' and St. Mark's is otherwise lacking. All three churches are on the old Bristol Turnpike and located within a short distance of each other. The vestry of Emmanuel seems to have used the architect of St. James as well as its design.

No. 110: June 21, 1857, S & S, *E*(Ea)

COMMISSION
Upland Normal School (later Crozer Theological Seminary, Pennsylvania Military Academy, and "Old Main" of Crozer-Chester Medical Center), northwest of Chester in the borough of Upland, Chester, Pa., for John P. Crozer.

DOCUMENTATION

Addison Hutton, letter to "Mollie" dated "6th mos. 21st., 1857," HP. (2) George Smith, *History of Delaware County, Pennsylvania* (Philadelphia: Henry B. Ashmead, 1862), p. 380. (3) "Crozer Theological Seminary," *History of Delaware County, Pennsylvania*, ed. Henry Graham Ashmead (Philadelphia: L. H. Everts & Co., 1884), pp. 433–434. (4) "Tracing Crozer-Chester Medical Center's History/Part 1, 1802–1897," *Close-up*, published by Crozer-Chester Medical Center, Autumn 1977, pp. 16–21.

NOTE: The author is indebted to Richard I. Ortega of Media, Pa., for bringing this building to his attention and researching most of the documentation. Mr. Ortega also provided the measured drawings of the building prepared by Edward T. Hinderliter, AIA, and John M. Dickey, AIA, Media, Pa., 1976.

ILLUSTRATION

Photograph, c. 1865, floor plan and view of temporary wards of USA General Hospital at Chester, 1862–65, and exterior of 1st floor of Crozer Building, "Tracing Crozer-Chester Medical Center etc.," op. cit., p. 18. (2) Photographs, color, extant building, collection of the writer, gift of Richard I. Ortega.

DESCRIPTION

History of Delaware County etc., ed. Ashmead, op. cit., p. 434.

HISTORY

Commissioned c. Spring 1857; opened Fall 1858; classes suspended Winter 1861; converted to emergency government hospital by John J. McArthur Jr. which opened June 18, 1862; temporary medical buildings torn down Aug. 1865 and property returned to Crozer; leased by Pennsylvania Military Academy Dec. 1865; dedicated as Baptist Theological Seminary Oct. 2, 1868; additions 1871–1950; extant, much altered internally, as "Old Main" of Crozer-Chester Medical Center.

No. 111: Autumn 1857–Winter 1858, S, *RE*(E)

COMMISSION

"Longwood," Oriental villa, Natchez, Miss., for Dr. Haller Nutt.

NOTE: The documentation, illustration, and history of this building are to be found on pp. 67–71 and notes 12–17 of Chapter 7, of this study. So many photographs, lithographs, and line drawings of "Longwood" have been published (and republished) that a listing of them would be excessive and confusing. The best illustrations of the building, as conceived, are the original design plans, now hanging in the building itself, and its presentation in Sloan's *The Model Architect*, while the best photographs of the building in its present condition are those in the collection of the Natchez Garden Club. The television-film of "Longwood," prepared for educational television, documents the building as it now is.

No. 112: Nov. 14, 1857, S & S, *RE*(Ud)

COMMISSION

Tabor Mission Sabbath School and Chapel, 17th and Fitzwater Sts., Philadelphia, Pa., for the Calvary Presbyterian Church.

DOCUMENTATION

PPL, vol. 44, no. 48, Nov. 14, and no. 68, Dec. 8, 1857. (2) *First Report of the Missionary Association of the Calvary Presbyterian Church* (Philadelphia: Henry B. Ashmead, 1858), pp. 12, 20. (3) *PCP*, pp. 33, 126–127.

ILLUSTRATION

Wood engraving, perspective, *First Report etc.*, op. cit., cover.

DESCRIPTION

PPL, Dec. 8, 1857, "of 2 stories, in brick, Itallian style with round-headed windows and brick pilasters, building 70' deep."

HISTORY

Sloan was a member of the church and of the Missionary Association; plans were a gift from the firm of Sloan & Stewart; site selected Apr. 1857; construction almost completed Nov. 1857; first services Spring 1858; building sold to become First African Presbyterian Church 1891; subsequent history unknown; demolished date unk.

No. 113: Dec. 8, 1857, S & S, *M* and *E*(Ea)

COMMISSION

Pennsylvania Training-School for Feeble-Minded Children, Elwyn, Middletown Township, Delaware County, Pa., for the State of Pennsylvania.

DOCUMENTATION

Proceedings at the Opening of the Pennsylvania Training School (Philadelphia: Henry B. Ashmead, 1859), collection of HSP. (2) *Fifth, Twenty-third, Thirty-Sixth, and Forty-Fourth Report(s) of the Board of Directors of the Pennsylvania Training School for Feeble-Minded Children* (Philadelphia: Henry B. Ashmead, 1858, 1875, 1888, 1896). (All the report(s) from the first through the fiftieth are in the collection of HSP.) (3) *PPL*, vol. 44, no. 68, Dec. 8, 1857, no. 140, Mar. 3, 1858; vol. 46, no. 123, Feb. 10, 1859; vol. 47, no. 48, May 20; no. 49, May 21, 1859; vol. 48, no. 27, Oct. 26; no. 34, Nov. 3, 1859; vol. 50, no. 122, Feb. 14, 1861.

ILLUSTRATION

Wood engraving, perspective, *Fifth Annual Report etc.*, 1858, op. cit., frontispiece. (*Note*: This perspective continues to be used until the [2] *Twenty-Third Annual Report*, 1875, when a different engraved view, signed, F. [or L.] B. Schell and printed by "JAHINGEN.SNYDER SC" is substituted for the frontispiece.) (3) Photographs, five views, "Department of Training School," plate 1, and one view, "The Main Building," plate 3, *Forty-Fourth Annual Report*, 1896. (4) Photograph, front elevation, "Department of the Training

School: Main Building," *Fiftieth Annual Report*, 1902, n.p. (5) Engraving, perspective, dated 1878, CC-FLP, vol. 27A, p. 6.

HISTORY

Site selected 1857; commission Dec. 1857; construction begun 1858; main building and one wing completed by Sept. 1859; official opening Nov. 3, 1859; second wing added before 1875; cupola removed before 1896; ten additional buildings were added to the complex between 1877 and 1892, eight more between 1899 and 1931; building extant, restored.

No. 114: Apr. 18, 1859, S, *RE*(E)

COMMISSION

First Baptist Church (second building), Front St., Wilmington, N.C., for the building committee of the church.

DOCUMENTATION

"Minutes of the Building Committee, First Baptist Church, Wilmington, April 1859," ms., collection of the church. (2) Marcus Kester, *Historical Sketch of the First Baptist Church, Wilmington, N.C., 1808–1933*, 125th anniversary edition, April 12, 13, 1933 (n.p.), p. 21. (3) "Historical Notes," *First Baptist, One of the Great and Historic Churches of Wilmington, N.C., 1852–1871* (Wilmington, N.C.: Wilmington Printing Co., 1952), n.p.

ILLUSTRATION

Photographs, collection of the church and the New Hanover County Historical Society.

DESCRIPTION

Kester, op. cit., "On April 18, 1859, the building committee recommended that a Mr. Sloan of Philadelphia be the architect and that the church be modeled after the Fredericksburg church. The model finally decided on was Early English Gothic, with two towers, a high tower and a lower one." (2) "Historical Notes," op. cit., "1859—Voted to build a church that would seat 600 downstairs, 200 in the gallery, have four aisles. Style, Early English Gothic with two towers, a high and low one. Estimated cost, $20,592."

HISTORY

Commission c. Apr. 1859; ground broken last of April or first of May 1860; construction under way May 7, 1859; construction halted 1862; construction resumed 1869; dedication May 1, 1870; building extant (1974).

No. 115: Summer 1859, S, *RE*(D)

COMMISSION

The First Presbyterian Church (second building), Third and Orange Sts., Wilmington, N.C., for the officers of the congregation.

DOCUMENTATION

Finley Hutton, "Memoir," HP. (2) *Memorial of the First Presbyterian Church, Wilmington, N.C.* (Richmond, Va.: Whittet and Shepperson, 1893), p. 16.

(3) Andrew J. Howell, *A History of the First Presbyterian Church, Wilmington, North Carolina* (Wilmington, N.C., 1951), pp. 3ff.

ILLUSTRATION

Lithograph, "Old First Presbyterian Church," *Memorial etc.*, op. cit., p. 16.

HISTORY

Commission c. Summer 1859; dedication Apr. 28, 1861; burned Dec. 31, 1925; present building designed by Hobart Upjohn.

NOTE: From Nov. 1, 1874, to Apr. 1, 1885, the pastor was Joseph R. Wilson, father of Thomas Woodrow Wilson.

No. 116: June 9, 1859, S, Competition

COMPETITION

The Sheppard Asylum (later Sheppard and Enoch Pratt Hospital), Towson, Md.

RESULTS

ICIUSC, p. 560, "The prizes for the plans were awarded in the following order; to Thomas and James Dixon, of Baltimore, to Samuel Sloan, of Philadelphia, and to Richard Upjohn and Co. of New York, in conjunction with D. D. Tilden Brown, medical superintendent of Bloomingdale Asylum. While the third prize was awarded to plans made under the advice of Dr. Brown, as will be subsequently seen, these formed the nucleus of the plans which, developed by Mr. Clavert Vaux, a well-known Architect of New York, were finally adopted."

No. 117: Jan. 1860, S.M(Ea)

COMMISSION

Hospital of the Protestant Episcopal Church in Philadelphia, southeast corner Lehigh Ave. and Front St., Philadelphia, Pa., for the Hospital Committee of the Diocese.

DOCUMENTATION

"Report of the Building Committee for January 1860," quoted by Israel W. Morris, *FWMV*, pp. 632–647. (2) *PPL*, vol. 40, no. 15, Apr. 11; no. 53, May 25, 1860; vol. 50, no. 20, Oct. 17, 1861; vol. 52, no. 15, Oct. 19, 1861; vol. 52, no. 92, Jan. 8, 1862. (3) *The Hospital of the Protestant Episcopal Church in Philadelphia: Its Origin, Progress, Work, and Want* (Philadelphia: J. B. Lippincott & Co., 1870), chap. 11, p. 16; chap. 3, p. 26. (4) *ARABJ*, vol. 2, Mar. 1870, pp. 514–523. (5) Joseph Jones, *Hospital Construction and Organization* (Baltimore, 1875), Introduction (a letter to the Committee on Construction for the Johns Hopkins Hospital). (6) W. Gill Wylie, *Hospitals: Their History, Organization, and Construction* (New York: D. Appleton & Co., 1877), p. 211. (7) Israel W. Morris, "The Hospital of the Protestant Episcopal Church in Philadelphia," *FWMV*, pp. 632–647. (8) *W-PP*, p. 328.

ILLUSTRATION

Engravings and photographs, all of the sources given under "Documenta-tion." (2) Photographs, 1955–60, collection of the author.

DESCRIPTION

ARABJ, op. cit., complete description by architect. (2) Morris, op. cit., de-scription of changes and alterations to 1909. (3) W-*PP*, op. cit., as of 1976.

HISTORY

Hospital first proposed May 3, 1851; commission Jan. 1860; chapel and one wing completed May 24, 1862; work suspended Spring 1862; work re-sumed Mar. 1869; building completed 1874; additions and alterations 1889, 1892, 1933, 1964; building extant, altered.

No. 118: Apr. 13, 1860, S, C(D)

COMMISSION

Farmer's Market, Market St. between 11th and 12th Sts., Philadelphia, Pa., for Farmer's Market Co.

DOCUMENTATION

PPL, vol. 49, no. 8, Apr. 13; no. 40, May 10; no. 117, Aug. 9, 1860. (2) *ARABJ*, vol. 2, Apr. 1870, p. 581. (3) "Reading Terminal Market Is Lar-gest," clipping, identified *Philadelphia Inquirer*, Nov. 18, 1935, Scrapbook of William Ives Rutter, collection HSP (We 282).

ILLUSTRATION

Photograph, dated 1860, PC-HSP, box 20. (2) Lithograph, and drawing, perspective and plan, *ARABJ*, vol. 2, Apr. 1870, pp. 592–593. (3) Photo-graph, "Market Street, East From 12th, c. 1880," Looney, *Old Philadelphia in Early Photographs, 1839–1914* (New York: Dover Publications, 1976), plate 88, p. 92, original in collection of FLP.

DESCRIPTION

PPL, op. cit., Apr. 13, 1860, "In mixed Itallian style, with marble base and brick above, arched doors and windows. 'Most of the roof, which will be supported by solid truss rafters, will be of glass.'"

HISTORY

Construction begun Apr. 1860; completed Aug. 1860; purchased by the Reading Rail Road Co. 1890; torn down and replaced by Reading Terminal and Market, which opened Feb. 1892.

No. 119: Apr. 26, 1860, S, P(D)

COMMISSION

Courthouse for Lycoming County, Lots 177–180 of the original plot of the city, bounded on the south by W. 3rd St. and on the west by Pine St. (later 3rd and Mulberry St.), Williamsport, Pa., for the Commissioners of Lycom-ing County.

DOCUMENTATION

The Commissioners' minutes prior to 1889 were destroyed in the flood of that year. The only contemporary documentation is the stone tablet removed from the southwest wall of Sloan's building and remounted in the courtyard of the new (1970) courthouse, with the inscription:

1860

Michael Sypher
Thomas Lloyd   Commissioners
Samuel Harris
                      Samuel Sloan, Architect
                      D. S. Rissell, Builder

(2) *History of Lycoming County, Pennsylvania* (Philadelphia: D. J. Stewart, 1876), pp. 42–44. (3) *History of Lycoming County, Pennsylvania*, ed. John F. Meginness (Chicago: Brown, Runk & Co., 1892), pp. 271–273. (4) *Evening News*, Williamsport, Pa., Nov. 20, 1903, p. 3. (5) Anne Lynn Cheyney, "Jacqueline's Letters to the Home Folks," *Williamsport Sun-Gazette*, vol. 2, Dec. 13, 1930. (6) "Lycoming County, the Largest County in the Commonwealth of Pennsylvania," *Commonwealth: The Magazine for Pennsylvania*, vol. 6, no. 6, Nov.–Dec., 1852, pp. 2–3. (7) Mark Peter Marer and Ruth Rosenberg, *A Picture of Lycoming County* (Naparsteck, 1978), vol. 12, pp. 185–186.

NOTE: The author is indebted to Mr. and Mrs. Emerson J. Probst, of Montoursville, and Mr. Samuel J. Dornsife and Miss Rebecca Huss, of Williamsport, for the majority of this documentation.

ILLUSTRATION

Lithograph, frontispiece, *History etc.* (D. J. Stewart), op. cit. (2) Photograph, in color, cover picture, *Lycoming County: Its History and Government*, pamphlet (n.p., n.d.). (3) Photograph, postcard, "Lycoming County Court House," Vannucci Fotos of Williamsport, Pa. (4) Photograph, *Dedication, May 1971, Lycoming County Courthouse*, program (n.p., n.d.), p. 4. (5) Photographs in the collection of Samuel J. Dornsife and the author, and supplied to the author by Mr. Emerson J. Probst Jr. of Towson, Md.

DESCRIPTION

Sloan building, "116' 11" × 60'; first story floor-to-floor height 12' 6", which contained all the county offices and a chamber for the presiding judge; second story contained main courtroom and jury room; third story contained jury rooms, rooms for the meetings of the institutes and storage; Cost $41,030," *History etc.* (D. J. Stewart), op. cit.

HISTORY

Commissioned Apr. 26, 1860; construction begun Spring 1860; occupied Mar. 1861; alterations 1895, 1903, 1920, 1933; demolished May 1969.

No. 120: Spring 1860, S, *RS*(D)

COMMISSION

Private dwelling (later known as Elliot Place), southeast corner of W. 4th and Elmira St., Williamsport, Pa., for William H. Armstrong.

DOCUMENTATION

History of Lycoming County, Pennsylvania, ed. John F. Meginness (Chicago: Brown, Runk & Co., 1892), p. 820. (2) John F. Meninness, *Resources and Industries of the City of Williamsport and Lycoming County*, by order of the Board of Trade (1886). (3) Samuel J. Dornsife, letters to the author, 1981, recording personal knowledge of the building and its later owners.

ILLUSTRATION

Engraving, "Residence of W. G. Elliot, West Fourth Street," ed. Meginness, op. cit. (2) Photograph, n.d., James V. Brown Library, Williamsport, Pa. (3) Photographs, collection of Samuel J. Dornsife, Williamsport, Pa.

HISTORY

Commission Spring 1860; sold to William G. Elliot 1884; at Elliot's death sold to Congregational Church; sold "about the end of World War One" (Dornsife) to the YMCA, which demolished the building and used the site for the erection of their new building.

No. 121: May 22, 1860, S, *RS*(E)

COMMISSION

Country villa, known as "Delta Place," at the juncture of Buffalo Creek and the Susquehanna River, Lewisburg, Pa., for the Hon. Eli Slifer, Secretary of State of the Commonwealth.

DOCUMENTATION

Samuel Sloan, letter and "Estimate of Items" for building, to Eli Slifer, n.d., Slifer Papers, Dickinson College Library, Carlisle, Pa. (2) *PPL*, vol. 49, no. 50; May 22, 1860, p. 3, "Architecture of the Country." (3) *Union County Star and Lewisburg Chronicle*, whole no. 842, June 1, 1860, p. 1. (4) *S-HA*, 1st ed., 1861, pp. 249–50. (5) *Godey's Lady's Book*, vol. 65, Dec. 1862, p. 615. (6) *ARABJ*, vol. 1, Mar. 1869, pp. 555–557. (7) *Delta Place, 1769–1976* (Mifflinburg, Pa.: Mifflinburg Telegraph, 1976), p. 7.

ILLUSTRATION

Engraving, *S-HA*, op. cit., p. 249. (2) Engraving, *ARABJ*, op. cit., p. 454. (3) Photographs, prints, and engravings, collection of Slifer House Museum, Lewisburg United Methodist Homes, Lewisburg, Pa. (4) Photographs, collection of the author.

HISTORY

Site, "Delta Place," purchased c. 1850; commission c. Spring 1860; occupied Autumn 1861; sold, purchaser unk., 1907; sold, Evangelical Association, for use as a hospital 1915–53; restoration begun 1975 by Slifer House Restoration Committee (building then on grounds of Lewisburg United

Methodist Homes); entered on National Register of Historic Places June 18, 1975; opened as historic house museum July 24, 1976.

NOTE: The documentation and restoration of this building was largely the work of Mrs. David L. Reed, wife of the administrator of the Lewisburg United Methodist Homes, to whom the author is greatly indebted.

No. 122: June 12, 1860, S, RE(D)

COMMISSION
First Baptist Church, Chestnut and Margaretta (36) Sts., West Philadelphia, Pa., for the building committee of the church.

DOCUMENTATION
PPL, vol. 47, no. 147, Mar. 15, 1860; vol. 49, no. 66, June 12, 1860; vol. 50, no. 37, Nov. 6, 1860. (2) CC-HSP, vol. 15, "Churches," newspaper clipping, n.p., dated in ink "11/22/61," and clipping, n.p., dated in ink "3/6/63."

ILLUSTRATION
Lithograph, in color, "First Baptist Church, West Philadelphia, Pa.," Duval, Williams & Duval, Philadelphia, 1860, 18" × 22½", signed "Samuel Sloan," copies in the collections of HSP and the author. (2) Wood engraving, CC-HSP, op. cit., perspective of building from southeast.

DESCRIPTION
PPL, op. cit., Nov. 6, 1860. (2) CC-HSP, op. cit., full description.

HISTORY
Property purchased c. Mar. 1860; commission c. Nov. 6, 1860; church occupied c. Autumn 1863; demolished date unk.

No. 123: Aug. 30, 1860, S, P (Competition, unexecuted)

COMMISSION
Competition for the New Public Buildings, Central Square (also Penn Square), Philadelphia, Pa., for the City of Philadelphia.

DOCUMENTATION
Letter, Samuel Sloan to Committee on New City Buildings, Aug. 30, 1860, Common Council Documents, New City Buildings, 1860 (Philadelphia: King & Baird, 1860), vol. 3, p. 20. (2) PPL, vol. 46, no. 123, Feb. 10, 1859; vol 49, no. 139, Sept. 4; no. 142, Sept. 7, 1860; vol. 50, no. 3, Sept. 27; no. 4, Sept. 28; no. 6, Oct. 1; no. 24, Oct. 22; no. 46, Nov. 16, 1860; vol. 50, no. 149, Mar. 18, 1861. (3) S&W, vol. 1, p. 735. (4) Jackson, vol. 2, p. 466. (5) John Mass, communications to the author reporting his researches in the City Archives of Philadelphia.

ILLUSTRATION
None known to the author. A description of Sloan's entry in PPL, vol. 49, no. 139, Sept. 4, 1860, gives: "The front elevations of the plans of Mr. Sloan are very elaborate and appear to partake more of the Byzantine style. As in the plan of Mr. McArthur, there is a centre building with columns and

wings, less ornamented. There is a steeple on the municipal building as in the other noticed."

HISTORY

Ordinance to provide New Public Buildings presented to Select Council Feb. 10, 1859; competition advertised Aug. 1860; plans received Sept. 1, 1860 (only three Philadelphia architects submitting: Sloan, McArthur, and George S. Bethel); McArthur's plan unanimously selected by the Committee on Public Buildings Sept. 6, 1860; Sloan received second prize (the competition was for two separate buildings to be located at the intersection of Broad and Market St. [Central Square or Penn Square]); arguments in Councils as to the site, the award, and the contract for erection Sept. 25– Oct. 22; resolution to elect a "City Architect" for supervision of all buildings passes City Council Oct. 1, 1860; action on the New Public Building tabled Nov. 16, 1860.

No. 124: Oct. 5, 1861, S, RE(E)

COMMISSION

"Woodland Terrace," twenty-two attached suburban dwellings, on both sides of the street between Woodland and Baltimore Ave., West Philadelphia, for Charles M. S. Leslie.

DOCUMENTATION

PPL, vol. 52, no. 12, Oct. 5, 1861, p. 2, col. 2, "Improvements in West Philadelphia." (2) Edward Teitelman and Richard W. Longstreth, *Architecture in Philadelphia: A Guide* (Cambridge, Mass.: MIT Press, 1974), p. 199. (3) W-*PP*, pp. 199, 218. (4) Roger Miller and Joseph Siry, "The Emerging Suburb: West Philadelphia, 1850–1880," *Pennsylvania History*, Apr. 1980, pp. 112ff.

ILLUSTRATION

Photographs, eight exterior (1973), National Register of Historic Places. (2) Photograph, CC-FLP, vol. 4.

HISTORY

Project initiated 1857 by Leslie, who began to buy property; commission 1861 before Oct. 5, when announcement in *PPL* first made; certified by Philadelphia Historical Commission 1963; Pennsylvania Register 1971; National Register 1973; extant in part, restored or adapted.

No. 125: 1861, S, RS(U)

COMMISSION

Private dwelling, "the head" of Norwood Ave., Chestnut Hill, Pa., for Charles Taylor.

DOCUMENTATION

H-*AM*, p. 452.

NOTE: This documentation was given to the author by James C. Massey, to whom he is indebted. It is the only report of the building yet found.

ILLUSTRATION

Wood engraving, "Residence of Colonel George H. North, Norwood Avenue," H-*AM*, p. 454.

HISTORY

Commissioned by Charles Taylor 1861; sold "in the fall of that year" to Horace Brown; sold date unk. to Dr. Bolling; sold to Col. North 1883; further history unk.

No. 126: 1862, S, *RE*(E, 1976)

COMMISSION

North Broad Street Presbyterian Church, northeast corner of Broad and Green Sts., Philadelphia, Pa., for the building committee of the church.

DOCUMENTATION

PPL, vol. 54, no. 66, Dec. 6, front page, col. 1; no. 67, Dec. 8, front page, col. 5; no. 69, Dec. 10, front page, col. 3. (2) Westcott, p. 280.

ILLUSTRATION

Wood engraving, perspective, Westcott, p. 279.

DESCRIPTION

Westcott, "Building of brownstone, in the Norman-Gothic style, 70 feet front on Broad Street, 115 feet deep. Steeple, 222 feet in height."

HISTORY

Commission c. Apr. 1862; cornerstone June 9, 1862; dedicated 1863; occupied 1875 (Westcott, p. 280); listed as extant 1976, W-*PP*, p. 375, n. 52.

No. 127: 1863, S or S & H, *RE*(E)

COMMISSION

Great Island Presbyterian Church, W. Water St., Lock Haven, Pa., for the Construction Committee, C. A. Mayer (chairman).

DOCUMENTATION

Historic Lock Haven: An Architectural Survey, ed. Dean R. Wagner (Lock Haven, Pa.: Clinton County Historical Society, 1979), p. 70.

ILLUSTRATION

Three photographs (1979 and before), *Historic Lock Haven*, op. cit., p. 70.

DESCRIPTION

NOTE: From *Historic Lock Haven*, op. cit., p. 70, "The walnut cabinet work was put up and partly constructed by N. J. Sloan and Bro. The ill-fated tower was 145 feet high. The roof of the original tower of this church was pierced with sharp gables and the cornice was decorated with an arcaded corbel table."

HISTORY

Commissioned, "early part of" 1863; chapel (sanctuary) complete July 1865; entire building completed 1872; steeple removed 1950; building extant, altered.

No. *128*: Feb. 23, 1864, S & H, *RE*(Ud)

COMMISSION

Enlargement, St. Mark's Evangelical Lutheran Church, Spring Garden and 13th Sts., Philadelphia, Pa., for the congregation.

DOCUMENTATION

S & W, vol. 2, p. 1430. (2) Westcott, p. 268.

DESCRIPTION

S & W, vol. 2, p. 1430, "At a congregational meeting, held Feb. 23, 1864, it was resolved to enlarge the church edifice. Plans prepared by Sloan & Hutton, architects, were adopted. An entire new front of brownstone, with central tower and lofty spire, was erected, the side walls were strengthened, and a new roof was put on, the audience room considerably lengthened, the ceiling raised, and side-galleries put in."

HISTORY

Commission Feb. 23, 1864; completed Nov. 5, 1865; in use 1875; not listed in W-*PP*, presumed demolished, date unk.

No. *129*: Nov. 30, 1864, S & H, *P*(D)

COMMISSION

(Pirated design) Northumberland County Courthouse, on "the 'state house' lot and lot No. 8, konwn as the Snyder lot," Sunbury, Pa., for the Commissioners of Northumberland County.

NOTE: The design, which was that of the Lycoming County Courthouse, Williamsport, Pa., with the tower moved to the northwest side of the front elevation, was used by the builder (D. S. Rissel, who built the Williamsport building) without the architects' permission.

DOCUMENTATION

"Minutes of the Commissioners," 1863–66, Northumberland County, entry for Nov. 30, 1864. (2) "Presentment," Quarter Sessions Docket, 1860–66, Grand Jury of Northumberland County, Jan. sessions, 1864. (3) *History of Northumberland County, Pennsylvania*, ed. Herbert C. Bell (Chicago: Brown, Runk & Co., 1891), pp. 161–162. (4) "The 27th Senatorial District," *Commonwealth: The Magazine for Pennsylvania*, vol. 5, no. 1, Jan.–Feb. 1951, pp. 2–4.

ILLUSTRATION

Photograph, from the northwest, "The 27th Senatorial District," op. cit., p. 2. (2) Photographs (1955 and 1962), collection of the author.

HISTORY

Proposed Nov. 30, 1864; contract (D. S. Rissel) Jan. 5, 1865; occupied Mar. 27, 1866; enlarged (wing to southern end) 1913; demolished c. 1979–80.

No. 130: Feb. 1, 1865, Addison Hutton of S & H, *E*(Ea)

COMMISSION

Swarthmore College Building (later Parrish Hall), ten miles west of Philadelphia at Westdale Post Office, later Swarthmore, Pa., for the building committee of the board of managers of Swarthmore College.

DOCUMENTATION

"Minutes of the Board of Managers of the College, 5th month 10th, 1866," which records the employment of Sloan & Hutton. (2) Addison Hutton, letter to Finley Hutton, dated "2mo.1, 1865," HP. (3) *Specifications for the Erection of Swarthmore College Building (etc.) . . . Architects, Sloan and Hutton (etc.)*. (Philadelphia: Merrihew & Son, 1866). (4) Edward Parrish, *An Essay on Education in the Society of Friends* (Philadelphia: J. B. Lippincott & Co., n.d.), p. 76. (5) *Minutes of the Nineteenth Annual Meeting of the Stockholders of Swarthmore College Held Twelfth Month Fifth, 1882* (N.p.), p. 64. (6) *Specifications of Workmanship and the Materials to Be Used in the Erection and Construction of the Swarthmore College Building*, bound together with citation no. 5 in the collection of the Friends Historical Library, Swarthmore College. (7) *History of Delaware County, Pennsylvania*, ed. Henry Graham Ashmead (Philadelphia: L. H. Everts & Co., 1884), pp. 158–159. (8) Yarnall, p. 42 and n. 6, p. 42.

ILLUSTRATION

Lithograph, "Swarthmore College," CC-FLP, vol. 27A, p. 41. (2) Engraving, frontispiece, *Eleventh Annual Catalogue of Swarthmore College, Swarthmore, Pa.*, 1879–80. (3) Wood engraving, *Guide-Book to the West Chester and Philadelphia Railroad* (Philadelphia: Sherman & Co., 1869), p. 64.

DESCRIPTION

Edward Parrish, op. cit., original description; Hutton letter, op. cit., development. (2) Yarnall, op. cit., final form of building.

HISTORY

Commission c. Feb. 1866; cornerstone May 10, 1866; opened Nov. 8, 1869; largely destroyed by fire Sept. 25, 1881; rebuilt by Addison Hutton; reopened Sept. 1882; building extant and in use.

NOTE: The author is indebted to Mr. Albert W. Fowler, Associate Director of the Friends Historical Library, Swarthmore College, for the major part of this documentation.

No. 131: Spring 1865, S & H, *RE*(D)

COMMISSION

Third Presbyterian Church, 6th Ave. and Cherry Alley (Grant St.) (later 5th Ave. and Nagley St.), Pittsburgh, Pa., for the building committee of the church.

DOCUMENTATION

Finley Hutton, "Memoir," HP, reference to 1865 commission. (2) *Dedicatory Services of the New Edifice of the Third Presbyterian Church of Pittsburgh, Penn'a with some account of the History of the Church from its Organization together with a full Description of the Present Building and its Appointments* (Pittsburgh: W. G. Johnson & Co., 1869), pp. 16–21. (3) *Historical Volume of the Third Presbyterian Church of Pittsburgh* (Pittsburgh: W. G. Johnson & Co., 1869), pp. 17, 19, 22, 27. (4) *ARABJ*, vol. 1, 1868, pp. 97–99. (5) The Rev. Louis H. Evans and the Rev. William L. McEwan, *The Third Presbyterian Church of Pittsburgh, Pa.: A Century's History, 1833–1933*, printed by order of the Session (n.d.), pp. 22, 27.

ILLUSTRATION

Engraving, church as proposed, perspective, "The Third Presbyterian Church at Pittsburgh," frontispiece, *Dedicatory Services etc.*, op. cit. (The same rendering appears in the *ARABJ* article, op. cit. *Note*: The names V. Aningen-Snyder appear in the lower right-hand corner of the perspective. (2) Engraving, plan of auditorium level, ibid., last page. (3) Photograph, church as realized (steeple of tower never built), Evans and McEwan, op. cit., p. 33.

HISTORY

Commission c. Spring 1865; cornerstone June 1, 1866; dedication Nov. 29, 1868; new site purchased Aug. 27, 1896; erection of chapel on new site May–Oct. 1897; last service in Sloan Church Oct. 1897; property and Sloan building sold 1901; building demolished and William Penn Hotel erected on site 1915.

NOTE: The documentation for this building was provided in large part by the Pittsburgh History and Landmarks Foundation.

No. 132: Mar. 1865, S & H, *P*(D)

COMMISSION

Horticultural Hall, Broad and Lardner Sts., Philadelphia, Pa., for the Pennsylvania Horticultural Society.

DOCUMENTATION

Transactions of the Pennsylvania Horticultural Society for the Year 1866 (Philadelphia: *Gardner's Monthly* office, 1867), report of Feb. 1866 meeting. (2) *Fiftieth Anniversary of the Pennsylvania Horticultural Society held at Horticultural Hall, Friday, December 21st, 1877* (Philadelphia: Harper & Brother, 1878), pp. 18–19. (3) S & W, vol. 2, pp. 621–622. (4) E. P. Oberholtzer, *Philadelphia: A History of the City and Its People* (Philadelphia: Clark, n.d.), vol. 2, p. 400. (5) James A. Boyd, *A History of the Pennsylvania Horticultural Society, 1827–1927* (Philadelphia, 1929), pp. 194, 198, 200, 225, 232. (6) "Old Horticultural Hall," *Inquirer*, Jan. 14, 1959, clipping in the collection of HSP.

ILLUSTRATION

Photograph, first building, *PE*, p. 44. (2) Photograph, building after fire of 1881, Oberholtzer, op. cit., p. 400. (3) Photograph, undated, SRL, vol. 18, p. 35, item no. 139. (4) Newspaper cut, identified in ink "Ledger, 1922," CC-HSP, vol. 16, "S. Broad."

DESCRIPTION

Fiftieth Anniversary etc., op. cit., "The structure consisted of a basement comprising a banqueting hall, kitchen, restaurant, dressing-room, storerooms, etc.: on the first floor were the Directors' room and library, ladies' dressingroom, and main hall and stage, with a gallery on both sides, opening into the foyer on Broad Street." Scharf and Westcott, op. cit., "the dimensions were 75 ft. front by 200 ft. depth."

HISTORY

Submission Mar. 1865; commission Feb. 1866; opened May 29, 1867 (*Note*: The *Program* gives Sloan entire credit for the design); burned Jan. 31, 1881; rebuilt (Addison Hutton) 1881; burned May 27, 1893; rebuilt and sold 1917, and Shubert Theatre built on site; theater opened Aug. 26, 1918.

No. 133: Apr. 4, 1866, S & H, *RE*(Ea)

COMMISSION

The Diocesan Seminary of St. Charles Borromeo, on 137 acres of the former Remington estate, Overbrook, Pa., for Bishop Wood acting for the see of Philadelphia.

DOCUMENTATION

Daniel H. Mahony, *Historical Sketches of the Catholic Churches and Institutions of Philadelphia* (Philadelphia, 1895), p. 170. (2) H-*RP*, pp. 53–54. (3) *The Philadelphia Seminary of St. Charles Borromeo* (Philadelphia: Catholic Standard & Times Publishing Co., 1917), p. 63. (4) *St. Charles Seminary, Overbrook* (Philadelphia: Jeffereies & Manz, 1943, p. 53.

ILLUSTRATION

Engraving, perspective, *PE*, p. 87. (2) Photographs, engravings, and lithographs, collections of HSP, FLP, and TLC.

DESCRIPTION

Westcott, p. 174, "A few years ago the ground at Overbrook, four miles and a half from the city, was purchased, and a fine building of greystone in the Itallian style of architecture erected. The edifice has a front of three hundred and eighty-four feet, with wings and pavilions. A high dome, with cross and lantern, surmounts the central building. Towers surmounted with crosses are upon the end buildings." (2) H-*RP*, p. 54, "The building contains a beautiful chapel, with elaborate decorations. The Library Room is large, and contains a valuable collection, and I was pleased to see the abundance of light from several windows. This institution has cost nearly a million dollars."

HISTORY

Commission c. Autumn 1865; cornerstone Apr. 4, 1866 (laid by Bishop Wood); first students admitted 1871; building extant (1963), altered.

NOTE: Sources Nos. 2 and 3, under "Documentation" above, give the architects as "Samuel T. Sloan and Addison Hutton." These are the only sources known that give Sloan's middle initial as "T," and they are all quoting from an unidentified "sketch" of the Seminary published in 1891.

No. 134: Oct. 16, 1866, S & H, RE(Ud)

COMMISSION

Bethany Presbyterian Church, 22nd and Shippen (Bainbridge) Sts. (also given as southeast corner 22nd and Bainbridge to Pemberton Sts.), Philadelpia, Pa., for the building committee of the church.

DOCUMENTATION

PPL, vol. 57, no. 12, Oct. 16, 1886. (2) "Sermon on the History of Bethany Presbyterian Church preached July 2, 1876," ms., collection of Presbyterian Historical Society (Ks51 B46Y), Philadelphia, Pa. (3) Bethany's Illustrated Year Book and Church Members' Guide for 1880, pamphlet (n.p.), p. 32, collection Presbyterian Historical Society. (4) Westcott, pp. 277–80. (5) PCP, pp. 132–135.

ILLUSTRATION

Engraving, "Bethany Church and Sunday-School," Westcott, p. 278. (2) Photograph, original church in left background, PCP, p. 132.

DESCRIPTION

The church complex was largely rebuilt in 1874, Sloan & Hutton's building being overshadowed by the new "Sabbath School." Only one description of the church prior to 1874 has been found. Westcott gives a lengthy description of the building as reconstructed, giving the dimensions of the original building as 112' × 185' and adding, "It is built of Trenton brownstone, is plainly but substantially finished, and can seat two thousand persons."

HISTORY

Church founded 1865; commission c. 1866; dedicated Feb. 13, 1868; greatly enlarged 1874; not listed in W-PP, presumed demolished date unk.

No. 135: Dec. 31, 1866, S & H, E(Ud)

COMMISSION

Tasker School, 9th and Tasker Sts., Philadelphia, Pa., for the Controllers.

DOCUMENTATION

RCPS, Dec. 31, 1866, pp. 26ff. (2) PSP, vol. 3, pp. 125–128. (3) Charles Robson, Biographical Encyclopaedia of Pennsylvania of the 19th Century (Philadelphia: Galaxy Publishing Co., 1874), p. 33.

ILLUSTRATION

Photograph, PSP, op. cit., p. 125. (2) Engraving, Robson, op. cit., plate 22.

DESCRIPTION

PSP, op. cit., "ten classrooms in 2 stories; partitions do not slide."

HISTORY

Contract let Sept. 14, 1866; building accepted 1867; extant 1916; not listed in W-*PP*, presumed demolished date unk.

No. *136*: Dec. 31, 1866, S & H, *E*(Ud)

COMMISSION

Reynolds School, southwest corner 20th and Jefferson Sts., Philadelphia, Pa., for the Controllers.

DOCUMENTATION

RCPS, Dec. 31, 1866, pp. 26ff. (2) *PSP*, vol. 3, pp. 137–140.

ILLUSTRATION

Photograph, p. 137; plan, p. 140, *PSP*, op. cit. (2) Woodcut, Custis, *Public Schools of Philadelphia* (Philadelphia: Burk & McFetridge Co., 1897), p. 477.

DESCRIPTION

PSP, op. cit., "16 class-rooms and assembly room; cost, $24,225."

HISTORY

Contract let Sept. 26, 1866; building accepted 1867; extant 1916; not listed in W-*PP*, presumed demolished date unk.

No. *137*: Dec. 31, 1866, S & H, *E*(Ud)

COMMISSION

Morris School, south side of Morris St. east of 2nd St., Philadelphia, Pa., for the Controllers.

DOCUMENTATION

RCPS, Dec. 31, 1866, p. 26. (2) *PSP*, vol. 3, pp. 129–132.

ILLUSTRATION

Photograph, *PSP*, op. cit., p. 129; plans, p. 132.

DESCRIPTION

PSP, op. cit., "10 class-rooms; except for the entrance, this school is identical with the Tasker School."

HISTORY

Contract let Sept. 14, 1866; building occupied 1867; extant 1916; not listed in W-*PP*, demolished date unk.

No. *138*: ?, S & H, *M*

COMMISSION

Additions, New Jersey State Lunatic Asylum (after 1893, New Jersey State Hospital), Trenton, N.J.

QUESTIONABLE DATE: (1855?) 1863, 1866

This work is referred to in the *First Biennial Report of the Commissioners to Build the Western Insane Asylum of North Carolina at Morganton, N.C.* (Raleigh: News Job Office & Book Bindery, 1876). However, firm documentation is extremely fragmentary, existing as vague references in the *State Papers* of the New Jersey legislature. The extent and nature of the work is undetermined, and although payment is recorded, the exact work paid for is not clear.

No. 139: Autumn 1866, S & H, *M*(Ea)

COMMISSION

The General Hospital for the Insane of the State of Connecticut (later Connecticut Valley Hospital), on 230 acres near Middletown, Conn., for the State of Connecticut.

DOCUMENTATION

"Report of the Superintendent to the Board of Trustees of the General Hospital for the Insane of the State of Connecticut," *First Annual Report of the Connecticut General Hospital for the Insane* (Hartford, Conn., 1867), pp. 10–15. (2) *Connecticut Hospital for the Insane*, reprint of reports of the trustees and superintendents from 1868 to 1895 (Hartford, 1895), pp. 5–7, 10–15. (3) *ARABJ*, vol. 2, July 1869, p. 64. (4) *ICIUSC*, vol. 3, p. 103. (5) The Rev. Alvin D. Johnson, *Connecticut State Hospital, 1866–1890*, pamphlet (n.p., n.d.), supplied by Mildred Asbell, Medical Librarian, Hallock Medical Library, Connecticut Valley Hospital, together with other documentary material for which the writer is indebted. (6) Finley Hutton, "Memoir," HP.

ILLUSTRATION

Original drawings, six sheets, entitled "Connecticut Hospital for the Insane, Middletown, Conn.," signed "Sloan & Hutton, arch'ts," collection of The Athenaeum, Philadelphia, Pa. (2) Engraving, cover of Johnson's *Connecticut State Hospital*, op. cit., taken from the *First Annual Report*, op. cit., perspective, original design of building. (3) Engravings and photographs, collection of the Hallock Medical Library, Connecticut Valley Hospital.

HISTORY

Joint Select Committee appointed by General Assembly 1865; "Act to Create a Hospital for the Insane" passed the General Assembly June 29, 1866; first meeting of the Trustees of the hospital July 20, 1866, appointed committee on "site and plans" (committee visited installations at Trenton, N.J., Philadelphia, Pa., and Utica, N.Y., and consulted with Dr. Kirkbride); Trustees meeting Oct. 15, 1866, appointed D. Abram Marvin Shew (of the hospital in Trenton, N.J.) superintendent; Dr. Shew retains Sloan & Hutton immediately upon his appointment, with the recommendation of Dr. Kirkbride; cornerstone June 20, 1867, in the presence of Dorothea Lynn Dix; construction of center building and one wing 1867–1869; second wing added 1871–72; additions and alterations 1880–81, 1893; of the original building there is extant (1983) the center building (now called Shew Hall), one wing (largely empty, no patients housed), and only a few bays of the opposite wing.

NOTE: Dr. Shew was a member of the staff of the Trenton, N.J., hospital when it was undergoing additions and alterations by Sloan. Also, a letter from Addison Hutton, recorded in the "Report of the Trustees" for 1868 to the board (dated Mar. 13, 1868), documents that Hutton had taken over full supervision of construction and responsibility for the additional plans, when required.

No. 140: Dec 30, 1867, S & H, M(Ea)

COMMISSION

St. Peter State Hospital, St. Peter, Minn., for the Board of Trustees of the hospital.

DOCUMENTATION

Samuel Sloan, letter "To the Board of Trustees, Hospital for Insane, Minn.," reprinted in *Second Annual Report of the Trustees and Officers of the Minnesota Hospital for the Insane for the fiscal year ending Nov. 30, 1868* (St. Paul: State Printers, 1869), p. 10. (2) *Seventh Annual Report etc. . . . for the fiscal year ending Nov. 30, 1873*, pp. 2–12, and "Report of the Building Committee," pp. 13–15. (3) *ARABJ*, vol. 2, June 1870, pp. 712–717.

ILLUSTRATION

Original drawing of the building, collection of the museum of the St. Peter State Hospital. (2) Photographs, front and rear views, *Seventh Annual Report etc.*, op. cit., 1873. (3) Engravings, perspectives and plans, *ARABJ*, op. cit., pp. 713, 715.

DESCRIPTION

Architect's description of original design, *ARABJ*, op. cit. (2) Description of building as realized, *Second–Fifth Annual Reports of the Trustees etc.*, 1869–74, op. cit.

HISTORY

Commission 1867; cost estimate for erection (Sloan) Dec. 30, 1867 (after a visit to the site); construction of north wing and part of center building 1868–70; partial construction, south wing, 1870–71; completion of center building and additional section of south wing 1871–72; addition of portico to center building and completion of service buildings 1873; numerous modifications and alterations 1880–1967; north and south wings demolished 1967–68; center building extant (1981).

NOTE: The author is indebted to Dorothy Sheehan, coordinator of Volunteer Services, St. Peter State Hospital, for the majority of this documentation.

No. 141: July 1867, S & H, P(E)

COMMISSION

Court House for Clinton County, Pa., southeast corner Water and Jay Sts., Lock Haven, Pa., for the County Commissioners.

DOCUMENTATION

Original specifications of the building as drawn by E. H. Welch, in the possession of Mrs. Isabel W. Pons (photocopy in the collection of the Annie Halenbake Ross Library), Lock Haven, Pa. (2) *Historic Lock Haven: An Architectural Survey*, ed. Dean R. Wagner, Clinton County Historical Society (1979), p. 80.

ILLUSTRATION

Photographs, two views of entrance facade, *Historic Lock Haven* op. cit., p. 80. Engravings and photographs, collection of the Annie Halenbake Ross Library, Lock Haven, Pa.

HISTORY

Commissioned July 1867; accepted 1869; extant and in use.

NOTE: The author is indebted to Mrs. Isabel W. Pons, Librarian, Annie Halenbake Ross Library, Lock Haven, Pa., for the majority of this documentation.

No. 142: Feb. 1868, S & H, C(D)

Banking House of the Philadelphia Saving Fund Society, Walnut St. and Washington Sq., Philadelphia, Pa., for the building committee of the Society.

NOTE: Although the plans and specifications for this building bear the signature "Samuel Sloan & Addison Hutton," the design and construction of the Banking House was the work of Addison Hutton alone. See "Report of the Building Committee to the Board of Managers of the Philadelphia Saving Fund Society, Feb. 1868," collection of HSP, and Yarnall, pp. 42–43.

No. 143: Aug. 1868, S & H, C(Ud)

COMMISSION

Commercial building, the Samuel S. White Manufacturing Co., dental supplies, southeast corner Chestnut and 12th Sts. (918 Chestnut St.), Philadelphia, Pa., for Samuel Stockton White.

DOCUMENTATION

ARABJ, vol. 1, Aug. 1868, p. 90. (2) *PE*, p. 26. (3) *Philadelphia and Notable Philadelphians*, ed. Moses King (New York, 1901–2), p. 46. (3) *A Century of Service to Dentistry, 1844–1944*, pamphlet (Philadelphia: S. S. White Dental Mfg. Co., 1944), p. 7, collection of HSP (Wm*682).

ILLUSTRATION

Photographs and engravings, collections of HSP, FLP, TLC. (2) Photograph, file "From 1844 to 1911," HSP, Wm*68, v. 2, reproduced in Kenneth Finkle, *Nineteenth Century Photography in Philadelphia* (New York: Dover Publications, 1980), plate 111, p. 105. (3) Engraving, Brenner Scrapbooks, HSP 33:70.

DESCRIPTION

ARABJ, op. cit., full description, particular attention to construction system of post-and-beam in wrought and cast iron, together with illustration of system, with a claim as to the "fire-proof" nature of the construction.

HISTORY

Commissioned 1867; occupied Sept. 10, 1868; alterations 1876–79; demolished before 1944.

NOTE: The first dental school in Pennsylvania was held on the second floor of this building.

No. 144: Aug. 1868, S, *RE*(E)

COMMISSION

West Presbyterian Church (now First Presbyterian Church), "on the West side of the river," Bridgeton, N.J., for the Presbytery of West Jersey.

DOCUMENTATION

ARABJ, vol. 1, Aug. 1868, p. 88, and Feb. 1869, pp. 191–195. (2) Thomas Cushing and Charles E. Sheppard, *History of the Counties of Gloucester, Salem, and Cumberland, New Jersey* (Philadelphia: Everts & Peck, 1883), p. 602. (3) *Art Issue of the Bridgeton Evening News*, ed. William B. Kirby, 1895, p. 21. (4) "The History of the 'West Presbyterian Church' (of the Presbytery of West Jersey) organized A.D. 1869, Bridgeton, N. Jersey," pamphlet (n.p.), collection of HSP (Mx5). (5) *One Hundredth Anniversary, 1869–1969*, pamphlet, collection of the Cumberland County Historical Society.

ILLUSTRATION

Engravings, perspective and plan, *ARABJ*, op. cit., Feb. 1869, pp. 491–495. (2) Photograph, *Art Issue*, op. cit., p. 22. (3) Photographs, exterior and interior, *One Hundredth Anniversary*, op. cit.

DESCRIPTION

Cushing and Sheppard, op. cit., "The Chapel is of grey Chester stone with Trenton Brownstone facings. It is divided by means of glass partitions into two apartments. The Church proper is of the Gothic order of architecture, constructed of like materials." The dimension is given as 153' in length with a semi-circular recess at rear end measuring 22' × 12', the chancel having a fine rose window, the church proper seating 600.

HISTORY

Organized Mar. 5, 1868; construction of chapel begun Aug. 11, 1869; cornerstone of church July 3, 1869; chapel dedicated July 4, 1869; church dedicated Apr. 11, 1878; building extant, in good state of repair and in use.

NOTE: The author is indebted to Carl L. West of the Cumberland County Historical Society for the majority of this documentation.

No. 145: Apr. 15, 1869, S, *P*(Competition, not constructed)

COMMISSION

[Second] Competition for the New Public Buildings, Independence Sq., Philadelphia, Pa., for the City and County of Philadelphia.

DOCUMENTATION

General Directions to Architects who may prepare plans for the New Public Buildings to be erected on Independence Square in the City of Philadelphia, pamphlet (Philadelphia, 1869), collection of FLP. (2) *Philadelphia Bulletin*, Apr. 5 and Sept. 28, 1869. (3) John Mass, communications to the author relative to researches in the Philadelphia City Archives. (4) Jackson, vol. 2, p. 466.

HISTORY

Competition advertised Apr. 15, 1869; prizes announced Sept. 28, 1869 (McArthur, first prize; Sloan, second prize); arguments as to site from Dec. 1869 until public "election" of Oct. 11, 1870, which determined the site to be Central Square (Penn Square); all entries returned to competitors in fall of 1869.

NOTE: Neither of McArthur's first-prize designs (1860 or 1869) was used in the design of the final building.

No. 146: July 1869, S, *RE*(Ud)

COMMISSION

Trinity Reformed Church, 7th St. below Oxford St., Philadelphia, Pa., for the building committee of the church.

DOCUMENTATION

Fiftieth Anniversary of the Organization, Trinity Reformed Church, Fifth Anniversary of the Dedication of the New Church, Philadelphia, Apr. 22, 1916 (which states, under the heading "First Building," "the architect was Samuel Sloan"). (2) *ARABJ*, vol. 2, July 1869, pp. 74–76. (3) CC-HSP, vol. 15, "Churches," newspaper clipping, n.p., n.d., notice of sale of "Old Trinity Reform Church."

ILLUSTRATION

Engraving, perspective, *ARABJ*, op. cit., p. 74. (2) Photograph, *Fiftieth Anniversary*, op. cit., n.p.

HISTORY

Commissioned May 1869; cornerstone June 26, 1869; dedicated Apr. 7, 1872; sold to congregation of Ohav-Zedka Synagogue 1910; not listed in W-*PP*, presumed demolished date unk.

No. 147: July 1869, S, *RE*(D)

COMMISSION

Chapel, Calvary Presbyterian Church, south side of Locust St. above 15th St., Philadelphia, Pa., for the building committee of the church.

DOCUMENTATION

Z. M. Humphrey, *Discourse Delivered at the Dedication of the Chapel of Calvary Presbyterian Church*, pamphlet (Philadelphia, 1871), p. 23 and n. 1. (2) *Dedication Services of the Chapel of Calvary Presbyterian Church*, 1870. (both documents in the collection of the Presbyterian Historical Society, Philadelphia, Pa.). (3) *ARABJ*, vol. 2, July 1869, pp. 74ff.

ILLUSTRATION

Engraving, perspective, Humphrey, op. cit., frontispiece. (2) Wood engraving, perspective, *Dedication Services etc.*, op. cit., back cover. (3) Engravings, perspective and plans, *ARABJ*, op. cit., pp. 74, 75.

DESCRIPTION

ARABJ, op. cit., architect's description. (2) Humphrey, op. cit.

HISTORY

Commission Spring 1869; dedication Dec. 25, 1870; in 1930 the congregation of First Presbyterian Church amalgamated with Calvary; not listed in W-*PP*, demolished date unk.

NOTE: Sloan was the chairman of the building committee and gave plans to the church, his entire family being members. The plans were a reduced version of Trinity Reformed Church.

No. 148: Mar. 10, 1870, S, *RE*(D)

COMMISSION

Second Presbyterian Church, southeast corner of Hanover and Pomfrey Sts., Carlisle, Pa., for the building committee of the church.

DOCUMENTATION

Samuel Sloan, letter to James Hamilton, Carlisle, Pa., Mar. 10, 1870, Special Collections, Dickinson College Library, Carlisle, Pa. (2) Original contract with John C. Comfort for the erection of the Second Presbyterian Church, ms. dated Nov. 21, 1870, "according to the plans, drafts or schemes, with specifications annexed, made, drawn and furnished by Samuel Sloan, Architect," collection Dickinson College Library, Carlisle, Pa. (3) "Account Book of Treasurer for Building Committee, 1870–1874, 2nd Presbyterian Church, Carlisle, Pennsylvania," ms. on loan to the Dickinson College Library. (4) *American Volunteer*, Carlisle, Pa., June 16, 1870; Apr. 20, 1871; Mar. 28, 1872, all p. 2. (5) *Carlisle Herald*, Carlisle, Pa., June 16, 1870; Apr. 20, 1871; Mar. 28, 1872. (6) Richard L. Arnold, *A Sesquicentennial Review of the Second Presbyterian Church, Carlisle, Pennsylvania, 1833–1983* (1982), pp. 37–68, 327–335.

ILLUSTRATION

Photographs, measured drawings, delineations, and paintings, collection of Richard L. Arnold, Carlisle, Pa. (many reproduced in *Sesquicentennial Review, etc.*, op. cit.).

HISTORY

Commission between June 16 and July 14, 1870; contract Nov. 21, 1870; cornerstone c. Apr. 1871; chapel completed Mar. 31, 1872; dedication May 29, 1873; demolished Jan. Feb. 1973.

NOTE: The building has been exhaustively documented and recorded from primary sources by Richard L. Arnold of Carlisle, Pa., to whom the author is greatly indebted for supplying most of the material for this entry.

No. 149: June 12, 1870, S, *RS*(D)

COMMISSION

"Aldie," suburban villa, near Doylestown, Pa., for Mrs. T. Bigelow Lawrence.

DOCUMENTATION

Letter from Mary Mercer to her husband William Fonthill, June 12, 1870, Fonthill Papers, uncatalogued ms. collection of the HSP. (2) *Bucks County Intelligencer*, Mar. 14, 1871. (3) Helen Hartman Gemmill, *E. L.: The Breadbox Papers* (Bryn Mawr, Pa.: Dorrance & Co., Bucks County Historical Society, Doylestown, Pa., 1983), pp. 182–184. (4) Letters, clippings, etc., Fonthill Papers, op. cit.

ILLUSTRATION

Photographs, front and garden loggia, Gemmill, op. cit., pp. 182, 183.

HISTORY

Commissioned c. Fall 1869 or Spring 1870 (there is correspondence in the Fonthill Papers, op. cit., that records a difference of opinion about the design of the house between the architect and the owner, which necessitated changes in the construction documents at an advanced stage in their production); occupied late spring or early summer 1871; demolished 1927.

No. 150: Sept. 17, 1870, S, *E*(E)

COMMISSION

Cumberland Valley State Normal School (now Shippensburg State College, "Old Main"), Shippensburg, Pa., for the Building Committee.

DOCUMENTATION

Shippensburg News, Sept. 17, 1870; May 13, 20, June 3, Oct. 21, Nov. 25, 1871; Apr. 5, 19, 1873. (2) *Tribune*, Altoona, Pa., Apr. 5, 1873. (3) John Hubley, *The Shippensburg Story, 1730–1970: An Anniversary Publication* (Shippensburg Historical Society, Shippensburg, Pa., News Chronicle Co., 1970), pp. 130–131.

ILLUSTRATION

Drawing, newspaper cut, front elevation, *Shippensburg News*, June 10, 1871. (2) Photograph, from Earl St. (1879), *Shippensburg Story*, op. cit., p. 131.

DESCRIPTION

Shippensburg News, Apr. 19, 1873, full description giving all dimensions, equipment, decoration, and names of all persons connected with the design and erection of the building.

HISTORY

Commissioned Sept. 24, 1870 (or Sept. 17, 1870); cornerstone May 31, 1871; dedication Apr. 15, 1873; "Old Main" closed as dormitory May 13, 1976; renovation by Venturi, Rauch, & Scott Brown Oct. 1981; extant as business office of college.

NOTE: The author is indebted to Richard L. Arnold, Carlisle, Pa., for the documentation of this building.

No. 151: Nov. 18, 1870, S(Competition)

Competition for the new city hall, City Hall Reservation, Yorba Buena Park (also Yerba Buena Park), San Francisco, Calif., for the Commissioners appointed to provide for the erection of a city hall in the City and County of San Francisco.

DOCUMENTATION

San Francisco Municipal Reports, 1870–1916 (1917), p. 519.

HISTORY

Competition advertised June 23, 1870; entries received, first date Nov. 1 extended to Nov. 15, 1870; opening Nov. 17, 1870; selection was Fuller & Laver, Albany, N.Y., first premium; second premium to Butler and Hochkoffer; third premium to S. H. Williams & Son; fourth premium to Wright & Saunders; fifth premium to to P. J. O'Conner. "In addition, the Commissioners decided that three other sets of designs and plans were of such merit that the sum of $500 was awarded to the author of each—viz. to Messrs. Laguerfeld and Attwood of Boston, Messrs. Patton & Jordan of San Francisco, and Mr. Samuel Sloan of Philadelphia."

NOTE: The author is indebted to John Mass of Philadelphia for the documentation of this competition.

No. 152: Mar. 17, 1871, S, P(Ea)

COMMISSION

Alterations and additions to the New Jersey State House, Trenton, N.J., for the legislature of New Jersey.

DOCUMENTATION

Daily State Gazette, Trenton, N.J., Mar. 18, 1871, p. 1. (2) *Daily True American*, Trenton, N.J., Apr. 19, 1871, p. 1. (3) "Senate Bill No. 362," *Journal of the Senate* (of the State of New Jersey), Mar. 31, 1871, p. 1253. (4) John O. Raum, *History of the City of Trenton, New Jersey. . .* (Trenton, 1871), p. 320. (5) John O. Raum, *The History of Trenton, New Jersey* (Philadephia: John E. Potter & Co., n.d.), pp. 214–217. (6) Zara Cohan, "A Comprehensive History of the State House of New Jersey and Recommendations for Its Continuation as a Historic Site," thesis, May 1969, Newark State College (now Kean College), pp. 87–103.

ILLUSTRATION

NOTE: All illustration references are taken from the Cohan "thesis."

Lithograph, "Aerial View of Greater Trenton Proper and Chambers-burgh." H. J. Toudy & Co., litho. and printer, Dolton's Block, Philadelphia, pub. by Fowler & Bailey (this shows Sloan's Senate and Assembly chambers, the 1866 library wing, and the alterations to the 1792 building). (2) Diagrams, "Assembly" and "Senate," showing layout of desks and other furnishings, *Manual of the Legislature of New Jersey* (Morristown, N.J.: F. L. Lundy, corrected to Jan. 1, 1874). (3) *Atlas of the City of Trenton and Suburbs, New Jersey*, engraved by A. H. Mueller of Philadelphia: E. Robinson, New York, 1881, Plate C (showing in outline the Sloan additions and alterations).

HISTORY

There is a possibility that Sloan's first association with the State House occurred in 1858, when "improvements" to its ventilation were made (*New Jersey State Records*). Sloan and his longtime client Samuel A. Harrison had become specialists in heating and ventilating equipment by 1855 because of Dr. Kirkbride's requirements for the new insane hospitals Sloan was designing. Commissioners for new work appointed Mar. 31, 1871 (Senate Bill No. 362); Sloan retained as architect Apr. 19, 1871; work included creation of larger meeting rooms for legislature, committees, remodeling of south wing to include a library and executive suite, and modifications to the 1792 Statehouse senate wing; work begun May 1, 1871 and continued to Nov. 18, 1873, when additional appropriations were made to alter John Notman's 1846 facade of the State House; all work completed and accepted by 1877; the State House largely destroyed by fire Mar. 1885; majority of Sloan's work demolished in rebuilding after fire; rebuilding campaign continued 1885–95, with some additions in the twentieth century; very little of the Sloan work survives.

NOTE: The Zara Cohan thesis, op. cit., contains a detailed and exhaustive history of the Sloan work at the State House, with all contemporary documentation.

No. 153: (Apr. 14, 1868, or before), Mar. 31, 1871, S & H, *M*(Ea)

COMMISSION

The State Asylum for the Insane (later, "Greystone Park State Hospital," "Dr. Buttolph's Hospital," Morris Plains Division, New Jersey State Hospital for the Insane, and today Greystone Park Psychiatric Hospital), one and a half miles from the Morris Plains Station, Hanover Township, Morris County, N.J., for the State of New Jersey.

DOCUMENTATION

Finley Hutton, "Memoir," HP, "in the office of Sloan & Hutton." (2) "An Act Appointing Commissioners to Examine Sites, Prepare Plans, &c, for Another State Lunatic Asylum," approved Apr. 14, 1868, *Laws of New Jersey*, 1868, p. 997. (3) *ARABJ*, vol. 1, Mar. 1869, pp. 551–554. (4) *Annual Re-*

ports of the Managers and Officers of the New Jersey State Lunatic Asylum at Trenton for the Year 1869, pp. 323–337. (5) "An Act to Provide Additional Accommodations for the Insane of This State," approved Mar. 31, 1871, *Laws of New Jersey*, 1871, p. 72. (6) *Report of the Commissioners Appointed to Select a Site and Build an Asylum for the Insane of the State of New Jersey, December 22d, 1874* (see esp. "Architect's Report," pp. 15–16). (7) There are, in addition, Commissioners' reports, legislative committees' reports, building superintendents' reports, and architects' reports for every year from 1872 to 1876, when the building opened, all of which are in the collection of the New Jersey State Library, 185 W. State Street, Trenton, N.J.

ILLUSTRATION

Engravings, plans and perspectives, *ARABJ*, vol. 1, Mar. 1869, pp. 551–554. (2) These same illustrations appear in "Documentation" references Nos. 4 and 6 (above). (3) Engraving, large "Bird's-Eye View," "State Asylum for the Insane, at Morristown, N.J.," *Report of the Commissioners . . . 1874*, op. cit., opposite p. 17.

HISTORY

If, according to the Finley Hutton "Memoir," HP, the commission was "in the office of Sloan & Hutton," it would have to have been given before the Jan. 1868 dissolution of the firm. This is substantiated by the publishing of plans and perspectives for the building in the Mar. 1869 issue of *ARABJ* which are identical with those printed in "Documentation" reference No. 4 (above), which states that a plan, by Sloan, was submitted to the Managers in 1868. In 1871 a new act was passed, and new Commissioners appointed, which advertised a competition to selected architects (among them, Richard Morris Hunt), one of the judges being Dr. T. S. Kirkbride. Sloan chosen and continued as the architect of the building until it opened in 1876. Although many minor alterations were made in the building's exterior between its first representation in 1868 and its accepted appearance in 1872, the plan remained almost unchanged. Alterations and additions have been made since 1876, but the body of the building is very much as Sloan designed it.

No. 154: Jan. 16, 1873, S, C(D)

COMMISSION

The Bank of New Hanover, northwest corner of Front and Princess Sts., Wilmington, N.C., for the board of directors of the bank.

DOCUMENTATION

Morning Star, Wilmington, N.C., vol. 11, no. 49, Nov. 19, 1872, p. 1; no. 99, Jan. 16, p. 1, no. 154, Mar. 21, p. 1, 1873; vol. 12, no. 99, July 17, 1873, p. 1; vol. 16, no. 67, June 9, 1875, p. 1; vol. 34, no. 103, July 22, 1884, p. 1. (2) Andrew J. Howell, *The Book of Wilmington* (Wilmington, N.C., 1955), n.p. (3) Correspondence with William M. Reaves of Wilmington, to whom the author is indebted for the documentation of this building.

ILLUSTRATION

Photographs in the collection of the New Hanover County Museum, Wilmington, N.C., spanning the years 1880–1910. (2) Photograph, J. S. Reilly, *Wilmington Past Present and Future* (Wilmington, 1884).

DESCRIPTION

Morning Star, vol. 11, no. 99, Jan. 16, 1873, p. 1, "When completed, according to the plan adopted by the Board of Directors, it will be the handsomest building in Wilmington, if not in the entire State. The whole of the ground floor will be occupied by the bank, and embraces the banking house proper, a cashier's room, director's room, closets &c. The second and third floors will each have six rooms for offices, all of which will probably be rented to lawyers and other gentlemen of the professions. The whole will be surmounted by a magnificent Mansard roof, ornamented with the latest architectural improvements, making the structure a credit alike to our city and the prosperous institution that projected it."

HISTORY

Commissioned c. Nov. 1872; ground broken Mar. 20, 1873; completed c. late 1873; building occupied by the Peoples Savings Bank at some date prior to 1955; demolished shortly thereafter.

No. 155: Aug. 8, 1873, S(Competition)

COMMISSION

Competitions (first and second) for the buildings proposed for the Centennial Exhibition of 1876; first competition advertised Apr. 1, 1873, judged July 15–Aug. 8; second competition announced Aug. 8, received Oct. 10, 1873, competition issued by the Committee on Plans and Architecture of the Centennial Commission.

DOCUMENTATION

First competition: (1) *Report of Committee on Plans and Architecture of the United States Centennial Commission*, Aug. 8, 1873, pamphlet (n.p.). (2) *PPL*, vol. 75, no. 117 and 118, Aug. 8 and 9, 1873, p. 2, "Plans for Centennial Buildings." (3) George B. Tatum, *Penn's Great Town* (Philadelphia: University of Pennsylvania Press, 1961), pp. 103–104. Second competition: (1) *Description of Design and Drawings for the Proposed Centennial Buildings, to be erected in Fairmount Park, presented by Samuel Sloan, Architect, Philadelphia*, October 10, 1873 (Philadelphia: Lippincott, 1873; Philadelphia: King & Baird, 1873) (*note*: This version has no date on the Salutation to the Committee). (2) Samuel Sloan, *Bill of Quantities for the Centennial Buildings* (Philadelphia: Lippincott, 1873). (3) Theo B. White, *Fairmount: Philadelphia's Park* (Philadelphia: Art Alliance Press, 1975), p. 62. Tatum, op. cit.

ILLUSTRATION

Original drawing, perspective, Art Gallery, Philadelphia City Archives. (2) Original drawing, "Elevation of North and South Fronts [Memorial Hall] Showing the Permanent, Temporary Buildings as Connected and Coverway

Crossing Belmont Avenue to Machinery Department," collection of HSP. Both these drawings are from the entry to the second competition. (3) Photographs (reduced) of competition drawings for the Centennial buildings, "Scrapbook of T. U. Walter," Library of the School of Fine Arts, University of Pennsylvania (*Note*: This latter collection contains the only known illustration of Sloan's first competition submission, "Americanus.") (4) *Description of Design etc.*, King & Baird, op. cit., illustrations of entries in second competition, "Perspective View of Art Gallery," opp. p. 16, "Elevation of East Front of Permanent and Temporary Buildings Connected," opp. p. 4, etc.

HISTORY

Competition advertised Apr. 1, 1873; first competition closed July 15, 1873, forty-three designs received; Sloan among the ten selected for second competition with an award of $1,000; second competition announced Aug. 8, 1873, to be received Sept. 20, extended to Oct. 10; Sloan's entry awarded second prize and $3,000.

No. 156: Mar. 14, 1874, S, *RE*(Ea)

COMMISSION

Presbyterian Church in the Forks of the Brandywine (later, Brandywine Manor Presbyterian Church, and Forks of the Brandywine United Presbyterian Church), Glen Moore, Pa., for the board of trustees of the church.

DOCUMENTATION

James McClune, *History of the Presbyterian Church in "The Forks of the Brandywine," Chester County, Pa. (Brandywine Manor Presbyterian Church) from A.D. 1735 to 1885* (Philadelphia, 1885), pp. 48–49. (3) *Schedule of Services, Forks of Brandywine Presbyterian Church*, pamphlet (n.d.), sections "Historical Landmarks" and "Brandywine Presbyterian Church." (4) Letters (copies in possession of the author) from the Rev. John A. Kauffroth, former pastor of the church, to Richard L. Arnold, Carlisle, Pa., May 25, 1976, and May 18, 1977, giving results of document search in church records.

ILLUSTRATION

Engraving of drawing, perspective, showing building as of 1953, artist H. T. MacNeill.

HISTORY

Sloan hired by board of trustees Mar. 14, 1874, to examine the old building; Sloan reported that building was beyond repair; commission for new building Mar. 24, 1874; cornerstone Aug. 7, 1875; dedication Dec. 14, 1876; bell tower added from design of William M. Potts (who paid for its construction) at some time after 1884; building, as altered, extant and in good condition.

No. 157: Oct. 1, 1874, *S*, Attribution *M*(U)

COMMISSION

Additions (four wings) to the Insane Asylum of North Carolina (called "Dix Hill," later State Hospital for the Insane), Raleigh, N.C., for the board of directors of the asylum.

DOCUMENTATION

Report of the Board of Directors and the Superintendent of the Insane Asylum of North Carolina (Raleigh: State Agricultural Journal Book & Job Office, 1874), pp. 39–42. (2) L. L. Polk, *Handbook of North Carolina* (Raleigh: Raleigh Steam News Book & Job Printers, 1879), pp. 178–180. (3) *RN&O*, vol. 17, no. 170, Sept. 26, 1880, p. 4.

HISTORY

This commission and its results, if any, are highly conjectural; however, the *Report of the Board of Directors*, cited above, is very specific in its request for enlargement of the Raleigh building and gives an exact cost ($60,000) for the wings they wish added. Both Polk's *Handbook*, op. cit., and K-*H* imply that Sloan is at work on alterations at Raleigh at the same time he is constructing the new asylum at Morganton. There are, however, no state papers to support work by Sloan at the Raleigh institution known to the author.

No. 158: Mar. 20, 1875 (Oct. 31, 1874), S, *M*(E)

COMMISSION

Western North Carolina Insane Asylum (later, Broughton Hospital), Morganton, N.C., for the State of North Carolina.

DOCUMENTATION

This building has been exhaustively documented, described and its history given by C. Greer Suttlemyre and Jim Sumner in the "National Register of Historic Places Inventory—Nomination Form" prepared by them, as representatives of the Division of Archives and History of the North Carolina Department of Cultural Resources, submitted by them Mar. 10, 1977. The only documentary references that might be added to theirs are (1) L. L. Polk, *Handbook of North Carolina* (Raleigh: Raleigh Steam News Book & Job Printers, 1879), pp. 180–181, which describes the site in detail, and (2) *RN&O*, vol. 17, no. 170, Sept. 26, 1880, p. 2, which reports that the building (first building program) is almost finished and "the cost of the work thus far, strange to say, has fallen below the original estimate of the architect"; and *RN&O*, vol. 20, no. 59, Nov. 23, 1882, p. 1, which reports, "The Western Asylum is now about ready to be occupied." (5) William B. Bushong, "A. G. Bauer, North Carolina's New South Architect," *North Carolina Historical Review*, vol. 60, no. 3, July 1983, pp. 306–313 and all footnotes.

ILLUSTRATION

Photographs, plans, etc., in the collections of the Division of Archives and History, North Carolina Department of Cultural Resources, Raleigh, N.C.;

the National Register, National Park Service, U.S. Department of the Interior; and the North Carolina Collection, University of North Carolina Library, Chapel Hill, N.C.

HISTORY

Bill providing for the establishment of the facility passed by General Assembly of North Carolina Mar. 20, 1875; commission appointed to choose the site, select an architect, and begin construction; Sloan given commission after consultation with a number of hospital superintendents, including Dr. Kirkbride (it is possible that Sloan had been suggested by Kirkbride to the board of directors of the asylum in Raleigh before their request for enlarged facilities in 1874); construction of "centre" building and "main" (south) wing under Sloan's direction 1875–82; north wing designed by A. G. Bauer, completed Oct. 1, 1886; main building (Sloan design) still in use and, externally, relatively unchanged, although interior changes have been made.

No. 159: 1876, S, RE(Ea)

COMMISSION

"Rocklynne," suburban villa on the Main Line of the Pennsylvania Railroad near Radnor, Pa., for Theodore D. Rand.

DOCUMENTATION

H-RP, pp. 229–230. (2) Benjamin F. Stahl Jr., owner of the house in 1960, photographs, measurements, and history.

ILLUSTRATION

Photographs, taken by Mr. Stahl, op. cit., in the collection of the author.

HISTORY

Hotchkin, H-RP, who documents the date of the house, also records that Mr. Rand was the "first citizen who built a country-seat" in that vicinity and that Rand was a native of Philadelphia, a well-known geologist and collector of minerals; the original frame and clapboard-cladded house was altered in 1909 (addition of wing) and 1914 (exterior stuccoed); purchased by Mr. Stahl in 1950; house extant, altered.

No. 160: Aug. 12, 1882, S & B, P(D)

COMMISSION

County jail, Craven County, N.C., Broad St., Newbern (also New Bern), N.C., for the County Commissioners.

DOCUMENTATION

Supplement to The Newbernian, Aug. 12, 1882, p. 1. (2) *Sanborn Fire Insurance Maps*, 1885–1931.

ILLUSTRATION

No photograph or other representation of this building is known.

DESCRIPTION

Supplement, op. cit., "The building is of brick, one story high, 33 feet wide by 72 feet 7 inches long (containing 4 cells). The cells in size are 6 feet 7 inches long and 7 feet 11 inches high, composed entirely of iron, with grated fronts, making them airy and comfortable, and affording sufficient light to read the finest print." (The description continues in detail.)

HISTORY

The *Supplement*, op. cit., describes the jail as already erected, "since the last report made to you by the Commissioners." It must therefore have been commissioned in 1881. The same source contains the following: "The arrangements and design of the building were gotten up by the Commissioners, a sketch and explanation of the same furnished to Messrs. Sloan & Balderston, architects, of Philadelphia, who supplied the working drawings, had the cells made and furnished such other material as was needed from that city, in its construction." The building was demolished in 1907 and replaced by the present jail in 1908.

NOTE: The existence of this building, and its documentation, was discovered by Mr. Peter B. Sandbeck of New Bern, N.C., and the material kindly supplied to the author by him.

No. 161: Apr. 3, 1883, S[? S & B], *P/RE*(E)

COMMISSION

The "new" governor's mansion of the State of North Carolina, Burke Square (Blount St.), Raleigh, N.C., for the state legislature.

DOCUMENTATION

Documentation of Sloan's initial connection with this project has not been found. *RN&O*, vol. 21, no. 24, Apr. 13, 1883, reported that the legislature on Apr. 3 had directed the governor to employ an architect. Ibid., no. 36, Apr. 27, reported that Sloan arrived in Raleigh on Apr. 26 with the design for the mansion. It would seem, therefore, that Sloan had been approached by some person or agency prior to the legislature's sanction of the project. (2) The *RN&O* published a continuing series of reports covering the construction of the building and its vicissitudes from Apr. 1883 until the opening of the mansion on Jan. 13, 1891. The most important of these, other than those cited above, are ibid., June 19, 1883 (beginning of foundation excavations June 18); and the issue of Jan. 14, 1891, reporting the opening. (3) V. M. Mulholland, "North Carolina's Gingerbread Whitehouse," *North Carolina Education*, vol. 24, no. 3, Nov. 1957, pp. 10–11, 26–29. (4) William B. Bushong, "A. G. Bauer: North Carolina's New South Architect," *North Carolina Historical Review*, vol. 60, no. 3, July 1983, pp. 309–311 and all footnotes. (5) Letter, Thomas J. Jarvis to William L. Saunders, Sept. 20, 1887, William Laurence Saunders Papers, State Archives, Raleigh, N.C., P.C. 271, 16 pages written from Rio de Janeiro (the most intimate and complete personal document of the mansion's construction).

ILLUSTRATION

Engraving, 1895, files of the Division of Archives and History, North Carolina Department of Cultural Resources, Raleigh, N.C. (2) Photograph, exterior detail, cover, *North Carolina Education*, op. cit. (3) Photographs, twelve, in color, four exterior, eight interior, by Paul G. Beswick, *Southern Accents*, vol. 5, no. 4, Fall 1982, pp. 66–73. (4) Photographs in the collection of the College of Architecture, Clemson University, Clemson, S.C., and of the author.

HISTORY

Commissioned (uncertain date) 1883; design accepted May 8, 1883; construction begun June 17, 1883; many changes in materials and details over the process of construction, but exterior remained essentially as designed; building completed by A. G. Bauer after Sloan's death (1884); mansion first occupied 1889 (Governor Fowle); official opening Jan. 13, 1891; renovation 1925; Executive Mansion Fine Arts Committee appointed 1965; major renovation 1970–73; building in excellent condition, only slightly altered.

No. 162: June 20, 1883, S(Bauer), E(U)

COMMISSION

St. Mary's School, new building addition, 784 Hillsboro St., Raleigh, N.C., commissioners unknown.

DOCUMENTATION

RN&O, vol. 21, no. 83, June 20, 1883, p. 4, "Observations" (a full description including dimensions, style, and furnishings).

NOTE: No substantiating documentation for this building has been found, but the description referenced above is so detailed and explicit that there is reason to assume that it was constructed. The author has not found an illustration of the building, nor any subsequent history of it.

No. 163: Nov. 27, 1883 (Nov. 27, 1882) S(Bauer), M(Ea)

COMMISSION

Centre Building (later Babcock Building) South Carolina Lunatic Asylum (later South Carolina State Hospital), Bull Street, Columbia, S.C., for the State of South Carolina.

DOCUMENTATION

This building has been exhaustively documented, illustrated, and its history given in a "National Register of Historic Places Inventory—Nomination Form" prepared by John E. Wells of the South Carolina Department of Archives and History, 1403 Senate St., Columbia, S.C., and submitted by him in July 1981; Wells lists all the state papers relative to Sloan's commission, together with supplemental contemporary references. (2) Bauer Papers, 17-page "memoir" and other material, in the possession of Mrs. Ruth O. Brumbaugh, North Canton, Ohio (electrostatic copy on deposit at the Archives, Division of Archives and History, North Carolina Department of Cultural Resources, Raleigh, N.C.) (3) William B. Bushong, "A. G. Bauer *etc.*" (4) Carmine Andrew Prioli, "The Indian 'Princess' and the Architect: Origin of a North Carolina Legend," *North Carolina Historical Review*, vol. 60, no. 3, July 1983, pp. 284–286.

ILLUSTRATION

Photographs and drawings in the collections of the South Carolina Department of Archives and History and the South Carolina Department of Mental Health. (2) Photographs, collection of Mr. Russell Maxey, Columbia, S.C. (3) Photographs, collection of the College of Architecture, Clemson University, Clemson, S.C., and of the author.

HISTORY

Commission, prior to Dec. 1882 (the state financial report for 1882–83 lists a disbursement to Sloan for "Ach't drawing &c" in Dec. 1882); building completed Aug. 1885 (a year after Sloan's death); alterations and additions 1898, 1904, 1910, 1919; however, the Centre Building remains essentially as designed and in good condition.

No. 164: June 22, 1883, S(Bauer), *E*(D)

COMMISSION

Swain Memorial Hall, auditorium on the campus of the University of North Carolina, Chapel Hill, N.C., for the State of North Carolina.

DOCUMENTATION

RN&O, vol. 21, no. 85, June 22; no. 87, June 24; no. 91, June 28; no. 131, Aug. 19, 1883; vol. 22, no. 122, Apr. 17, 1884. Kemp Plummer Battle, *History of the University of North Carolina from Its Beginning to the Death of President Swain, 1789–1858*, vol. 1; *1868–1912*, vol. 2 (Raleigh: Edwards & Broughton, 1907, 1912), vol. 2, pp. 245–252, 315–316. (3) Archibald Henderson, *The Campus of the First State University* (Chapel Hill: University of North Carolina Press, 1949), pp. 198–199 and nn. 29, 32. (4) John McKee, "Spooky Architectural Monstrosity," *Carolina Magazine*, vol. 64, May 1935. (5) William B. Bushong, "A. G. Bauer *etc.*," pp. 311–313 and all footnotes.

ILLUSTRATION

Photographs and drawings, Southern Historical Collection, Library of the University of North Carolina, Chapel Hill, and Division of Archives and History, North Carolina Department of Cultural Resources, Raleigh, N.C.

HISTORY

Commission first mentioned in connection with Sloan June 28, 1883; plans approved by building committee Aug. 19, 1883; construction halted because of cost overruns Nov. 1883; construction recommenced early 1884 and in progress at the time of Sloan's death (July 19, 1884); construction continued under the supervision of A. G. Bauer; dedication June 3, 1885; condemned as unsafe 1929 and demolished 1930; present Memorial Hall built on site.

No. 165: July 24, 1883, S(Bauer), *E*(D)

COMMISSION

Centennial Graded School, Fayetteville St. (site of the "old Governor's Mansion"), Raleigh, N.C., for the Board of Aldermen of Raleigh.

DOCUMENTATION

RN&O, vol. 21, no. 115, July 24; no. 122, Aug. 1; no. 132, Aug. 14; no. 136, Aug. 18; vol. 22, no. 104, Nov. 4; no.125, Nov. 28, 1883. (2) William B. Bushong, "A. G. Bauer *etc.*," n. 7, pp. 307–308.

ILLUSTRATION

Photograph, Carolina Collection, Library of University of North Carolina, Chapel Hill, N.C.

HISTORY

Commission awarded to Sloan Aug. 1, 1883; construction begun Nov. 1883; construction completed after Sloan's death (July 19, 1884) by A. G. Bauer, demolished 1931; site now occupied by Memorial Auditorium.

No. 166: Aug. 1, 1883, S(Bauer), *E*(U)

COMMISSION

Additions to Peace Institute (later Peace College), Peace St. at the head of North Wilmington St., Raleigh, N.C., commissioners unknown.

DOCUMENTATION

RN&O, vol. 21, no. 122, Aug. 1, 1883; vol. 22, no. 138, May 1; no. 152, May 13, 1884.

NOTE: Aside from the Aug. 1, 1883, report in the *RN&O*, which gives the commission to Sloan, and a brief report on May 1, 1884 (*RN&O*), that the building "will be completed by the next term in September," the author has been unable to find any illustration of the Sloan work or any subsequent history of the building.

No. 167: Aug. 1, 1883, S(Bauer), *E*(U)

COMMISSION

Rebuilding of St. Augustine Normal School (later St. Augustine College), Raleigh, N.C., commissioners unknown.

DOCUMENTATION

RN&O, vol. 21, no. 109, July 18; no. 122, Aug. 1, 1883; vol. 23, no. 136, Aug. 17, 1884.

NOTE: No illustration of the Sloan work is known to the author.

HISTORY

Commission awarded some time before Aug. 1, 1883; work not begun on the rebuilding of the school, which was destroyed by fire in Mar. 1883, until Aug. 1884. It can be assumed, therefore, that Sloan's death (July 19, 1884) delayed completion of construction documents. There is no documentation that this building, or the new addition at Peace Institute, was completed by A. G. Bauer. Subsequent history of the Sloan designs at St. Augustine is unknown to the author.

No. 168: Nov. 3, 1883, S(Bauer) (W. J. Hicks), *P*(D)

COMMISSION

State Agricultural Exposition Building, grounds of the State Fair, Raleigh, N.C., for the State of North Carolina.

DOCUMENTATION

RN&O, vol. 21, no. 103, Nov. 3; no. 104, Nov. 4; no. 105, Nov. 6; no. 132, Dec. 6, 1883; vol. 22, no. 107, Mar. 25; no. 132, Apr. 24; no. 138, May 1, 1884; vol. 23, no. 24, June 11; no. 35, June 22, 1884. (2) *Plans of Building, Rules and Regulations Governing Exhibitors at the North Carolina State Exposition, Raleigh, N.C., October 1st to October 28, 1884* (Raleigh: Edwards, Broughton & Co., 1884), "Main Building," n.p. (3) *Visitors' Guide to the North Carolina State Exposition and City of Raleigh* (Raleigh, 1884), pp. 71ff.

ILLUSTRATION

Engraving, perspective of building, "The State Exposition: View of the Main Building," *RN&O*, vol. 23, no. 35, June 22, 1884. (2) Identical engraving, *Plans of Buildings*, op. cit., "Main Building," n.p. (3) Photographs and graphic illustrations in the North Carolina Collection, Library of the University of North Carolina, Chapel Hill, N.C.

HISTORY

Commission received early Dec. 1883; Sloan associated with W. J. Hicks as joint architect, A. G. Bauer executed the drawings; foundation work in progress by May 13, 1884; building complete by Oct. 1, 1884; demolished date unk.

No. 169: June 17, 1883, S, *E*(E)

COMMISSION

Graded School (also known as the Bell Building and the "Second" New Bern Academy Building; later Central Elementary School), 517 Handcock St., New Bern, N.C., for the trustees of the New Bern Academy.

DOCUMENTATION

RN&O, vol. 21, no. 81, June 17, 1883, credits Sloan with the design of "The Graded School at Newbern." (2) Trustees of the New Bern Academy, Records, vol. 3, Aug. 8, 1882, to Apr. 30, 1886, files of the New Bern City Schools administration, Jones-Roberts House, New St., New Bern, N.C. (3) Mary Pickett Ward, "New Bern Academy," ms., n.d., collection of New Bern Historical Society, New Bern, N.C. (4) "National Register of Historic Places—Nomination Form," prepared by John Wells, Survey and Planning

Unit staff, State Department of Archives and History, 109 East Jones St., Raleigh, N.C., and presented July 8, 1971.

NOTE: This is a disputed attribution. The *RN&O* credits Sloan with the design both on June 17, 1883, and in his obituary, June 20, 1884 (vol. 23, no. 56). This is also the case with Sloan's obituaries in two of the Philadelphia newspapers, which state, however, that they copied the Raleigh announcements. Wells, in the HABS "Nomination Form," cited above, says, "An architect, a Mr. Carroll, was asked to submit a design, which was soon approved." This attribution is seemingly supported by the trustees' records and the Ward ms., op. cit. However, the trustees' records also show that in 1883 they had expressed an "earnest desire . . . to erect suitable buildings for the *graded school* as recommended" (italics added). "Graded School," not "Academy," is the name given by the *RN&O* to the Sloan commission. Moreover, Sloan had a long association with merchants in New Bern. There are in the Romulus Armstead Nunn Papers, Perkins Library, Duke University, Durham, N.C., two letters: one from Samuel Sloan to Mr. B. Ellis of "Newbern" dated Aug. 14, 1866, and a reply from Bryan Richardson of "Newbern" dated Aug. 29, 1866, in regard to the purchase of a large consignment of wood flooring and its shipment, by coastal vessel, to Philadelphia. Sloan is firmly documented as the architect of the Craven County Courthouse in New Bern. It is therefore the contention of the author that the design of the "Newbern Graded School" was that of Samuel Sloan.

ILLUSTRATION

Photographs, collection of the New Bern Historical Society, New Bern, N.C.

HISTORY

Commission, probably in the early fall of 1883; finances for the construction secured by Mar. 14, 1884; groundbreaking May 8, 1884; cornerstone June 13, 1884; building accepted June 30, 1885; building extant, externally as designed.

No. 170: (Exact date unknown), 1883, S & B, *P*(Ea)

COMMISSION

Courthouse for Craven County, N.C., Broad St., New Bern, N.C., for the County Commissioners.

DOCUMENTATION

Minutes of the Board of County Commissioners of Craven County, N.C., 1882, 1883. (2) Marble plaque, Broad St. entrance to building, records "Sloan and Balderston, Architects" and the year "1883."

NOTE: As the firm name, Sloan & Balderston, is given, rather than that of Sloan alone, it can be assumed that this building was designed in the Philadelphia offices of the firm, not in Sloan's Raleigh, N.C., office. There is no record of Balderston having come to North Carolina at any time; therefore, supervision of the building's construction must have been done by Sloan.

ILLUSTRATION
Photographs in the collection of the New Bern Historical Society Foundation, 511 Broad St., New Bern, N.C. These photographs and a few additional ones of the courthouse are now in the permanent collection of the New Bern–Craven County Photo Archive, New Bern–Craven County Public Library, 400 Johnson St., New Bern. There are presently ten views of the courthouse in this collection, dating from about 1900 to 1957. (2) Photograph, by Dan Maxhimer, *Sun Journal*, New Bern, Jan. 6, 1983, Section B, p. 1.

HISTORY
Commission uncertain, 1882 or before; builder John B. Lane; dedication 1883; building remodeled 1958; partial restoration 1983–84; extant, good condition.

No. 171: Mar. 30, 1884, S (Bauer), E(D)

COMMISSION
Gymnasium and ballroom, campus of the University of North Carolina, Chapel Hill, N.C., for the University Gymnasium Association (incorporated Oct. 29, 1883), which gave the building to the university.

DOCUMENTATION
Alumni Quarterly, Chapel Hill, N.C., vol. 1, no. 2, Jan. 1895, pp. 56–57. (2) Archibald Henderson, *The Campus of the First State University* (Chapel Hill: University of North Carolina Press, 1954), p. 249. (3) William B. Bushong, "A. G. Bauer: Architect for the State of North Carolina, 1883–1898," ms. in the possession of its author, p. 8, n. 20.

ILLUSTRATION
Photographs, Carolina Collection and Southern Historical Collection, Library of the University of North Carolina, Chapel Hill, N.C.

HISTORY
Association incorporated Oct. 29, 1883; lot purchased "adjoining the campus and just opposite the old Mitchell dwelling, now occupied by Prof. Gore" (*Alumni Quarterly*, op. cit.) early in 1884; "Mr. Sloan, the architect of Memorial Hall, prepared the plans and the Gymnasium was rapidly erected" (ibid.); building remodeled in 1898 and used as Commons Hall; demolished 1915–16.

DIVISION II: ATTRIBUTED COMMISSIONS WITH MINIMAL DOCUMENTATION

The following commissions, with locations, are attributed to Samuel Sloan, but with only minimal documentation.

No. 1: School building (unnamed) at 4th and Lombard Sts.,
Philadelphia, Pa. (1851).

DOCUMENTATION

PPL, vol. 31, no. 6, Apr. 2, 1851.

No. 2: Secondary school (unnamed), north side of Mary St. below 2nd St.,
Southwark, Philadelphia, Pa. (1851).

DOCUMENTATION

PPL, vol. 31, no. 65, June 10, 1851.

No. 3: Villa for Charles F. Abbott (after the design of "Bartram Hall"),
"near the Queen Lane Reservoir," Philadelphia, Pa. (1852–53).

DOCUMENTATION

CC-HSP, vol. 99, newspaper clipping (n.p., n.d.), "A Noted House Burned,
The Eastwick Mansion." (*Note*: "Bartram Hall" burned May 29, 1896; this
article must therefore be provisionally dated May 30 or 31 of that year.)
(2) Research by Mark Frazier Lloyd, Director, Germantown Historical Society, disclosed: the reservoir site was approved by City Council on Mar. 24,
1892; if the land acquired for the reservoir (as shown on the ward maps after
1896) is compared with the Hopkins Ward Atlas of 1875, it shows that the
northeastern half of the estate of "Charles F. Abbott" was included in the
land purchases; the existing portion of the property is occupied today by the
Medical College of Pennsylvania (formerly Women's Medical College) with
the address 3300 Henry Ave.

NOTE: It is reasonable to conclude that this was the site of the Abbott
villa. The date of the building's demolition is not known but is some time
prior to 1930, when the college was built.

No. 4: Warren Grammar School, Robertson St.,
Philadelphia, Pa. (1852–53).

DOCUMENTATION

Henry Barnard, *School Architecture* (New York: Charles B. Norton, 1854),
p. 111. (2) *AJE*, vol. 13, Mar.–Dec., 1863, p. 828.

NOTE: Neither of these references attributes the building to Sloan directly
and by name. However, it is listed along with other schools documented as
by Sloan without any differentiation, and hence it is assumed that the building was attributed to Sloan.

No. 5: Remodeling, South-East Grammar School (address not given),
Philadelphia, Pa. (1859).

DOCUMENTATION

PPL, vol. 47, no. 134, Aug. 30, 1859. The report gives Sloan as the architect; the building to be ready by Sept. 5; alterations include installing
sliding, glazed partitions and improving the ventilation.

No. 6: Protestant Episcopal church (name not given), Lehigh Ave. near
Front St., Philadelphia, Pa. (1860).

DOCUMENTATION

PPL, vol. 49, no. 14, Apr. 19, 1860.

NOTE: It has been suggested that this could refer to the Church of St.
John the Evangelist, which was at Reed and Front Sts.; first listed in the city
directories in 1863; after 1885 no longer listed; presumed demolished.

No. 7: "Cherokee," suburban villa for Robert Jemison,
Tuscaloosa, Ala. (1860).

DOCUMENTATION

Gray D. Boone, "Life in Landmark Is Unmatchable Treat," *Antique Monthly*,
Tuscaloosa, Ala., Dec. 1979, p. 4a, with a photograph of the house.

NOTE: This is the same city as the Alabama Insane Hospital site, and it
was characteristic of Sloan that he accepted private commissions wherever he
was given state commissions.

No. 8: House for Henry G. Morris, S. Broad St., Philadelphia, Pa. (1865).

DOCUMENTATION

Finley Hutton, "Memoir," HP.

No. 9: Villa from Design XXXII of *Sloan's Homestead Architecture*,
Ann Arbor, Mich. (before 1867).

NOTE: This is the design for the Slifer villa in Lewisburg, Pa., of 1860.

DOCUMENTATION

S-HA, 1st ed., pp. 107–110.

NOTE: Janice G. Schimmelman of Ann Arbor and Professor Charles E.
Brownell of Oakland University, Rochester, Mich., both attempted to research this attribution, with only marginal success. It was their conclusion
that if the Sloan house was constructed it was probably the Chauncey H.
Millen house, southeast corner of Washtenaw and Hill Sts., which was demolished 1920. A photograph of the building appeared on the cover of the
Michigan Gazette, University of Michigan, no. 6, June 1971.

No. 10: Morris City School, 26th and Thompson Sts.,
Philadelphia, Pa. (1866–67).

DOCUMENTATION

RCPS, Dec. 31, 1866, pp. 26–28. (2) *PSP*, vol. 3, pp. 141–144.

NOTE: This is not the same building as the Morris School. The address is different. Sloan's name is not specifically given in the Controllers' report; however, the building is grouped with two others, which are identified as by the firm of Sloan & Hutton.

No. 11: Oxmead Farm, alterations of the main house (1866–67), possible changes to south front as early as 1860, gatehouse 1858, barn 1860, complex located on Oxmead Rd., near Burlington Township, Burlington County, N.J., for George Dillwyn Parrish of Philadelphia.

DOCUMENTATION

National Register of Historic Places Inventory—Nomination Form, prepared by Terry Karschner, Department of Environmental Protection, Historic Preservation Section, State of New Jersey, 1982.

NOTE: Dillwyn Parrish was one of Sloan's earliest clients; as a member of the combine that developed Riverton, N.J., he had known Sloan since 1852.

No. 12: Villa erected from Design IV of *Sloan's Homestead Architecture*,
"in Germantown, near Philadelphia" (before 1867).

DOCUMENTATION

S-HA, 1st ed., pp. 80–86.

No. 13: "American Bracketed Villa," erected "near Philadelphia"
(before 1869).

DOCUMENTATION

ARABJ, vol. 1, Mar. 1869, pp. 556–557.

No. 14: Banking House for Elliot and Dunn, 3rd St. below Chestnut,
Philadelphia, Pa. (before 1868).

DOCUMENTATION

ARABJ, vol. 1, Dec. 1868, p. 362. (2) Wood engraving, newspaper cut, CC-HSP, vol. 89, "3rd and 4th Sts."

NOTE: No listing for this building, or firm, is given in Westcott's 1875 *Guidebook to Philadelphia*; however, the same address is given for the Tradesmen's Bank (later Tradesmen's National Bank), which is described as follows: "Until within a few years the banking-house was at the south-west corner of Second and Spruce, and afterward in first story of the Commercial Exchange

building." It is reasonable to conclude, therefore, that the building was purchased by the Tradesmen's Bank before 1875. This clears up the problem of
the Tradesmen's National Bank, which can then be listed as:

No. 14A: Tradesmen's National Bank, 3rd below Chestnut St.,
Philadelphia, Pa., Sloan & Hutton.

DOCUMENTATION

PE, p. 20, and wood engraving. (2) CC-HSP, vol. 3, "Banks," newspaper cut
and article, identified in ink "Evening Telegraph, 3/23/1912." (3) Almost all
of Sloan's Philadelphia obituaries list this building, as does the obituary in
AABN, vol. 16, No. 449, Aug. 2, 1884, p. 49. The building was given up by
the bank in 1910 and was still extant in 1955. It is not listed in W-*PP* and
presumed demolished.

No. 15: Protestant Episcopal Church of the Incarnation, Broad and
Jefferson Sts., Philadelphia, Pa. (before 1870).

DOCUMENTATION

ARABJ, vol. 2, Aug. 1870, p. 70.

NOTE: The site given for this building is now occupied by the William
Penn High School. It is not listed under "Churches" in Westcott's *Guide*
(1875); however, it is mentioned, as worth seeing, in the walking tour outline given under "Six Days in Philadelphia," in Westcott, p. 399.

No. 16: Two wings added to the Insane Department of the Philadelphia
Almshouse ("Blockley Hospital for the Insane"), West Philadelphia, Pa.
(1870), Sloan.

DOCUMENTATION

S & W, vol. 2, p. 1063. (2) Charles K. Mills, "The Philadelphia Almshouse
and the Philadelphia Hospital from 1854 to 1908," *FWMV*, pp. 465–467.

NOTE: Both sources give this to Sloan by implication only; however, no
other architect has been found to be associated with the work.

No. 17: Consultant (possibly associate architect) for a building at
Bloomsburg State College, Bloomsburg, Pa., (1868, 1870, 1875), Sloan.

NOTE: The writer is indebted to Roger W. Fromm, College Archivist,
Bloomsburg State College, and Michael J. Lewis III, of Kingston, Pa., for
research into this confused attribution. The *Minutes* of the board of trustees
for June 23, 1868, call Sloan an "advisory architect" in connection with the
"new building." This "new building" could be a dormitory, plans for which
had been submitted to the board by Professor Henry Carver on April 15,
and accepted by the board, which agreed to execute a contract with Carver.

This building burned in Sept. 1875 and was replaced by Waller Hall (demolished 1974–75), which was designed and erected by Willis G. Hale, who had worked in Sloan's office. The conclusion is that Carver, not a professional architect, ran into difficulties with his construction plans and Sloan was called in as a consultant (or possibly even as associate); then, when the building was replaced in 1875, Hale, a Sloan trainee, was called upon as architect. There is an illustration of "a building" at Bloomsburg which was dedicated on June 25, 1868, in Engle's *History of the Commonwealth of Pennsylvania* (Philadelphia: E. M. Gardner, 1883), p. 584.

No. 18: "A Country Mansion," Kalamazoo, Mich. (before 1870)

DOCUMENTATION

ARABJ, vol. 2, Feb. 1870, pp. 453–455.

NOTE: This is identified as having the same plan as the villa "at Lewisburg, Pa." (Slifer villa), as was the earlier Michigan building at Ann Arbor. Professor Charles E. Brownell has researched this building, as he did the Ann Arbor attribution, but has been unable to identify any specific building, either extant or demolished, as being the one specified.

No. 19: Baptist Church (name not given) "in one of our Southern Cities" (before Aug. 1870), Sloan.

DOCUMENTATION

ARABJ, vol. 2, Nov. 1870, pp. 273–274.

NOTE: This could either be the church in Warrenton, Va. (for which the Virginia Historical Society, Richmond, has three sheets of original drawings), or a Baptist church in Louisville, Ky. (name unknown) to which Sloan refers but for which no other documentation has been found.

No. 20: Country residence (possibly "Berwick House") for Burnett Landreth, Bloomsdale, Pa. (possibly Apr. 15, 1874), Sloan.

DOCUMENTATION

Photograph of rendered perspective entitled "Residence of Burnett Landreth, Bloomsdale, Pa." and signed "Samuel Sloan, Architect," in "Scrapbook of T. U. Walter," collection of the Library of the School of Fine Arts, University of Pennsylvania, Philadelphia, Pa.

NOTE: This building was researched by Terry A. McNealy of the Bucks County Historical Society, Doylestown, Pa., who also provided a typescript copy of Burnett Landreth's memoir, "Reminiscences, 1886–1927." Neither McNealy's search nor the Landreth memoir mentions Sloan in a way that would substantiate the attribution; however, Berwick House was built in 1874–75, and the rendered perspective conforms to the style of building which Sloan was designing at that time. It could also be a presentation design, seeking the Landreth commission, which was not accepted.

No. 21: Workingmen's cottages, for a joint stock company, Philadelphia,
Pa., 1870, Sloan.

DOCUMENTATION

ARABJ, vol. 3, Sept. 1870, pp. 150–151, elevation opposite p. 150, plan
p. 151. "These workingmen's cottages are now about to become fixed facts
in this community, a number of gentlemen of Philadelphia having formed a
joint stock company for the building of one hundred of them as a beginning."

NOTE: These may have been from the designs made originally for Joseph
Harrison Jr. and never carried out.

No. 22: Women's Department (Central) Indiana Hospital for the Insane,
Indianapolis, Ind., 1875 and after.

DOCUMENTATION

K-H, 2nd ed., p. 35. (2) *ICIUSC*, vol. 2, pp. 327ff., Sloan consultant or in
collaboration with another architect.

NOTE: The architect of the building's original core and north wing was
Joseph Curzon (construction 1853–1867). Kirkbride specifically notes it as
based on his "system" and credits Sloan with the expansion of 1875; however, the records of the hospital do not mention Sloan. In 1875 the official
name of the institution was Indiana Hospital for the Insane; the addition of
"Central" to the title did not occur until 1889. The *ICIUSC* entry seems to
have been a restatement of the Kirkbride claim.

DIVISION III: ATTRIBUTED COMMISSIONS WITHOUT DOCUMENTATION

The following commissions are attributed to Samuel Sloan with no documentation other than inference, local tradition, or stylistic resemblance to
executed or published works by Samuel Sloan.

No. 1: Tuscan villa in Hightstown, N.J. (c. 1852), Sloan.

SOURCE

Mrs. M. P. Schuman, letter to the author, Feb. 26, 1968, "Our Jerseymen
Chapter at Peddie [School] is doing a research project on a house Samuel
Sloan built in Hightstown. . . . We think there might be some connection
between the Tuscan Villa of Sloan's and the Octagon House across the
street."

No. 2: Hospitals for the insane, built on the "Kirkbride system" and
advised on by Dr. Kirkbride himself in states for which there is no
documented hospital work by Samuel Sloan.

Kirkbride, in the 1880 edition of *Hospitals for the Insane* (K-H), states that there are examples of Sloan's hospital work in every state of the Union (as of 1875). "Development of Hospital Architecture," *ICIUSC*, chap. 4, p. 204, states: "The plans, as developed in a series of 26 propositions by Dr. Kirkbride, were formally adopted by the Association of Superintendents of Institutions, and, as a result, buildings were constructed on the Kirkbride plan in almost all the states of the Union. I can recall them without any effort in New Jersey, Ohio, Michigan, Illinois, Wisconsin, Kentucky, Tennessee, North Carolina, Georgia, Alabama, Louisiana, Mississippi, Texas, Iowa, Minnesota, Nebraska, Missouri, New York, Massachusetts, Connecticut, Maine, Utah and California."

NOTE: Those hospitals for the insane which have been associated with Sloan's name, through the agency of Dr. Kirkbride, are listed here, although primary credit for their design may have been assigned to other architects.

1. Missouri State Hospital, Fulton, Mo. (1852)
2. Augusta State Hospital, Augusta, Maine, wings added (1851–53)
3. State Insane Asylum, Asylum, Mich. (1852–56)
4. Georgia State Sanitarium, Milledgeville, Ga., additions (1851–58)
5. Taunton State Hospital, Taunton, Mass. (1853–54)
6. Spring Grove State Hospital, Spring Grove, Md., rebuilding (1853–56)
7. Western State Hospital, Hopkinsville, Ky. (original 1854, rebuilding 1864)
8. Illinois State Hospital for the Insane, Jacksonville, Ill., west wing (1857–58)
9. Mount Pleasant State Hospital, Mount Pleasant, Iowa (1855–61)
10. Osawatomie State Hospital, Osawatomie, Kans. (1860–66)
11. Central Indiana Hospital for the Insane, Indianapolis, Ind., additions (1866–75)
12. Buffalo State Hospital, Buffalo, N.Y. (date unknown)

No. 3: Courthouse, corner of Washington and Lawrence Sts.,
Montgomery, Ala. (1852–53).

Judge Walter B. Jones, "Off the Bench," *Montgomery (Ala.) Advertiser*, June 11, 1956. The article gives the dates of site purchase (Apr. 13, 1852); payment of "erectors" (May 4, 1853); changes in the plans by the building commissioners (May 16, 1853); and the authorization to employ John Stewart as "superintendent architect." It does not mention Sloan by name, but at this time the Alabama Insane Hospital at Tuscaloosa was being erected with Stewart as supervising architect, and it was the usual practice of Sloan &

Stewart to accept private and municipal commissions wherever they had large public commissions. This connection may also explain the commission for the J. S. Winter house in Montgomery. The "Old" Courthouse, as Judge Jones refers to it, was completed by Dec. 21, 1854, and was at the time of the Jones article "only a mass of ruins." The writer is indebted to Mr. Robert Thorington of Montgomery for this documentation.

No. 4: Masonic Hall, Lambertville, N.J. (1877).

SOURCE

The *Lambertville Record* (1875–77) which records the foundation of the Lodge in 1875 and the erection of the building (1877), which is said to have been designed and built by Sloan in association with Capt. James Bird; Bird is said, by local tradition to have "become an architect in 1880, and practiced in Philadelphia"; the Masonic Hall of Lambertville was "to be built like Taylor Hall, Trenton NJ." James Bird appears in the Philadelphia City Directory for 1880 as an architect; however, thereafter he is listed as a builder and contractor.

No. 5: "Mistletoe Villa," suburban dwelling for Col. Ike Young, Young Ave. at the intersection of Chavassee and Dorsey Aves., Henderson, N.C. (1883–85).

SOURCE

"National Register of Historic Places Inventory—Nomination Form," prepared by Michael Southern, Jerry Cross, and Catherine Bishir of the North Carolina Division of Archives and History, submitted Jan. 12, 1978. On p. 8, "the house is associated by family tradition with the architect of the North Carolina Executive Mansion, Samuel Sloan." The building is fully described and stylistically analyzed.

No. 6: "Dunleith," suburban villa for Robert P. Dick, 677 Chestnut St., Greensboro, N.C. (1856).

SOURCE

Mrs. Henry Zenke of Greensboro and the author. There is no documentary evidence for this attribution, which is based on the similarity of the design to that of the Michael E. Newbold villa in the outskirts of Mount Holly, N.J., which Sloan designed in 1854. The building has been demolished; however, a set of measured drawings by Irving A. Pearce and Scott J. Heacock are in the collection of the Preservation Society of Greensboro.

No. 7: Central National Bank (later the Sylvan Building), corner of Richardson (Main) and Plain (Hampton) Sts., Columbia, S.C. (1871).

The late John J. Seibels and the late Walter Petty, both of Columbia, S.C. Mr. Seibels, who died in 1962 at the age of ninety-one, recalled that the architect of the building was named "Sloan" (this recollection was without any prompting). The author has examined the building in detail and concurs with the attribution. It has been listed on the National Register of Historic Places. There is a strong probability that this building is a redaction of the Bank of New Hanover, Wilmington, N.C., which Sloan executed in 1872–73.

No. 8: West wing, South Carolina Institute for the Deaf and Blind, Spartanburg, S.C. (Feb. 22, 1884).

SOURCE

Minutes of the Board of Commissioners of the Institute, collection of the South Carolina Archives, ". . . drawings, plans and specifications and superintending of the west wing . . . was awarded to Mr. Sloan of Columbia for $250. . . ." At this time Sloan was still employed on the Centre Building for the Insane Hospital and maintained a "branch office" in Columbia. It is therefore entirely possible that he was retained for this addition.

No. 9: Nine "country churches," their location given as "in country towns in Pa. and N.Y. State" (only one of these has, possibly, been identified).

SOURCE

PPL, vol. 25, no. 62, June 3, 1853.

NOTE: This was at the time that Sloan was at the height of his popularity with the *Public Ledger* and when it was reporting his commissions with almost daily regularity. The only "country church" in Pennsylvania from this period (prior to June 3, 1853) could be the First Baptist Church of Germantown, Pa. All the rest, now known, were in Philadelphia. None, at any time, have been identified from rural New York State.

No. 10: Schoolhouses built from plans in *Pennsylvania School Architecture* (pub. 1855).

SOURCE

History of Venango County, Pennsylvania, ed. J. H. Newton (Columbus, Ohio: J. H. Caldwell, 1879), "Some twenty school houses have been built or remodeled from plans taken from the *School Architecture*, and doubtless many more will be in the ensuing year. Where directors are intelligent and interested, the *School Architecture* is generally brought into requisition, otherwise, cheapness is the only consideration, at the sacrifice of every advantage."

DIVISION IV: PUBLICATIONS OF SAMUEL SLOAN

Books

THE MODEL ARCHITECT

1. First issued as twelve of twenty-four projected paperback folios, appearing monthly from August 1851 (Philadelphia: E. G. Jones & Co.).
2. First edition, in two volumes, vol. 1 appearing in 1852, vol. 2 in 1853 (Philadelphia: E. G. Jones & Co.), 113 pages, 96 plates.
3. Second edition 1860 (Philadelphia E. H. Butler & Co.), 2 vols., 113 pages, 93 plates.
4. Third edition 1865 (Philadelphia: E. H. Butler & Co.) 2 vols., 113 pages, 93 plates.
5. Fourth edition 1868 (Philadelphia: J. B. Lippincott & Co.), 2 vols., 113 pages, 93 plates.
6. Fifth edition 1873 (Philadelphia: J. B. Lippincott & Co.), 2 vols., 113 pages, 93 plates.

NOTE: A pirated copy of the last edition (1873) with no publisher given is in the collection of the Boston Public Library.

THE CARPENTER'S NEW GUIDE

Sixteenth edition 1854, N. K. Davis revisor, Samuel Sloan editor and contributor (Philadelphia: J. B. Lippincott & Co.).

NOTE: Sloan contributed several designs for domes, circular stairs, etc.

CITY AND SUBURBAN ARCHITECTURE

1. First edition 1859 (Philadelphia: J. B. Lippincott & Co.), 104 pages, 136 plates.
2. Second edition 1867 (Philadelphia: J. B. Lippincott & Co.), 102 pages, 136 plates.

SLOAN'S CONSTRUCTIVE ARCHITECTURE

1. First edition 1859 (Philadelphia: J. B. Lippincott & Co.), 148 pages, 66 plates.
2. Second edition 1866 (Philadelphia: J. B. Lippincott & Co.), 148 pages, 66 plates.
3. Third edition 1873 (Philadelphia: J. B. Lippincott & Co.), 148 pages, 66 plates.

NOTE: A copy in the collection of the Carpenter's Company, Carpenter's Hall, Philadelphia, has no publication date or publisher and can be presumed to be a pirated edition.

NOTE: *Catalogue 57, 1957* Edward Moorhill & Son, Inc., Boston, lists a first edition with the following description: "Presentation copy from the author to Abraham Lincoln, Nov. 8, 1861. In 1868 the book was presented by Mrs. Lincoln to M. D. Dean, whose name is on the flyleaf."

SLOAN'S HOMESTEAD ARCHITECTURE

1. First edition 1861 (Philadelphia: J. B. Lippincott & Co.), 355 pages, 52 plates.

2. Second edition 1867 (Philadelphia: J. B. Lippincott & Co.), 355 pages, 51 plates.
3. Third edition 1870 (Philadelphia: J. B. Lippincott & Co.), 355 pages, 51 plates.

AMERICAN HOUSES: A VARIETY OF DESIGNS FOR RURAL BUILDINGS

1. First edition 1861 (Philadelphia: Henry B. Ashmead), 6 pages, 16 l, 29 plates (27 color).
2. Second edition 1868 (Philadelphia: Henry Carey Baird), 6 pages, 14 l, 26 color plates.

Pamphlets

1. Sloan & Hutton, *Specifications for the Erection of a Banking House for "The Philadelphia Saving Fund Society" Jointly Submitted by Samuel Sloan and Addison Hutton, Architects* (Philadelphia: J. B. Lippincott & Co., 1868), 16 pages.
2. *Description of Designs and Drawings for the Proposed Centennial Buildings, (etc.) Submitted by Samuel Sloan, Architect* (Philadelphia: J. B. Lippincott & Co., 1873), 8 pages.
   NOTE: This issue of the pamphlet is identified:

   "OFFICE OF SAMUEL SLOAN, ARCHITECT
   152 South Fourth Street
   Philadelphia, October 10, 1873"

   It contains no illustrations. Copy in the collection of the HSP.
2b. *Description of Designs and Drawings (etc.)* (identical title as above) (Philadelphia: King & Baird, 1873), 8 pages, 4 plates.
   NOTE: This issue of the pamphlet is identified:

   "presented by
   Samuel Sloan, Architect
   Philadelphia [no date]"

3. *Bill of Quantities for the Centennial Buildings, Submitted by Samuel Sloan, Architect* (Philadelphia: J. B. Lippincott & Co., 1873).
4. *Specifications of the Workmanship and Materials to Be Used in the Erection and Construction of the Western State Asylum for the Insane: at Morgantown, Burke County, North Carolina, Prepared by Samuel Sloan, Architect, Philadelphia* (Philadelphia: McLaughlin Brothers, 1875).

Periodicals

The Architectural Review and American Builder's Journal, ed. Samuel Sloan and Charles J. Lukens (Philadelphia: Claxton, Remson & Haffelfinger), vol. 1, July 1868–June 1869; vol. 2, July 1869–June 1870; vol. 3, July 1870–November 1870.

NOTE: Vol. 1 of the *Architectural Review* was reprinted in book form as *City Homes, Country Houses, and Church Architecture* (Philadelphia: Claxton, Remson & Haffelfinger, 1871), 792 pages, 82 plates.

Contributions, Designs, and Articles

1. *Godey's Lady's Book and Magazine*, ed. L. A. Godey, Philadelphia.
   Vol. 45 (July–Dec. 1852), pp. 400, 469, 488 (designs).
   Vol. 46 (Jan.–June 1853), pp. 83, 102, 291–292, 375, 473, (designs).
   Vol. 52 (Jan.–June 1856), p. 299 (design).
   Vol. 58 (Jan.–June 1859), pp. 277, 452, 471, 545 (designs).
   Vol. 59 (July–Dec. 1859), pp. 171, 181, 193, 289 (designs).
2. "Art. XV: Heat and Ventilation," *Church Extension Annual, including the Ninth Annual Report of the Board of Church Extension of the Methodist Episcopal Church for the Year 1874* (Philadelphia: Craig, Finley & Co., January 1875), pp. 38–44.
3. *Wooden and Brick Buildings with Details* (New York: A. J. Bicknell & Co., 1875); vol. 1, Design 17, plates 23–24; Design 18, plates 25–27; Design 19, plates 28–30.
4. "Art. XVI: Our Designs," *Church Extension Annual*, op. cit., pp. 44–63.
5. "Our Designs," *Minutes of the General Assembly of the Presbyterian Church in the United States of America with an Appendix*, n.s., vol. 4, 1877 (New York: Presbyterian Board of Publications, S. W. Green, Printer, 1877), pp. 11–16 of the Appendix.

Selected Bibliography

Included in this Selected Bibliography are works of general, rather than specific, reference. Those documenting specific buildings are found in the Catalogue, while those documenting specific events in the life of Samuel Sloan are found in the Notes. All works authored or edited by Samuel Sloan are listed in Division IV of the Catalogue.

American Journal of Education. Edited by Henry Barnard. Hartford, Conn. Vols. 1–13, 1852–63.

Barnard, Henry. *School Architecture*. 5th edition. New York: Charles B. Norton, 1854.

Boyd, James A. *A History of the Pennsylvania Horticultural Society, 1827–1927*. Philadelphia, 1929.

[Annual Reports of the] *Controllers of the Public Schools for the City and County of Philadelphia, [Thirty-Third (1851)–Forty-Eighth (1867)]*. Philadelphia: Crissy & Markley.

Edmunds, Franklin Davenport. *The Public School Buildings of the City of Philadelphia*. 3 vols. Philadelphia: Privately printed, 1913–17.

Engle, William H. *History of the Commonwealth of Pennsylvania*. 3rd edition. Philadelphia: E. M. Gardner, 1883.

Evans, D. Morier. *The History of the Commercial Crisis, 1857–1858, and the Stock Exchange Panic of 1859*. London, 1859 (reissued, New York: Burt Franklin, n.d.).

Founder's Week Memorial Volume. Edited by Frederick P. Henry. Philadelphia, 1909.

Freemasonry in Pennsylvania. Edited by Julius F. Suchse. Philadelphia: By order of the Grand Lodge of Pennsylvania, 1919.

Gleason's Pictorial Drawing Room Companion. Edited by F. Gleason. Boston, 1852–1962.

Gopsill's Philadelphia City Directory. Edited by Isaac Costa. Philadelphia: James Gopsill, 1869–1895.

Henderson, Archibald. *The Campus of the First State University*. Chapel Hill: University of North Carolina Press, 1954.

Hotchkin, S. F. *Ancient and Modern Germantown, Mount Airy, and Chestnut Hill*. Philadelphia: P. W. Ziegler & Co., 1889.

————. *The Bristol Pike*. Philadelphia: George W. Jacobs & Co., 1893.

————. *Rural Pennsylvania in the Vicinity of Philadelphia*. Philadelphia: George W. Jacobs & Co., 1897.

————. *The York Road, Old and New*. Philadelphia: Binder & Kelly, 1892.

Hutton Papers. Quaker Collection, Haverford College Library, Haverford, Pa.

Index of American Architectural Drawings Before 1900, American Association of Architectural Bibliographers. Charlottesville, Va., 1957.

Jackson, Joseph. *America's Most Historic Highway*. New edition. Philadelphia: John Wanamaker, 1926.

————. *Encyclopaedia of Philadelphia*. Harrisburg, Pa.: National Historical Association, vols. 1–2 (1931), vol. 3 (1932), vol. 4 (1933).

Jones, Joseph. "Report to the Committee on Construction for the Johns Hopkins Hospital." In *Hospital Construction and Organization*. Baltimore, 1875.

Kirkbride, Thomas S. *Hospitals for the Insane*. Philadelphia: J. B. Lippincott & Co., 1854 (1st ed.), 1880 (2nd ed.).

Mahony, Daniel H. *Historical Sketches of the Catholic Churches and Institutions of Philadelphia*. Philadelphia, 1895.

Manson, George Champlin. "Professional Ancestry of the Philadelphia Chapter." *Journal of the American Institution of Architects*, vol. 1, no. 9, Sept. 1913.

McElroy's Philadelphia Directory. Philadelphia: A. McElroy, 1837–67.

Miller, Roger, and Joseph Siry. "The Emerging Suburb: West Philadelphia, 1850–1880." *Pennsylvania History*, April 1980.

Nutt Papers, collections of (1) Duke University Library, Durham, N.C., and (2) Henry E. Huntington Library, San Marino, Calif.

Oberholtzer, E. P. *Philadelphia: A History of the City and Its People*. Philadelphia: Clark, n.d.

Official Guidebook to Philadelphia, 1875. Edited by Thompson Westcott. Philadelphia: Porter & Coates, 1875.

Philadelphia and Its Environs. Philadelphia: J. B. Lippincott & Co., 1874.

Philadelphia and Notable Philadelphians. Edited by Moses King. New York, 1901–02.

Philadelphia as It Is in 1852. Edited by R. A. Smith. Philadelphia: Lindsay & Blakiston, 1852.

The Presbyterian Church in Philadelphia. Philadelphia: Allen, Lane & Scott, 1895.

Proceedings of the [First and Second] Session of the National Convention of the Friends of Public Education. Philadelphia: E. C. & J. Biddle, 1849, 1850.

Proceedings of the First Session of the American Association for the Advancement of Education. Philadelphia: E. C. & J. Biddle, 1852.

Proceedings of the Select Council of the City and County of Philadelphia (1852–1864). Philadelphia: Crissy & Markley.

Scharf, Thomas J., and Thompson Westcott. *History of Philadelphia, 1609 – 1884*. 3 vols. Philadelphia: L. H. Everts & Co., 1884.
Van Vleck, George W. *The Panic of 1857: An Analytic Study*. New York: AMS Press, 1967.

Index